Everything Is Useful

Everything Is Useful

Turning Obstacles into Opportunities on the Road to Enlightenment

Garth J. Hallett

HAMILTON BOOKS
AN IMPRINT OF
ROWMAN & LITTLEFIELD
Lanham • Boulder • New York • London

Published by Hamilton Books
An imprint of The Rowman & Littlefield Publishing Group, Inc.
4501 Forbes Boulevard, Suite 200, Lanham, Maryland 20706
www.rowman.com

86-90 Paul Street, London EC2A 4NE, United Kingdom

British Library Cataloguing in Publication Information Available

Library of Congress Cataloging-in-Publication Data Available

ISBN 9780761873907 (paper : alk. paper) | ISBN 9780761873914 (ebook)

♾ The paper used in this publication meets the minimum requirements of American National Standard for Information Sciences—Permanence of Paper for Printed Library Materials, ANSI/NISO Z39.48-1992.

There is no such thing as a problem without a gift for you in its hands.

You seek problems because you need their gifts.

—Richard Bach, *Illusions*

A traveler is walking along a narrow foot-path at night. Suddenly he stops and steps aside terror-stricken, crying out, "A cobra! A cobra!" Regaining confidence, he grasps his bamboo staff firmly, strikes a light, and sees a coil of rope lying in the way. "Ah!" he says, "that is just what I need . . ."

—W. Y. Evans-Wentz, *Tibetan Yoga and Secret Doctrines*

To my teachers and guides—past, present, and future.

Contents

Acknowledgments

It has been said that no one succeeds alone; no book does either. With that understanding in mind, I hasten to acknowledge the support and encouragement of the following individuals: my magnificent mother, Gloria Hallett, who placed a book in my hands before my eyes could read, and my old teacher, mentor, and lifelong friend, Professor Daniel Buczek of Fairfield University. Both of these key individuals have now passed from this earth and beyond my sight. I long for the time when I will, in one form or another, meet with them again.

I also wish to extend my recognition to Professor Walter Petry of Fairfield University. He taught me (though not explicitly) that you can only understand one set of ideas against the backdrop of the ideas opposing them, and that simple solutions are for simple minds only; to my first cousin and "first teacher," Anne Gosain, who taught me how to tell time, so that I never had to ask her when the lesson was over; to Paramahansa Yoganada and the Self-Realization Fellowship line of gurus, who, along with Joseph Goldstein of the Insight Mediation Society, have been my greatest spiritual influences. I owe them a debt of gratitude I can never hope to repay; to Professor Emerita Shyamala Raman of the University of Saint Joseph, who gracefully encouraged my efforts with both this book and the last; to my editor, Brooke Bures, and formatter, Jasmine Harris, both of whom have been commendably patient with me as this project reached fruition; and, last, but not least, to my good wife, Christine, and charming daughters, Erin and Michelle. They've shown me the joy in life, with only a few minor bumps in the road as compensatory obstacles.

To all those I didn't mention who have had a role in shaping both this book and my life, I am grateful for your gifts and to have shared the journey with you.

Introduction

When I began writing Everything is Useful, the year was 2015. Then, this book was nothing more than a loose jumble of ideas, ideas that would come to me in the car on the way to work. Once I arrived there, I would furiously type them out and send them to myself in an email. By 2017, I had enough material to consider writing a book. By 2019, I was poised to send that book to market.

Then a catastrophe struck, a pandemic of seismic proportions, one that cast into doubt so many of our routine assumptions. Millions of people were out of work who, as adults, had always worked before. Our nation grew severely divided, our leadership stymied by the rapid onset of this unusual and comprehensive disaster. We found that our once prosperous future hung suddenly and precariously in the balance, as we navigated warily between the Scylla of economic dislocation and the Charybdis of a renewed plague.

In reviewing my completed manuscript against this tumultuous backdrop, I found myself revising, in an unexpected way, my basic description of society as it pertained but a few years ago. I edited into the past—or into the conditional—many previously unchallenged assumptions. Much that I thought would never change, had already been rapidly transformed. Such basic activities as going to the gym or sharing an intimate lunch with a friend had been seriously called into question, as the world I once knew seemed light years away.

Yet even in the depths of this colossal upheaval, my book's basic theme remained relevant. Living under COVID's shadow shifted the bulk of the media's attention from predatory gossip to more substantive issues, issues that actually meant something, issues of life and death. Our mandatory seclusion gave us time to think and to reexamine our personal goals and priorities. We had a renewed opportunity to better connect with our precious families and friends. And as the skies literally cleared on our global environment, many of us discovered, in this perilous interval, our own innate capacity for kindness and heroism. All this attests to the truth, as valid now as it ever was, that everything is useful.

HOW IT BEGINS

Imagine there is a man who owns a dog. Each day, when he comes home, the man visits the place where the dog is kept. On most days he pets the dog, and the dog is delighted; but on other days, for no apparent reason, and without advance warning, the man beats the dog brutally. This torments the dog all the more, in being as unexpected as it is out of keeping with the man's typical behavior at more ordinary times. After each such incident, the dog is in shock, but eventually recovers. This pattern is found, however, to repeat itself without end. Ultimately, the dog finds his situation intolerable, and looks for a way out.

If this description sounds familiar, it should, for in the above analogy the man is the world and we are that beaten dog. Though the scenario it portrays is brutal, it is no more so than the opening scene of the Hindu Bhagavad Gita, in which the Avatar, Krishna, enjoins his star pupil, Arjuna, to engage in a savage battle. That story too, as Gandhi and others assure us, is merely an analogy, a representation of the spiritual struggles each of us faces in the arena of our everyday lives.

On most days, if we are fortunate, everything goes well, and we have reason to declare ourselves happy; then suddenly, and without warning, something harsh and unexpected occurs: the loss of a job, the death of a parent, the close of a long-term relationship, the departure of a much-valued friend. There are travails even rarer, that we have reason to hope we may never experience at all: the death of a sibling or child, a debilitating accident or illness Yet the sheer variety of such misfortunes is so great, life itself so uncertain, our bodies so changeable and fragile, that the odds increase with time that one or more of these less likely tragedies will occur to us as well. Some difficult experiences will be peculiar to us. Others, like the pandemic that continues to rage at the time of this writing, are an inherent part of the human condition. There is loss; there is death; there is disappointment. All of us have known or will know them, and though we may proceed through life as if we are immune, there are truly no exceptions. Nor is the dawn of adversity made easier by the pleasure that went before, for as with the beaten dog, the greater the contrast, the greater the pain. As with the loss of someone we love, or the end of a gratifying career, our greatest suffering is often founded on the joy that went before. At times, it seems that our troubles never end, while the good things in life we hope for, forever come and go.

The conclusion that many of us draw, is that the world is a bad master. And in our pain and disappointment, our disillusionment and distress, we seek a better one in God, Source, or Spirit. We long for an alternative to our "quiet desperation"—if not to our outright screaming agony. We seek a positive and realistic way to add fullness, security, and meaning to our lives. Yet we find, along the way, that we are confronted with numerous obstacles, some without, the greater part within.

The Buddha stated that "if one man conquer in battle a thousand times a thousand men, and if another conquers himself, he is the greatest of conquerors." (Babbitt verse 103, location 249) On that crowded battlefield, filled with 1000 times 1000 men, the opponents we face will be varied and numerous. This book makes no pretense to identifying them all. But it does look at some of the more prominent ones in a way that should be helpful to those on a spiritual path, as well as to the rest of us just trying to muddle our way through. Its central objective, as such, is not scholarly, but practical. And while it may sit neatly in the stacks alongside other books within the general success category, it is distinguished in the following way: It assumes that we are spiritual beings with a spiritual reason for being.

We may own the best-designed car available. But if it remains parked in our garage or driveway, it hasn't fulfilled the purpose of its design, which is to enable us to joyously and efficiently travel. We may have all the money in the world. We may have degrees and the respect of our peers. Our family lives may be idyllic havens of domestic enjoyment, free of any noteworthy struggle or strife. But if we don't realize our purpose in life, the goal of our spiritual natures, then we will have lived in vain.

One thing is clear, from the reported experience of those who've gone before, should you proceed on a spiritual path, in whatever form it takes, through whatever tradition you respectfully honor, you will be challenged, and challenged in a way that you never were before. Such challenges will demand that you grow, and grow in a balanced way. Spiritual practices such as focused prayer or mindfulness meditation will untie many internal knots that can bring troubling memories or other cathected material to the surface. These internal challenges will, in turn, send you trucking off to the gym or to the yoga studio, to develop the strength and stamina you need to work through them; and your newly-developed meditative skills will help you, in turn, to accomplish more at the gym. This one leg after another approach is the balanced way in which spiritual development, and indeed all enduring progress in life, occurs.

With respect to the external obstacles, it is clear that, though we live in a land of abundance and choice, it remains a troubled utopia, one characterized by a hyper-emphasis upon the commercial and the material to the detriment of all else. It has been said that "before a wish is realized it is a hope, and then afterwards, a responsibility." In modern times, our lives have become littered with the wreckage of numerous hopes fulfilled. We have been left overwhelmed, in the midst of any outward prosperity, with an interminable array of forms to complete, lawns to mow, roofs to repair, emails to answer, taxes to pay, and with many "obligatory"—and costly—events to celebrate, the inordinate cost of which has hurled us back along the treadmill of pain in a dubious attempt to catch up. So overwhelmed are we with the trivial and the mundane, that we have occasion to wonder, as our exhausted heads hit our pillows at the end of the day, whether anything of real value has actually been accomplished. The further we advance, the more we appear to lag, as we continue to pay the price for those benefits to which we have grown accustomed, but which, having lost their original luster, no longer offer us much notable joy. Too often, what we obtained becomes a source of fear, while no longer adding much excitement or meaning to the context of our lives. More and more of us feel like we have been living at the top of a Tetris board, with additional pieces being mercilessly piled on.

To sustain us in this daily strife, the food we eat contains, on average, numerous ingredients we can't even pronounce, colorfully packaged to add to its specious appeal. We bleach the nutrients out of standard white bread, only to add them back in at the end of the process, calling the result "enriched." Even those foods we would favor as being naturally grown, have, more often than not, been coated with pesticides or have been genetically altered. Others laden with processed sugar are so ubiquitous that obesity and diabetes have become national epidemics. In this domain, as in others, in the pursuit of what cannot ultimately satisfy, we have lost our more basic and vital connection to what we most need, to ourselves and to our living Source.

As if this were not enough, and despite the complexity of these and other problems, we, as a society, feel the need to continually dumb ourselves down, hesitating in even a rudimentary way to think creatively or independently beyond the pattern of the norm. America is a young nation, not yet at that point where, finished with conquering the world—at least not economically—we can hope to give equal weight to more enduring cultural accomplishments; and for those of intellectual or artistic bent, the endless, mindless pursuit of the "practical" at the expense of the profound can be positively maddening.

Our corporate institutions, through which we shoulder our way to earn our daily bread, have become veritable laboratories of morally unsound behavior in which people, day-by-day, are gaining their worlds by losing their souls, advancing their material causes through the spiritually unsound means of treachery, cruelty, and deceit. Many people, even more so now than before, are uneasy and uncertain. Knowing no other way to cope, they make it uneasy and uncertain for many of those around them. In this hypercompetitive environment of mutually-inflicted strife, many of them readily conclude that the only way they will ever mount the saddle of their success is upon the bowed backs of others, with a bloated advertising industry dedicated to extracting the potential inherent in that false and pessimistic assumption. As PT Barnum is reputed to have observed, "there is a sucker born every minute," with our foolishness and false hopes matched by an endless array of morally corrupt—yet perfectly legal—enterprises ready and willing to "whisper sweet nothings" into the ears of those already bereft of any real hope. While the Covid-19 crisis has brought out the best and the worst in us, the worst in what it's revealed is already quite familiar, and continues to pertain.

We have, in sum, become a land of inordinately pestered people, people whose frustration has grown in direct proportion to the number of wants they have—wants that seem to be never-ending and ever-increasing. As we are callously driven by greed and fear, we demand too much of ourselves and others. We plaintively yearn for what we don't have. And we have been wretchedly consumed, in our daily encounters, with pettiness, wrath, and spite.

Too often people with spiritual commitments wonder how they can make it in the world as it is. They question how they can do what they need to do, and still preserve the larger part of their integrity. Here our challenge and task are to think for ourselves, to leverage the positive elements of freedom and prosperity we continue, despite challenges, to enjoy, and to produce outcomes that will help us to forgo the common fate.

Though the landscape in view may thus seem less than rosy, the obstacles need not discourage us, for they, more than anything else, provide the means to attaining the happiness we seek. While in Shakespeare, "the play is the thing," (Shakespeare Act 2, Scene 2, p. 119) in life, the obstacles are; and in the various "plays" we find ourselves in, we participate with others in a dynamic process of growth aimed at overcoming our flaws. It is a process by which we are, whether we realize it or not, continuously, and systematically growing, fulfilling the purpose of understanding and love for which we came to this earth to begin with. Rather than freezing in pain and terror, each time such obstacles appear, we must learn to play judo with them, to transmute their ostensibly negative energy into fuel for achieving our goals, and thus pave the way to our ultimate enlightenment and happiness.

This book is thus intended to be practical about a topic that would not seem, to some, to be very practical at all, but which constitutes our greatest need. That topic is spirituality. Most people exhaust themselves amidst life's standard routines. They rarely, if ever, question the value of those "normal" activities our society takes for granted. They settle for prescribed or limited goals that can never truly satisfy them, or that are contrary to their natures. Even if they gain what they seek, deprived of peace, character, and a connection to their Source, they inevitably end up jaded and unhappy.

It also deals with what spiritual people typically perceive as being some of their greatest obstacles, but which are really opportunities in disguise, for no weight lifter ever grew strong by merely pumping excuses, but by pitting his strength and will against the heavy weights opposing him. No contender in any competitive game or sport ever won greatly except by losing greatly at first, relinquishing pride, and doing what it takes to properly perform and thus to better achieve. It is the same with life and its obstacles.

Chapter 1

Obstacles and Order

Jesus once observed that "not" (a sparrow) "falls on the ground apart from your Father's will. . . ." (Bible Hub, n.d., World English Bible, Matt., 10:29) Einstein, in a matching assertion, claimed that "God doesn't play dice." In an orderly universe, where, to paraphrase Shakespeare, the obstacles are the thing, the ones we individually face are not likely to be arbitrary. The larger ones, at least, will be cater made for us. The aging beauty, obsessed with her waning charms, who finds herself working at a Home for the aged. The macho military officer who sires an intelligent and creative son, one who also happens being gay. The brilliant History or English major, always at or near the top of his class, who, upon leaving academia, must make his way in a utilitarian world where his best abilities are underemphasized, and who is, at the outset at least, overshadowed by others better equipped with those skills the world values more. Such inferences do not constitute proof of a great universal order; but they do provide good circumstantial evidence, are observable, and reveal living processes that, at first glance, can seem harsh, or even devastating. But this is not about God, Life, or our Source being deliberately cruel, but about our overcoming all that essentially limits us. Here clinging unwisely to our blessings can be as obstructive as cherishing our flaws in inhibiting our plunge into Infinity. It is at our weakest link that life will directly challenge us. Our attitude should then, and must then be, if we are ever to have a chance to be happy, to regard our obstacles as opportunities, and to honorably contend with them as we brave the battle of life. Since "all that we are is the result of what we have thought," (Babbitt 2012, location 46, verse 1) when our thoughts are random and chaotic, our experiences will seem that way too. When our thoughts become ordered, through meditation or other spiritual practices, the patterns of growth inherent in life begin to more clearly emerge.

On the spiritual path, we confront two basic kinds of experiences, those that directly and those that indirectly benefit us. The first causes us to receive what is an energetic match for our fondest hopes and desires; through it, we

obtain exactly what we want. The second, which encompasses all the obstacles we must inevitably face, demands that we grapple with our demons in
the form of what we do not want—but nonetheless need—for our continued
development.

Ram Das, among others, observed that all what we generally experience
in life is what we desire, what we fear, and what we can learn from. Neutral
experiences, like "ships that pass in the night," don't make it within the range
of our personal radar. Even when a part of our experiential backdrop, they
make little to no impression on our minds.[1] There is an order and beauty to
this process, as we interact with others in a spiritual exchange by which we
provide them with the lessons they need, and they do the same for us. We
expand our capacity to receive by surmounting our limitations and discharg-
ing our debts. Into the seemingly negative category fall all those unwelcome
experiences we need to grow, all the "cruel to be kind" aspects of Nature and
existence.

To transform our obstacles into opportunities is the lightning road to happiness and growth. The mechanism by which this unfolds is the energy of our
thoughts. Amidst the workings of this cosmic process, the second category
of experience can benefit us as much as the first. In fact, it can typically help
us more, in increasing our capacity to receive and thus ultimately to expand
and to develop.

When I look back on my individual history, I see that God or my Source
has given me most of what I have asked for, and in most cases, in a way
better than I had originally asked for it. This occurred most effectively and
efficiently once I had made a commitment to my own spiritual development.
The only wishes left unfulfilled were those that were denied in favor of a
higher end, or that in a way unbeknownst to me at the time, would have
caused myself or another harm.

If a toddler loves sand trucks, it is unlikely that a solicitous parent would
allow him to play at a construction site where trucks and other heavy vehicles
are actively maneuvering. But that same parent would gladly give his child
a toy that would capture the essence of the joy his child seeks from that
experience.

As human beings, we rarely see all ends; hence, God will likely preserve
us from the effects of our most destructive wishes. We are also unlikely to
see wishes fulfilled that will violate life's pre-established order—though
you never know, some of those may come true, as well. If we wish to fly,
it may not happen; yet there have been Tibetan yogis, for example, who are
reputed to have acquired that ability, who have risen above the game of life
to such an extent as to have, in essence, transcended its laws (or, more likely,
what we know of such laws). Yet all of them, I am sure, realized such skills,
only at a time, and at a stage in their development when they were unlikely

to exhibit such talents promiscuously, or to interfere pridefully with Life's universal order.[2]

If, beyond that point, we remain insistent in our misguided demand for something, we are then likely to "get what we want," in not having been "careful of what we wished for." Life will also send us trials to accompany our fulfilled wishes. As stated in Biblical terms, "And Jesus . . . said, Verily I say unto you, there is no man that hath left house, or brethren, or sisters, or father, or mother, or wife, or children, or lands, for my sake, and the gospel's, / But he shall receive an hundredfold now in this time, houses, and brethren, and sisters, and mothers, and children, and lands, with persecutions; and in the world to come eternal life." (Bible Hub, n.d., King James Bible, Matt. 10:29–30)

There is a sound and beneficial reason why this battery of trials appears, and it is not to pull the carpet out from under our happiness. It is not to cheat us out of our legitimate hopes, or to make us feel that the objects of our dreams can never be obtained. It is because those intent on a spiritual path, whether they fully realize it or not, are, no longer satisfied with droplets of pleasure or whirlpools of fleeting satisfaction; they want to bathe in the ocean of joy at its Source. Hence trials and obstacles come to lead them home.

We will also be tested on the quality and durability of our wishes, some of which may be satisfied at a time when we are no longer so interested in their fulfillment. This may seem like God or the universe toying with us; yet the delay is, in effect, just Life's way of asking, "Is this what you want—I mean, really, really want?" In treading what the Buddha called the Middle Way, the way that eliminates superfluous desires, we discover what we want from life a lot better, as our experience puts what we genuinely need into its proper perspective.

Ultimately, we discover that none of what we desire from life, its pleasures and satisfactions, is evil unless it is destructive of ours or another's happiness, or perverted beyond its natural role and measure. God is the source of all wealth, be it material or spiritual, and the two are not separate but one.

There is certainly no virtue in poverty. All that poverty can provide that wealth cannot is freedom from material distractions. In forgoing lesser pleasures, we may be liberated, as a result, to pursue happiness in its direct and highest form. Yet poverty can be as much of a distraction as wealth, one that will prey on our minds if our basic needs are unmet. With respect to material things, they are a legitimate part of life; thus, to hate something because it tempts us demonstrates only our weakness, not the value of an impoverished situation.

For certain, advanced souls, like Job, God may take everything else away to satisfy the need for liberation, for unity with one's Source. Job overcame his trials by acknowledging the goodness of God amidst the harshness of his experiences. Through the denial of those lesser things we generally pin our hopes on, whether it be fame, wealth, or possessions, he was left with what was best and most important, with what could not, by any evil or obstacle, ever be taken away—the light of God's love. But amidst more ordinary circumstances, which is where most of us tend to be, the good things in life are still Good. Even our obstacles are ultimately Good, as well.

NOTES

1. As Ram Das specifically noted, "The universe is made up of experiences that are designed to burn out our reactivity, which is our attachment, our clinging, to pain, to pleasure, to fear, to all of it. And as long as there are places where we're vulnerable, the universe will find ways to confront us with them. That's the way the dance is designed. In truth, there are millions and millions of stimuli that we are not even noticing, that go by in every plane of existence, all the time. The reason we don't notice them is because there's no attachment to them in us. Our desires affect our perception." (Das, Grist for the Mill 1987, 83)

2. The power of wingless flight was reputedly possessed by Tibet's Great Yogi, Milarepa, as described in his biography by the same name. (Evans Wentz 1969, 212)

Chapter 2

Why We are Here

In the Kabballah, there is a concept known as "the bread of shame." (Y. Berg 2004, 62) This has little to do with shame, in the ordinary sense of fidgety red-faced embarrassment. Rather, it is what we experience when we attempt to "grab the prize" without "running the race," where we refuse to face our challenges and obstacles head on. Such obstacles exist, not to humiliate or to destroy us, but to render the prize of our ultimate victory that much sweeter in the end. As metaphorically described by Yahuda Berg, imagine a Little League pitcher named Bobby. As Berg portrays him:

> If Bobby could have one wish . . . it would be to pitch a ballgame that would fill his parents with pride and joy . . . And the little boy doesn't disappoint. He throws a no-hitter and sets a record for the most strikeouts in a game.
> After the game, Bobby discovers something rather shocking. It seems that his dad made a prior arrangement with both coaches and both teams to throw the game for his son. . . . The entire game was fixed . . . How does Bobby feel now? (Y. Berg 2004, p. 61)

According to the Kabballah, from the hand of God, we originally received everything, everything, that is, except the impression that we had earned it. By overcoming our signature obstacles, we obtain that critical sense of accomplishment as well. The Bhagavad Gita, one of the sources repeatedly mentioned in this book, has, as its introductory line, "on the field of Truth, on the battlefield of life." (Mascaro 1974, p. 23) This compelling opening comparably sets the stage for our own herculean struggles to surmount our own specific challenges.

The "bread of shame" scenario further begs the question as to why we are here and what, if anything, we are meant to accomplish. According to Hinduism, each person exists to express a unique aspect of divinity before returning to the Cosmic One. Like raindrops meandering down a windshield, each individual's path is—and is intended to be—unique. Even within the identifiable context of a particular religious tradition, each of us has his own imagery to represent those values to which our group collectively adheres. We then employ that imagery as an aid, to help us to overcome our own specific challenges, and to successfully make our way through. As proclaimed in Eastern lore, "the ways to the One are as many as the lives of men." (Humphreys 1962, p. 135) It is only the dictators and oppressors of the world who, out of fear and a lust for power, seek to enforce a false religious or ideological uniformity.

I remember being slightly amused, years ago, upon seeing a religious portrait on a sidewalk in New York, within the general vicinity of Grand Central Station. Its caption read "the real last supper." Each of the twelve apostles and Jesus were portrayed as African-American. My first thought on viewing that curious rendition was "why?" What did it matter whether Christ was Black or Jewish? The thought that quickly ensued was "well, why not?" for don't we all discover and relate to truth through the context with which we are most familiar? What serves one may not serve another quite as well. Even Santa Claus could—and should—be Black too.

As we advance towards enlightenment, we are also quite arguably, on different stages of the soul's overall path. The well-known entertainer, Jackie Gleason, reflecting back on a dissolute life of chain smoking, pool playing, and gluttony, arose, at the end, from his overflowing plate to declare, "how sweet it is." For someone who had experienced too many of the world's vicissitudes already, arguably, and as suggested by some, through the course of numerous lifetimes, that sweetness might show its sour side more quickly. It all depends on who, what, and where we are. The apparent harshness of particular practices associated with certain religious traditions reveals how, for at least some of their practitioners, ordinary material life has become such a burden that they need a more hard-core method of releasing themselves from it.

The Tibetan practice of exchanging oneself for others is a perfect example. Through it, we are instructed to ritually bestow all our blessings and benefits on others while agreeing to take on all their burdens and pains. Most of us would shrink from committing to such a task, even mentally. It's just not where we are at our current level of development. And of course, by the Law of Karma, such a practice wouldn't harm us either, as the more we do for others, the more we stand to benefit ourselves. That being said, it may not be the right practice for us—just a more rigorous way for some of us to make our way through. Still, the reincarnational standard central to Buddhism suggests the possibility, one worth considering from the perspective of a spiritual logic in which justice is truly meant to reign, that we have been at this game a very, very, very long time. In that very long time, the monotony of the process, for some, may finally have become too much, and they may just now be stretching their distracted wings, looking for deeper challenges, for further opportunities, for higher planes of evolutionary experience, or for just a more respectable way out.

All these different approaches to religious understanding should serve as a pointed reminder that we need to be tolerant of others and their views, for our intolerance may deprive the next person of just what he or she needs to progress. We should also manage our commitment to faith the way the founders of the great religions would if they were still here today. Do you really think that Christ and Buddha, were they to meet in the 21st Century, would be warming up on different sides of a ring, ready to box each other senseless over fine distinctions in doctrine or disputed shades in individual practices? They would be far more likely to sip tea together and to engage in a friendly discussion. So how could we, their lesser followers, presume be intolerant when acting on their behalf?

As we proceed through life, we venture through the territory of varying viewpoints and competing philosophical systems. Rather than being right or wrong, what may be a step forward for one, could well be a step backward for another. Maybe the larger purpose behind the Babel of these disparate views is ultimately to provide enough meaningful variety to satisfy all needs. To forcefully promote a materialistic utopia may not be as exalted as achieving peace and wholeness through love, but for some people, it could be a step up from an earlier mindless pursuit of material wealth. We often miss our targets in evaluating what is right for us; we are even less equipped to accurately evaluate the needs and nature of others.

It seems that when someone tries to teach us bigotry, suspicion, or intolerance, it is a lesson too-casily learned—whether its focus be Jews, Blacks, Muslims, Communists, males, females—or otherwise. There is something in our instincts that causes us to fear what is new or different, or to see what exists beyond the protective walls of our current, limiting identities as threatening. We should not hastily condemn ourselves for such feelings, while continuing to be mindful of them, for, as we dig deeper through introspection into our minds' sedimentary layers, we are likely to find many harsh and prejudicial tendencies, implanted there by Nature for some generalized purpose that reason and compassion can now more efficiently accomplish.

The sex instinct, for example, was implanted in us for a very specific and important end. But it is a blind mole-like imperative that cannot be unquestioningly pursued. When we gaze at an erotic photo on the Internet or in a magazine, there is, in truth, no reproductive opportunity there, just glossy paper, or a light image cast upon a screen. Yet our instincts don't know better. They tell us that this is what we want.

The sex instinct, immoderately and illegitimately pursued, has not only led to crimes, but has caused numerous people to be lured into unhappy relationships with partners who are unsuitable for them. None of this even begins to imply that the instinct itself has no point, or that it shouldn't have been there, to begin with. It is not simply some despicable abomination leading to hell; still, its blunt and unbridled tendencies do have to be modified by the subtler tones of our more-refined hearts and intellects to avoid becoming destructive. A wariness toward outsiders, of people whose customs or appearance, nationality, dress style, economic structure, etc. is somehow different from ours, is also an instinct planted in us by Nature for a generalized, inexact reason. It expressed itself in an ugly way during the 2016 Presidential race, and in its immediate aftermath, by dogmatists on both sides.

People find security in protective groups. They seek out those whose goals, tendencies, interests, and backgrounds mesh with their own identifiably, and after having "tested the waters," forge a solid protective bond with them. In primitive times, such protective groups attacked other groups in a competitive quest for food and other scarce resources. The concept of nationhood can itself be traced back to such rudimentary forms of defensive group security.

We witness this force in operation, when working groups are formed. When people are first thrown together, they begin to feel each other out. They not only look for things that can help them to accomplish the explicit goals of the team, but also those that identify common interests and congenial modes of thought. "Hey how about those Yankees! That was quite a game on Sunday night. A 7 and oh shutout." Some will heartily join in, responding to such cues with alacrity, while others will remain listlessly "on the sidelines." In the final stage of "conforming and norming" when the group's cohesiveness has all but fully formed, the unified membership will expel all who don't seem to belong as if they were a virus.

While this defensive group instinct, like the sexual one, has been planted in us by Nature, it can be just as easily misguided. Differences in religion, race and nationality are ultimately superficial, and we may easily find that we have more in common with those who are presumed to be different, than with members of our designated tribe.

Human beings collectively are evolving in a more spiritual direction, sloughing off those primitive instincts that do more to divide than unite us. Given advancements in technology which cause our more backward-leaning tendencies to threaten all life on earth, the current evolutionary trend is to prod us to a state beyond them, and beyond their now immeasurably more hazardous outcomes. This makes our physical instincts, as we develop in a more spiritual way, akin to evolutionary training wheels, wheels that we need to remove to progress.

In this cutting-edge process, it is precisely an accommodation to what is different that enriches our thought and enables us to grow. The greater the difference, the more we are compelled to stretch our spiritual tendons, and to challenge the stifling limits of our current understanding to grasp it; the more it reveals the flaws and challenges the deficiencies of our standard, more limited perspective, the better it is for us. It is an obstacle that becomes as a catalyst for growth. But since we know that we can only "bend so far before we break," we will want to retain our distinctive identities as well, and this is where our protective instincts tend to obstructively kick in. Like our other instincts, they developed for a reason, and like those other instincts, they are basic, blind, and inexact.

In describing my own approach to life, I am apt to say that the only thing I hate is hatred and the only thing I can't tolerate is intolerance, but even that, upon finer examination, is revealed to be a bigoted view, one that tends to serve my ego far more than the unvarnished truth. It is all too likely to send me on a vindictive rampage against those I feel are "intolerably intolerant," or obnoxious in some way, feeding, as such, into a deluded sense of superiority, into the isolating and limiting idea that my way of life or thought is fundamentally better than somebody else's.

As the Bhagavad Gita observes, "Facing us in the field of battle are teachers, fathers and sons; grandsons, grandfathers, wives' brothers; mothers' brothers and fathers of wives." (Mascaro 1974, 46). This literary backdrop provides the perfect metaphor for the start of our spiritual journey. We seek comfort and security, by nature, in that which is familiar, in that which is known, in that which is identifiably similar. Thus, we cling to our own family, our own tribe, our own race, our own country, blindly and unthinkingly. This blind allegiance, while associated at times with certain admirable qualities, does have its definite dark side. We take refuge in such things as ritual, custom, and family environment, while ignoring the needs of the larger human community. We build our walls high, while keeping our attitude toward outsiders cool. We join with those who look like us, while instinctively fearing—and sometimes even reactively hating—those who do not. And we have threatened all life on earth by viewing the unity of the nation rather than of the world as the supreme commonality. The Gita shows us, from the very outset of its drama, that we cannot ultimately take shelter in such partial and limited things. In the reinforcing language of the Dhammapada, "that is not a safe refuge, that is not the best refuge." (Babbitt 2012, verse 189, location 372). The prejudices engendered by instinct and by early life conditioning must be abandoned as we grow older and wiser, however tenaciously they may cling, no matter what obstacles we may face, or however fierce the battle that ensues in our strenuous effort to dislodge them.

Chapter 3

The Most Profound Religious
Statement of All

Arguably, the most profound religious statement of all time is not one derived from any religious book, but from Shakespeare, when he wrote "to thine own self be true." (Shakespeare, Hamlet 2012, Hamlet, Act 1, Sc.3, p.45) Each of us has a purpose (or more than one)—that is written upon our hearts. When we find it, we will know it; then we will recognize who we are, and what we are meant to accomplish. While mentors, guides, and books -certainly books like the Gita and the Bible (and hopefully, to some degree, this one as well)— can direct you to your heart's wisdom, they cannot live it for you. That you, alone, are properly equipped to do.

I remember attending college with a student who, whenever I asked him a question about life, would thumb furiously through the Bible looking for the appropriate answer. The Bible is a monumental work, one that, while derived from the humblest of origins, has served as the foundation value system for empires, nations, and kings, It is one that, as I fully believe, contains the inspired word of God. Yet another testimony to Christ's exalted nature is the near miraculous rise of the Christian faith, and the enduring nature of its message. Its spirit of humility has resounded through the ages as proud empires fell. But the Bible is meant to be employed as a guide and not as a crutch or shield; it should enrich our individual understanding, not "protect" us—or excuse us—from exercising it. To accomplish our purpose in life, we must feel and think our way through. We must "find our place in the orchestra,"[1] and read the language of truth as it is written upon our hearts, not merely in any separate work, however exalted. Spiritual texts are but a mirror that reflects the truth within, or alternatively expressed, they are lamps that illuminate the jewel of understanding, revealing where it can be mined; they don't mine it for us.

NOTE

1. An expression I previously used in Guideposts to the Heart. (G. Hallett 2011)

Chapter 4

Obstacles in General

Given that there are so many obstacles in life, how can we ever hope to overcome them? Is there a reliable map to progress, perhaps even more than one? Are there underlying laws with predictable effects, laws that govern our success, determine our progress, and that can help us to attain our goals? Thankfully, the answer to all of these questions is "yes," for we have been gifted, throughout history, with a number of faithful guides to progress. This book focuses on the practical wisdom contained in four of the most prominent: The Tao Te Ching, the New Testament of the Bible, the Dhammapada, and the (Hindu) Bhagavad Gita. It also includes, at key junctures, excerpts from a useful little work called *The Voice of the Silence*. It is recommended that you obtain a copy of each of these sources, if not several varied translations, not only to imbibe the message delivered here, but to directly absorb the wisdom that each of them independently contains. Together they comprise a depth of meaning and wonder that has inspired the rapt attention of millions for centuries.

There will be occasions when you are confused about something, about what you should do or about a particular point of doctrine, and one key passage from one particular translation will make the matter clear to you. It will do so in a way that the others won't. That doesn't necessarily mean this one translation is best, only better at clarifying that one particular point. So, having more than one translation is generally preferred.

Among the sources enumerated above, the Bible, as the cornerstone work of Western culture, needs no introduction. What may need to be further explained is why I have focused on the four gospels, rather than on the Bible, as a whole.

Organized Christianity, in its commonplace form, makes two routine assumptions: 1) that all parts of the Bible are equally inspired and 2) that prophesy and revelation ended with them. The first assumption should appear questionable to anyone who takes the time to read that unique and epic guide. In the earliest parts of the Bible, we see elements of a primitive

19

mindset at work in which animal sacrifice and the loose attribution of natural events to supernatural causes is rife. Moreover, the tenor of separate Old Testament chapters is different. The tone of "Exodus" is different from that of "Wisdom." And while, in "Psalms," we find some of the most beautiful passages in the Bible, there David praises God for providing him with the means to crush the necks of his enemies, a sentiment that falls vastly short of either Christ's tender mercy or the exalted precepts of Mahayana Buddhism. [1]

The God of the Old Testament, vs. the Christ of the New, is a God of wrath and jealousy who leads a primitive people out of bondage by constantly herding them into line. Yet perhaps the difference here between the Old and the New has less to do with God than it does with Man; in much the same way as an adult would speak differently to another adult than he would to a child, God relates differently to Man in the Old vs. New Testaments. The receptivity of Man to God's higher ways, in the early Old Testament, had yet to fully evolve; in Christ, it reached its culmination.

One time my cat, Oreo, captured and killed a mouse. Soon afterwards, he marched triumphantly into the living room and plopped the grisly offering in front of me. He then sat back on his haunches, positioning himself squarely behind the carcass of the dead mouse (so that I couldn't miss viewing both the remains and him together, unmistakably associating the one with the other). He held there for a time, sporting an indelible expression of comingled pride and affection on his furry face. Although I had no need for a dead mouse—and would have preferred to do without one—I knew that he had presented it to me out of love. He was thinking of me at the same time as he was providing for himself. So, the last thing I would have considered doing, under the circumstances, would be to deem his offering unworthy by yelling at him, or by chasing him and the mouse carcass away.

In Old Testament times when a lamb or calf was slaughtered, it would have been, without question, a very real sacrifice. Such commodities were hard to come by, and, in the raw and unforgiving environment of the ancient Middle East, were the basis upon which the individual's own life was precariously sustained.

In modern Christian rituals, and as part of the same linear tradition, the practice of animal sacrifice is implied in the notion of Christ as "the lamb of God." That being said, during the course of Sunday mass, we don't trot a lamb, calf, or goat up to the altar, there to ritually slit its throat, capture its blood, and burn its carcass. If we did, we would no doubt be doing so in the midst of some horrified parishioners, with the police and ASPCA as regular attendees! In modern times, the religious impulse has evolved beyond the barbaric slaughter of innocent life, a gruesome practice which we are most likely today to identify, along with the Tibetans, as the rough equivalent of feeding a mother her own children. The higher expressions of sacrifice, the ones we are accustomed to now, are the ones that developed later as civilization itself progressed.

So, regardless of any difference between the inspired nature of the Old and the New, a point that remains moot, in the life and teachings of Christ, we see exemplified and recorded for posterity the most refined essence of moral wisdom and compassion. It is a greater expression of truth, one divested of its underlying tradition's more primitive overtones, and of a sort that the modern world in the nuclear age, most desperately needs to survive. While we may not have been ready for it, in ancient times, in its direct and undiluted form, we desperately need it now.

Love God and love thy neighbor can be aptly described as the "E=MC2" of morality, while "the Sermon on the Mount" has been praised and admired by spokespeople of various religious traditions, most prominently by Swami Prabhavandanda in his inspired commentary.[2] Judaism and Islam both have their higher mystic traditions; the first can be found in the teachings of Sufism as exemplified by the writings of Hazrat Innyat Khan, and the second in the Kaballah. Each of these sources liberally references the works of other faiths, and is notably free of intolerance.

The second questionable assumption, noted above, effectively denies the validity of any subsequent revelation, such as that of Edgar Cayce, which has made a colossal contribution to spirituality, let alone to the beautiful and inspired writings of someone from a separate spiritual tradition, such as those of Ramakrishna. Here the two questionable assumptions would appear to promote the cause of religious authority far more than that of religious Truth.

This book makes the friendly and inclusive assumption that Truth, like sunlight filtered through a forest glade, casts its impression in different combinations of light and shade upon the legacy of various cultures. For some, the foliage is thick, the vision of Truth, itself, unclear, while with others the sun's rays are seen to burst through more openly. As *The Voice of the Silence* more explicitly observes, "The light from the One Master, the one unfading golden light of Spirit, shoots its effulgent beams on the disciple from the very first. Its rays thread through the thick dark clouds of matter. / Now here, now there, these rays illumine it, like sun-sparks light the earth through the foliage of jungle growth . . ." (Blavatsky 2011, 14, location 173)

To use a different analogy, let's say I have a good friend I decide to visit one day. I show up at his house wearing a T shirt and Khakis. He immediately recognizes me and greets me warmly; but when, the next day, I show up wearing a three-piece suit, instead of welcoming me, he says, "get out of here, right now; I don't know who you are!" We might conclude that my friend is shallow or deranged; the least that can be said is that he is not terribly perceptive. Yet it is much the same where the identical truth is clothed in different garbs, the garbs of distinct cultural legacies. There is but one Truth, but varying means to realizing it, different for different people of different religious temperaments, "different strokes, for different folks." There is but one Way, as Christ proclaimed, but multiple means of travel.

In my own quest for truth, I never properly understood the depth of spirituality buried within the Catholicism of my birth until I studied Hinduism and the teachings of Yogananda, never deeply fathomed the idea of karma, the process of sowing what you reap, until I encountered its more detailed description in Buddhism, never fully understood the opening line of the (Buddhist) Dhammapada, "all we are is the result of what we have thought," until I immersed myself in the contemporary New Thought literature. The supposition of One Truth, in various guises, casts the venerated works considered, not merely as guides to follow as we traverse our way through life, but as alternative reference sources for cross-checking the truth to verify how clearly and completely any one approach is grasping it.

There is a process by which our perception of Truth has been known to arise and decline. It has done so repeatedly in the lives of individuals and throughout the history of the world.

The founders of the great religions were unique visionaries who caught a glimpse of something beyond what most people know, typically through a transcendent means or exalted faculty beyond the grasp of ordinary people. That is why Christ spoke in parables. It is why Mara's recommendation to Buddha, on the eve of the latter's enlightenment that he should keep his discovery to himself (as no one else would understand it), was "the Great Tempter's" most convincing argument. (Smith 1991, 87).

Such ideas, bordering as they are to begin with, on the fringe of comprehension, are then codified as sacred texts, to be further represented (re-presented) through the flawed medium of language as intellectually graspable constructs. These constructs have, in turn, been filtered down to us through the hazy lens of time, perhaps bequeathed that way only after being subject to an untold number of questionable revisions, revisions whose marks would be traceless today, and whose motivating politics no longer pertains. The meaning of such dead issues would indeed be incomprehensible to us now, like the strange intonations of a lost foreign tongue, rendering the resulting modifications even more difficult to discern.

The contemporary Catholic Church, now confined to its role as a religious institution, was literally the "power behind the throne" of Europe's kings for centuries. During the Crusades, and on behalf of Christian ideals, ideals which emphasized mercy and love, "blood flowed ankle deep through the streets of Jerusalem." The Church is now benefiting greatly in no longer being distracted from its spiritual mission by an "absolute (secular) power (that) can easily corrupt absolutely." But the distortions we have just intimated have most likely occurred already, and would now be virtually untraceable.

The decline of spirituality within the life and soul of the culture parallels that which occurs in the life and soul of the individual, as described in the story of Genesis and its fall of Man:

1. At first, we have a reliable connection to our Source—to God, the Living Universe, or however we choose to identify the Ultimate Reality of Life. Because we have "sought first the kingdom of God"—or in the case of Adam and Eve, never (initially) left it, all else has been added unto us. We are overwhelmed with joy over benefits received, and our sincere and sustained gratitude opens the door to further boons yet to come. Our minds are clear, and that clear perspective, wise. We are attuned to our genuine needs and to the greater needs of Life. Because of this reliable attunement, we travel smoothly down the road to success.

2. A lesser pleasure or pursuit (an apple on the tree of knowledge) lures us away from our Source to become the main objective. Such lesser joys are not evil. Yet they were never intended to occupy center stage. When we substitute the lesser for the greater, we lose our reliable connection to our Source. Out of tune, our lives become broken instruments, unable to render the dulcet harmonies they were originally designed to emit.

3. While, in phase 2, we abandoned the state where we could realistically satisfy our needs by keeping our centers true, in phase 3 we move even further away from our Source. Our minds, by now, have become densely clouded by the undertakings associated with a false pursuit of happiness. Though what we are doing can never, in the long run, satisfy us, having lost the clarity of thought associated with a valid attunement, we are no longer equipped to appreciate our own predicament. We become easily angry and frustrated, as that anger and frustration increasingly become our prevailing state of mind.

4. At the culmination of this process, having become thoroughly frustrated, as we must now inevitably be, with our misguided pursuit of pleasure, and seeing all our original joys as cheats, we begin to feel that life itself has betrayed us. We become increasingly bitter and cynical. Separated from our Source and unable to find relief or joy in those pleasures that we have inordinately—and thus falsely—pursued, we reach the depths of degradation, taking solace in the only remaining refuge we are then able to recognize, that of cynicism, cruelty, and hatred. Our natures become demonic. Unable to realize any real happiness of our own, we begin to find, in the frustrated hopes of others, a perverted form of alternative satisfaction. As this approach is fully "adharmic," violating the truth of our oneness with others, and denying any compassion

for them, we sink deeper and deeper into lower and lower layers of desolation and unhappiness.[3]

Hopefully at or before this level, we begin to turn around. We have our own "road to Damascus" conversion. It is here that life will use pain and obstacles as an efficient goad to recovery. The wiser of the unwise will use the tools of this phase to mend their errant ways; but the thoroughly cruel will become even more stubbornly angry. Their hearts become hardened as the Pharaoh's was in Exodus.

Avoiding this trap is only achieved by a willingness to understand. When we can forgive life its trespasses, realize the value of those obstacles that have come our way, and recognize the truth that they have arrived due to our wandering away to begin with, we can reascend the ladder of moral refinement and initiate our return to phase one—to the recovery of what Yogananda described as our original nature as "a unified harmony or Eden." (Yogananda 2003, 38)

As we proceed on our quest for truth, we need to clear the debris from our minds and trust again in our hearts. We must seek validation, not in the siren call of custom or in a limited modern materialism, however validated it may seem to be by an outwardly-directed science, but in the Source of Truth within. This is different from arrogantly claiming that we already thoroughly know, or know better than the authors of the Dhammapada, the Tao Te Ching, the Gita, or the Bible. It is only that at the deepest layers of our being, as conscious members of a Living universe, we are always and forever one with Truth. It is within that this Truth will come to us in complete and living form. When our cups are empty, we need to return to that well, for even the most respectable religion is subject to a departure from its most essential principles.

Once we progress to some degree, along the spiritual path we have chosen, using the aforementioned aids or others, we realize that our relationship to Life is less the beaten dog's, and more like Man's to fire. Fire provided Primitive Man with warmth. It cooked his food. It was a weapon to wield against an abundance of natural enemies. Today, we use the equivalent of fire in much the same way, stoking our furnaces with oil to heat our homes. But, if we stick our hands into the flames—of a campfire or a furnace—we will inevitably get burned, and not just occasionally or randomly, but each and every time. Both the comforts and dangers of fire are experienced in a way that is lawful and consistent. So long as we respect it, and maintain a proper relationship to it, fire will always be our friend. We may accidentally transgress the laws associated with fire, but the consequences of that accident will be lawful and consistent nonetheless. It is the same with the circumstances of life, in how we relate to the boon of our material gifts. So long as we enjoy and experience them properly, they will remain beneficial. It is only those who have been burned by life through their improper relationship to it that tend, in the end, to disrespect their material treasures entirely. To realize success and happiness, we must understand and honor life's principles and laws, and proceed in accordance with them.

NOTES

1. As the full passage goes, "Thou hast also given me the necks of mine enemies, that I might destroy them that hate me." (Bible Hub, n.d., King James Bible, Psalm 18:40)

2. The Sermon on the Mount According to Vedanta. (Prabhavananda 1972)

3. What is "dharmic" is in keeping with the spiritual laws of existence; what is "adharmic" is opposed to them.

Chapter 5

The Spiritual Treasures of the Past

A large part of the fascination with such films as Raiders of the Lost Ark is the intriguing possibility that there may have been ancient civilizations more advanced, in key ways, than ours. Though less technologically astute, many were more spiritually wise. Having less of what is superfluous, they had more of what counts in a closer connection to Life and to creation's Source; it was a connection forged in an ancient realm of miracles, beneficently removed from the frenetic and coldly materialistic domain of our emotionally turbulent contemporary lives. Not everything, most assuredly, was better—and many things certainly worse. Those who lived then were nonetheless free of the modern and supremely hazardous imbalance that conjoins a vast—though still limited—knowledge with wisdom's precarious absence, a volatile combination that in the last century and during the Cold War most prominently, brought all life on earth to a nuclear brink of extinction. It may well do so again, given that the underlying cause in our persistent human failings remains consistently unaddressed. Yet there remains hope, for here, lying still and dormant, like one of Indiana Jones' proposed archeological digs, the wisdom of the past remains for us to mine, with many valuable treasures to uncover, containing perhaps, if we are fortunate, those crucial keys to Life and living that can save us in the end.

Chapter 6

The First Principle

The Principle of Flow

In a way reminiscent of the Bible's "my yoke is easy, and my burden is light," (Bible Hub, n.d., Matt. 11:30), the Tao Te Ching proclaims, "My words are easy just to understand:/ To live by them is very easy too; Yet it appears that none in all the world/Can understand or make them come to life." (Tzu 1983, verse 70, p. 146) There is no degree in Spirituality, as there is in Religion or Theology, nor should there be, for the truths of Spirit are not difficult to understand, only difficult to apply and to live. The truth that is plainest to see, yet hardest to accept is that of flow, of continuous change.[12]

Change is so ubiquitous, that we needn't look far to find it. Standing at a crosswalk on a Friday afternoon, you see traffic moving, people walking, shifting masses of clouds billowing overhead. Even those aspects of life that seem stable are constantly re-presenting themselves to our experience. Visual data is experienced as a stream of photons, sounds as sound waves. Even if what we observe were not visibly in motion, we, as the observers certainly are. All that doesn't change is our concepts, and it is this routine and unconscious substitution of concepts for reality, reinforced by the assurance of collective belief, that gives a deceptive "solidity" to what resembles, more than anything else, a 3-dimensional movie in which we are not merely observers but participants.[3] In the words of Herman Hesse from his novel, Steppenwolf, it is a ". . . MAGIC THEATRE—FOR MADMEN ONLY—PRICE OF ADMITTANCE -YOUR MIND." (Das, Remember: Be Here Now 1971, 102) The madness of ordinary living is in denying the truth of change.[4]

When Jesus said, "The foxes have holes and the birds of the air have nests; but the Son of Man has nowhere to lay his head," (Bible Hub, n.d., King James 2000 Bible, Luke 9:58) he might as well have been stating a metaphor for change in the human condition. Though we long inwardly for security, all we outwardly witness is perpetual transformation matched by a growing uncertainty, should we misread the change as permanence; here, amidst a swirl of transformation, sits revealed the great irony of our existence and what the Buddha described as the root of all of our suffering. Although, when we are standing still, we may appear not to change, our hearts continue to pump blood, our bodies relentlessly regenerate. We might look back on an earlier time and exclaim, "wow, was that really me!" Yet that change didn't occur in a single leap; it had been happening all along. In light of this fact, we would advance much quicker and save ourselves much unnecessary suffering if we were to be more proactive in our willingness and recognized need to change. We should say ahead of time, after we do what we must do, what can I do today that, while it may not be immediately necessary, accounts more amply for tomorrow, where tomorrow will be unavoidably different from today.

Acknowledging and coping with change is the key to a happy life. Those who see existence as a realm of suffering and those who view it as a journey of joy don't live in separate worlds; they experience the same world in different ways. One futilely looks to the change to satisfy the need for permanent joy and security. The other discovers the changeless amid the change, and can thus be entertained by the sensory realm's kaleidoscopic variety, knowing that the source of enduring happiness has been identified beyond it. This is the essential difference between the enlightened and the unenlightened perspective, between viewing Nirvana from the perspective of Samsara, and Samsara from the perspective of Nirvana.

The Stella Awards (comparable to the better-known Darwin Awards) tells an amusing story of an Oklahoma woman who, thinking that cruise control was autopilot, left the wheel unattended to head for the back of her Winnebago and make herself a sandwich. As the road on which the camper was travelling was fairly long and straight, there was no apparent problem for a while. But as soon as the gravel turned, the van veered off course, careening over the line and crashing. (The RV Forum Community n.d.)

Our customary approach to life and to happiness is similarly ignorant. Not noticing the change that occurs from moment to moment, we think that we are okay. We believe we can find permanence and stability in all those experiences that are forever passing away, and in continuous separation from our Source or God. But when change catches up to us, we find ourselves trapped in its snares. In the words of the Dhammapada, "Mara the tempter crushes you again and again."[5]

Buddhism refers to the reliable sources of security as the Buddha, the Sanga, and the Dharma. The Buddha, the ultimate source of security, is the equivalent in different terms of our Source or God. The Sangha is the group of people who are on the same path as we are, and who are determined to achieve the same goal. As noted by Napoleon Hill, it is only by joining with like-minded individuals that our personal aims can be efficiently accomplished. (Hill 2008, 1–59) The third is the Dharma, or Law of Life. It allows us to take refuge in the way things are, and represents for those who are honest and true, and who "hunger and thirst for righteousness," a release from the need to bow mindlessly before prevailing trends, for they find shelter under the canopy of laws that are set in stone by God and that proceed directly from Life.

It is amazing how many people make critical compromises on their ambitions or integrity because they feel compelled to supplicate before a domineering or corrupt external authority. They then continue through life as emotional amputees; part of their essential humanity—and any legitimate basis for self-respect—has been savagely stripped away. They are not drones; nor are they, any longer, complete people either; and the reminder of what they have lost is borne like a battle wound. Knowing that there is a higher law than what we arrogant, venal humans have created for ourselves gives us the courage to speak up where our principles are at stake, to take reasonable risks to improve our lots and lives, and to remain honorable and undiminished individuals.

To achieve harmony in our lives, it is essential to become one with the Flow. Alan Watts referred to the Tao, itself, as "the watercourse way," the fluid way that wends itself deftly around obstacles as is if they weren't even there. (Watts, Tao: The Watercourse Way 1975) It is a way that accounts fully for the ubiquitous nature of change. Perhaps the deeper truth behind the Christian ritual of Baptism through which we are transformed by "water and the Spirit" (Bible Hub, n.d., American Standard Version, John 3:5) refers to basically the same thing, to a return to "the watercourse way," to life's underlying flow from a state of delusion and clinging. It is a course that leads to a recovery of our genuine spiritual selves.

Everyone is wary of transitions. We all get invested, to one degree or another, in what and where we are. This is natural. It is even helpful and practical at times. But it is precisely what gives birth to our most characteristic obstacle, the obstacle of unwarranted attachment.

As we commute to work, to our own sphere of life and activity, we pass interminable lines of factories and shops that fall along our route. We don't usually give them a first—let alone a second—thought. Yet it is amazing to consider how each one of these locations is a mini-world in itself, a self-contained domain in which tight workplace dramas are enacted in a way comparable to our own. Each is a separate arena in which people, much like us, are as totally invested in their own limited situations, where they proceed, like us, as if that one corner of the universe is really all there is.

In *Seth Speaks*, Seth refers to the plenitude of plays—plays, yes, yet serious plays—which blanket the surface of our earthly reality. They are plays in which untold numbers of people are satisfying their desires, confronting their flaws, and realizing their dreams. (Roberts 1972, 53–69) Someday, maybe not today or tomorrow, but eventually and decisively, we will find ourselves in a place other than where we are now, with a different set of conditions and challenges. We tend to believe that, when we leave or are extracted from our current situation, there will be nothing left for us, that there is this one plan or situation or none, that we will either succeed with it or fall from a sphere of heightened creative activity and purpose into nothingness. Yet how we land, as in the martial arts, depends on how we fall. Life is infinitely creative, and that creative potential is astonishing. There are an untold variety of adventures waiting for us, more friends to meet, and, if we believe in reincarnation, to perhaps meet again, in other narratives yet to unfold. There may be promises we made to ourselves before our eyes first opened, of things we wanted—and needed—to do.

When circumstances do change for us, we are likely to find ourselves, through the natural unfolding of events in an ultimately benevolent universe, in one of two conditions: someplace we like that tightly corresponds to what we have imagined and desired, delivered to us through the Law of Attraction, or one in which we can learn and grow, so as to manifest a better reality more efficiently later on. That ultimately beneficent—though challenging—transition will, if it is utilized correctly, teach us to conquer our fears and overcome our failings. It will enable us to scale the even greater heights that face us, in this life and, as a developing soul, in the wondrous great beyond.

A practical way to confront the reality of change, and to break through the bubble of immediacy, is through memory review. By plunging into the briny depths of the past, we realize that where we are now is not where we have always been or will forever be. We will then begin to see life, in all its bewildering ups and downs, in its proper perspective. To recollect the past, and to learn from it, is to engage with and to live properly in the present.

The Bible speaks to an awareness of change, to the temporary nature of our limited life situations, in stating that, ". . . we are all strangers before you, and sojourners, as were all our fathers: our days on the earth are as a shadow, and there is no abiding." (Bible Hub, n.d., King James 2000 Bible, 1 Chronicles 29:15) This doesn't imply that our souls have no future, only that the passing scene will pass. Who we are essentially will move on, bearing upon the protean sculpture of our evolving souls the etchings of our prior actions and experiences. That we have starred in one play may make us, if we have acted well, better thespians in the next. If not, we are likely to find our spiritual futures decidedly more troublesome. Remarkably, this starting point to truth in a recognition of change is not achieved through any act of faith, but through keen and mindful observation, by what the Buddhists call, "bringing the mind face to face with reality," for the facts of our spiritual lives are as demonstrable to us as scientific ones are to an experimenter in his lab.

As the Bhagavad Gita proclaims, "the unreal never is, the Real never is not." (Mascaro 1974, 49) When mindfulness allows us to see change as change, when we stop trying to grasp Life's river in our tightly-clenched fists, in finally and fully letting go of what can never be held to begin with, we find ourselves smack dab in the middle of that which never changes, that which constitutes the foundational Truth, the ultimate reality of existence. It is a Truth that has never gone anywhere, a Truth that has always been. It is that Reality, that Truth, upon which we can rely, and ultimately nothing else—nothing else at all. This is another basic realization that is, at first, very difficult to accept, but ultimately beneficent in its workings. As stated by the Buddha, there is "an Unbecome, Unborn, Unmade, Unformed," by which we can escape from "that which is become, born, made, and formed." (Evans-Wentz, The Tibetan Book of the Dead 2000, 68) In realizing it, we will have followed the river to its oceanic end, and made our epic return home. It is there that we must dwell, as the changeless amid the change, if we are to live happily, peacefully and securely.

It is further worth noting that the change we fear in the Flow is in not necessarily negative either, for the transitions that brings loss, like fresh bubbling streams, also bring renewal. There are, nonetheless, times when we adamantly refuse to change; our lives then become stagnant ponds, that, in not coursing fluidly, turn fetid. We know we should move forward, and we don't. We take a blind and foolish refuge in a false and easy security, becoming attached to what we have, not recognizing such attachment itself as factually untenable. We accept the "not so good" as "not so bad;" in the process we ensure the doom of our noblest hopes, and affix a binding seal to the parchment of our continued unhappiness. Once we settle for being miserable, we deepen our negativity demonically. Recognizing no solution apart from that which we are fearfully unwilling to apply, we become hateful and cynical toward others and resentful of life, as a whole. Our cowardice glues us in place, as it did Arjuna on his eve of battle. Had he remained there, continuing to succumb to his reluctance, his destiny would have been quite different—ignominious and dark not bright and legendary, as it has since been memorialized.

The proper and positive relationship to life, one that unflinchingly acknowledges the Principle of Flow, was ideally encapsulated by Blake in the first stanza of his poem, "Eternity." As Blake wrote therein:

> He who binds to himself a joy
> Does the winged life destroy;
> He who kisses the joy as it flies
> Lives in eternity's sun rise.

To bind oneself to a joy is to become attached. It is to live in a way that is constricted, narrow and destructive. As the Tao Te Ching states, "grabbing misses . . ." (Tzu 1983, 138)

We experience this all too often in our romantic relationships where one person becomes desperate and possessive. This serves only, and contrary to his intent, to drive the object of his affection further away. "Kissing the joy as it flies" means that we experience and fully engage with life. We don't hold a cross up to it with quivering hand to chase away its demons. We buy into it all; we wholeheartedly express and receive love; we enjoy our time with our friends. But when the moment finally comes to let go, we learn to embrace it, and our own inevitable sadness, with lightness, courage, and love. We realize, In this way, through skillful interaction with the events of our individual lives, the brilliance of immortal love, what Blake calls "eternity's sunrise," shining behind the veil of all of our transitory and more limited experiences. This is indeed the best way to live.

The movie, *Terminator 2: Judgement Day*, featured a battle between two cyborgs from the future. The first was composed of the most solid tensile steel, the 2nd, more advanced, of an alloy that could go from solid to liquid, and then back again. Bullets would "splash" into this 2nd cyborg, then the liquefied metal would flow back into the "wound," as it were never there. At one point in this futuristic drama, the second, more versatile cyborg, is frozen by liquid nitrogen, then shattered into fragments. But once reheated, the fragments revert to their liquid state, and the cybernetic entity is enabled to re-form. The rigid structure of the first cyborg allowed for no such adaptability. Its mechanical arm mangled, it had no option but to proceed on its preprogrammed mission without it.

I often think these 2 cyborgs, and of the differences between them, when I ponder the fluid nature of the Tao. If we are like the Tao, we wend our way around obstacles, rather than being bluntly battered by them; when shattered by the harshness of circumstance, we fluidly re-form. Such fluidity is a tremendous advantage. It is not a sign of weakness but of strength to give in and to flow. Most—if not all—of our traditionally-defined virtues are, at basis, expressions of such fluidity, our vices, a denial of it.

When we are humble rather than proud, we flow by relinquishing a static self-image. We skillfully adapt to the course of change rather than clinging painfully to those ideas and circumstances that life has already contradicted. When we are patient, we proceed smoothly with the Flow rather than lurching prematurely forward. When we are loving, we are open to the free-flowing movement of energy between our engaged hearts. When we are untruthful, it is only because we are delusively clinging to something, something that no longer pertains, to a faded scene along life's riverbank, one that has already passed us by.

The "original sin" (in effect) for Buddhism is ignorance. We predicate our lives on a false premise, and thereby generate actions that rebound to our detriment. What we are specifically ignorant of is the fluidity of time, and the instability of the material world. Not that it is ever that difficult to see, only difficult to accept, for we have conditioned ourselves to look in only one direction—outward—for meaning and joy. Once convinced that we will never find it there, we believe that we will never find it anywhere; yet it is in the very absence of clinging that the greater value of life is allowed to emerge. When we are able, in the depths of mindfulness, to see and to accept the world as it is, we will automatically generate truthful causes that lead reliably to happiness. It is then that the beautiful, changeable things that the outside world presents will suddenly appear to be no less wondrous for being a transitory part of our experience, but rather more beautiful and treasured in their passing. When we let go instead of clinging, what we are left with is wonder and love, the essence of all of our experiences, a light that guides our way home.

Think of all the cataclysmic events that once took place where there is now only stillness and silence. How remarkable that such events should have impacted the globe so decisively, and now be mysteriously gone. We view in our minds the beloved images of departed relatives and friends now beyond our reach, lots and yards we played in as children, buildings we occupied and roads we travelled that we frequent now only in memories and dreams. We study wars and other sweeping events of the past upon whose pivotal ruins new creative structures have emerged, furnishing in their distinct social and architectural contours but a shadowy hint of all that once preceded them.

There may be planets and civilizations lost to time where lives much like ours played themselves out with not so much as a hint of their existence left to adorn the present stage. Yet perhaps their life still resonates through the music of the Akashic Records, where their wonder and beauty can be glimpsed once again.[6] And if God's Infinite Mind does exist, then what greater source of comfort can there be than that our lives and the lives of all others should be perfectly cradled in the womb of that incomprehensible vastness, in the light of an Intelligence so radiant it can't even be directly observed. As Yogananda states, "What more quickly liberating thought than 'God is' . . ." (Yogananda 2003, 153) Then we see that what we were so worried about, the loss of our cramped little selves, finds both its foundational fear alleviated, and its cause to matter less from the standpoint of a universe that is eternally conscious and permanently alive, a universe to which we forever belong.

On my shelf sits a collection of old CDs. Although a certain song may not be playing now, I know I can fire up my changer, pop in the appropriate disc, and play it whenever I want. The universe may work in a similar way.

Is it really so hard to believe that, in the Infinite Mind of God, nothing in truth is lost, that the song of our lives plays on, there in the Akashic Records, ready like Frosty the Snowman to, in due season, take form once again? It may just not be playing right now, with time being "Nature's way," as John Archibald Wheeler proclaimed, "of preventing everything from happening all at once." As Krishna says to Arjuna near the beginning of the Bhagavad Gita, ". . . we all have been for all time: I, and thou, and those kings of men. And we all shall be for all time, we all for ever and ever." (Mascaro 1974, 49)

Once we finish with life's fretful game, the set is returned to its shelf, but remains there still, ready for the next round. To awaken ultimately from that game-like state to the mind of God, is, as all who have experienced it affirm, to know the universe as perfect, to recognize nothing as ultimately lacking, with that underlying perfection rendered, miraculously and ironically, even more so by the imperfect play, the dreamlike drama, that preceded it. It is by acknowledging and overcoming the bread of shame and in clearing those obstacles that once seemed so intractably formidable which makes the end of our arduous road, that much more fulfilling and glorious.

NOTES

1. As noted by Christmas Humphreys, "life is flow." (Humphreys 1962, 28)

2. R. B. Blakney has likewise noted the similarity of these two passages in the commentary section of his Tao Te Ching translation. (Tzu 1983)

3. The subject of change receives similar treatment in my earlier book, Humanity at the Crossroads. (G. J. Hallett 2015)

4. The ultimate origin of this citation from Remember: Be Here Now is Herman Hesse's Steppenwolf.

5. The full quote is "Dig up the root of thirst, as he who wants the sweet-scented usira root must dig up the birana grass, lest Mara crush you again and again, even as a stream crushes the reeds." (Babbitt 2012, verse 337, location 643)

6. As described by the Edgar Cayce Association for Research and Enlightenment, "The Akashic Records," or "The Book of Life," can be equated to the universe's super-computer system. It is this system that acts as the central storehouse of all information for every individual who has ever lived upon the earth. More than just a reservoir of events, the Akashic Records contain every deed, word, feeling, thought, and intent that has ever occurred at any time in the history of the world. Much more than simply a memory storehouse, however, these Akashic Records are interactive in that they have a tremendous influence upon our everyday lives, our relationships, our feelings and belief systems, and the potential realities we draw to us. (Edgar Cayce's A.R.E. Association for Research and Enlightenment n.d.)

Chapter 7

Faith, Trust, and the Principle of Flow

Every transitional moment in life involves a leap of faith into the new and the unknown. Most often, when we take that leap, we don't plummet off a cliff or spin off into the stratosphere (even without our space cadet boots). That is because the currents of our purpose and destiny carry us invisibly along. It is only when we cling to the passing scenery that we add imbalance to the Flow. And the resulting distortions produce their karmic effects. The irony—a typical Taoist irony—is that it is only when we let go of what we are clinging to that our lives have a chance to work out the way we hope, for our dreams to be harmoniously fulfilled. Our attachments add only a false and delusive coloration to our thoughts, and an awkward imbalance to our actions that militate in favor of all the negative outcomes we definitely don't want. The Principle of Flow suggests that it is in our best interest to be "living life as life lives itself," (Humphreys 1962, 147, 156) that "God's will is Man's highest destiny." (G. Hallett 2011, 26) As Richard Bach states in *Illusions*, "Imagine the universe beautiful and just and perfect. Then be sure of one thing: The IS has imagined it quite a bit better than you have." (Bach 1977, 115) We assume, through pride, which is merely the product of our clinging at those points where we resist the flow, that we, ourselves, know best; but in truth we rarely, if ever, see all ends. In combatting the flow, we are only distorting reality to our detriment.

There is an old Chinese fable that graphically illustrates this point. As related by Derek Sivers:

A farmer had only one horse. One day, his horse ran away. His neighbors said, "I'm so sorry. This is such bad news. You must be so upset." The man just said, "We'll see."

A few days later, his horse came back with twenty wild horses following. The man and his son corralled all 21 horses. His neighbors said, "Congratulations! This is such good news. You must be so happy!"

The man just said, "We'll see." One of the wild horses kicked the man's only son, breaking both his legs. His neighbors said, "I'm so sorry. This is such bad news. You must be so upset." The man just said, "We'll see." The country went to war, and every able-bodied young man was drafted to fight. The war was terrible and killed every young man, but the farmer's son was spared, since his broken legs prevented him from being drafted. His neighbors said, "Congratulations! This is such good news. You must be so happy!" The man just said, "We'll see." (Sivers n.d.)

You would think that evading a battlefield death would be the definitive end to the story. Yet perhaps in living further, in not being killed, the son would have gone on to commit some heinous offense, one that would have landed him in a retributive hell, whereas his death in a battle, a battle such as the one Arjuna was called upon to fight in the Bhagavad Gita, would be the challenge that "opened the gates of heaven," the obstacle representing the greatest of opportunities.

We really don't see all ends, and "the IS" really does know better. To be truly happy, we need to accept life's guidance, to give God and the universe the benefit of the doubt. How many outright tragedies will we avoid through the lesser hardships we are currently experiencing? How many obstacles we confront to which we vociferously object are really just opportunities in disguise? Perhaps, if we look carefully enough, instead of yammering foolishly about them, we would see behind their masks.

Perhaps you lose a job in favor of one that pays less and is less immediately interesting, but landing there puts you within range of some fabulous person, one who rocks your world, maybe even the love of your life, or perhaps someone who helps you to repay a cosmic debt, one that would have otherwise been repaid more harshly, later on. Witnessing the quilt-like pattern of obstacles, growth and good fortune as they weave their way successively through our lives, we realize that our greatest good was typically formed through dramatic shocks and adjustments, frequently in the guise of loss. We are forever led to a greater joy through life's more limited pains to that juncture, where we can perceive and embrace, as part of our greater experience, something more enduringly valuable.

As we become increasingly one with Life's Flow, we progressively perceive how our lives and destinies are intertwined with those of others. As we pursue our separate agendas, we each play a role that mutually serves. As the Tao Te Ching states, "All things work together:/ I have watched them reverting / And have seen how they flourish/And return again, each to his roots . . . This I say, is the stillness/ A retreat to one's roots; Or better yet, return/ To the will of God,/ Which is, I say, to constancy/ The knowledge of constancy/

I call enlightenment and say/ That not to know it/ Is blindness that works evil." (Tzu 1983, 77)

Life is not always comfortable or convenient. There are irritating extremes of heat and cold; there is sadness, loss, and pain. But should we look closer, we are likely to see that the greater part of our suffering, "the full turkey with all of its trimmings," all our anguish, worry, anger, doubt, and fear is invariably caused by our clinging. And our clinging is informed by our delusion, by the belief that Life's Flow can be held, that the movie that proceeds on and on, across Reality's universal screen, can be paused at the pleasant moments or even stopped entirely. In this, the relative stability of things typically misleads us. But that doesn't mean that it is not all part of time's unceasing movement, and thus, inherently changeable by nature. By reaching such a pivotal understanding, we will begin to transform our obstacles and trials into challenges and opportunities, for they, more than our blessings or our more favorably-realized hopes, serve to beneficially remind us of this critically important truth.

The great disillusionment—the understanding that what we have relied on all along is not, in truth, reliable—leads us to let go into Life's Flow and to discover Spirit, that which can be depended on. To reemphasize what the Gita states, "the unreal never is, the Real never is not." (Mascaro 1974, 49) When you get down to it, only the One Ocean of Spirit is real, all else is but a relative projection; it is but sparkles glimmering off of Eternity's waves.

Chapter 8

Ego

As Christmas Humphreys observes, the ego, the false "I," what we mistake for our True Self, forms when we stop flowing. (Humphreys 1962, 165) The ego is comprised of elements of attachment and aversion that stubbornly resist the Flow, that cling to the riverbank instead, sending the raft of our existence spiraling into a precarious tailspin. Since the clinging is delusive anyway, our routine sense of self, as derived from it, is as well. We realize eventually, through such spiritual practices as mindfulness meditation, that this ego we cherish so much, because it is false from the outset, is our own worst enemy. In keeping us out of harmony, and in a delusive state of clinging, it prevents us from generating optimal outcomes for ourselves. All for something that, in the final analysis is neither real nor who we are. As with the Picture of Dorian Gray, in venerating it unduly, we short-change ourselves as appropriately-defined through the greater and more wondrous presence of our authentic spiritual Selves.

Pride, as exemplified by the Biblical fall of Lucifer, is the first sin, for you must first have the false ego, before generating all the false thoughts, motivations, and actions that inexorably proceed from it; you must have the room, before you can spot the furniture. When we cling to what is external, calling one thing or another "mine" we assume a process of ownership that Nature, herself denies.

By the world's physical laws, anything can still happen to anything we claim to own, whether we want it to or not, making our standard sense of ownership dubious at best, and troubling throughout. Still, while claiming to own things, we ordinarily have enough discernment not to equate our very selves with them. External possessions remain just that. But we do routinely form a sense of self out of all those internal objects that comprise our collection of concepts, experiences, motivations, and memories, materials no less ephemeral, yet which our minds deceptively solidify into something "permanent" and "real." And upon the ones we identify with most, the ones we most deeply cherish, we hang, like a hat upon a rack, the concept of "self."

Legend has it that a chela (spiritual aspirant) went before an exalted Master, seeking the truth of enlightenment. The student asked the Master, "Master what is my self?" The Master replied, "What would you do with a self?" (Humphreys 1962, 119) In that very instant, according to legend, his Master's truthful words penetrating to the core of his being, the student's mind was illuminated.

What we refer to as our "self," is but a measure of our separation from Life. It is a separation that is neither true nor real. It is not that we don't exist, only that we don't exist the way we think we do. We are as we are only in relation to everything and everyone else. In rediscovering our obscured unity with others, we reclaim our eternal consciousness. When we dig down to the root of our individual minds, we discover the Universal Mind, our "original face before we were born."[1] When we discover our true selves as inseparably one with Life, we realize that perpetually vibrant and unified essence, that ineffable perfection, that was there not only before we drew our first breath, but before the first stars were born. It is the foundation of who we are, and of everything else besides. When we act from this essence, we cease our egotistical posturing. We stop being like those called-out Biblical hypocrites who "whenever (they) fast . . . put on a gloomy face, for they neglect their appearance so that they will be noticed by men . . ." (Bible Hub, n.d., New American Standard Bible, Matt. 6:16), an ancient version of what in modern terms is generally called "advertising." As with the current state of the art, the less substance we find, the more style we must inject to compensate for its absence. In pursuing the contrary way of the Tao, we do our part without seeing it as anything other than what Joseph Goldstein calls (in specific reference to love), "the natural expression of . . . oneness."[2] We just do what needs to be done, then think little or nothing about it. It is the ego, the false self, that separates us artificially from the naturally simplicity of right action and from all that innate glory.

It also becomes easy to see, once we look closely enough, how pride causes us pain by pitting us against the Flow, by directing us routinely to contradict reality as we are experiencing it the moment. We want to be recognized at work, and receive a written warning instead. We want to be portrayed as beautiful; then someone tells us we're ugly. We envision ourselves as smart and capable; then someone says we're stupid and incompetent. And it is as if, each time we attempt to pit our egos against a contradictory reality through the influence of our attachments, we are reaching for a gigantic truck tire, spinning across the highway of our lives, and attempting to halt its forward movement with our hands—a futile and painful endeavor. This is why the Gita says that "You have a right to work, but for the work's sake only. You have no right to the fruits of the work." (Isherwood 1972, 40) The fruits will come, of course, and in an even better and more satisfying way, when we are not being so damned neurotic about them. We must, as hard as it may be, remain fluidly unattached—to outcomes, to other people's ideas, to our own limited views, and to the very space in which we dwell, unless we want the boat of our lives to be twirled about wildly in the side rapids of the Tao.

A natural amount of humility should further arise from the recognition that each of our minds and bodies, even more so than a cat's or a dog's, represents a complex level of design and functioning that we can't even begin to fathom, let alone manufacture from its cosmic blueprint. The best we can do is to work with that design and with the laws that formed it to accomplish what we intend. We know that, should we initiate a fitness routine, we will be working with laws that allow us to grow healthy and strong. If we exercise our minds, they will become more efficient. If we routinely develop a talent or skill, we are destined increase our proficiency. But we can neither weave that ability "out of whole cloth," nor alter the laws that govern its unfolding. Even if we wanted to, we could not independently conjure, out of its constituent elements, the life contained in one of our own fingernails.

In the Kena Upanishad, the following story is told with this specific idea in mind. It cogently identifies the sort of lend-lease relationship that exists between Life's power and our own capabilities, doing so in a way that should lessen our pride. As the Upanishad describes:

Brahman . . . obtained a victory for the gods; and by that victory of Brahman the gods became elated. They said to themselves: "Verily, this victory is ours; verily, this glory is ours only."

2) Brahman, to be sure, understood it all and appeared before them. But they did not know who that . . . Spirit was.

3—6) They said to Agni (Fire): "O Agni! Find out who this great Spirit is." "Yes," he said and hastened to It. Brahman asked him: "Who are you?" He replied: "I am known as Agni; I am also called Jataveda." Brahman said: "What power is in you, who are so well known?" Fire replied: "I can burn all—whatever there is on earth." Brahman put a straw before him and said: "Burn this." He rushed toward it with all his ardour but could not burn it. Then he returned from the Spirit and said to the gods: "I could not find out who this Spirit is."

7—10) Then they said to Vayu (Air): "O Vayu! Find out who this great Spirit is." "Yes," he said and hastened to It. Brahman asked him: "Who are you?" He replied, "I am known as Vayu; I am also called Matarisva." Brahman said: "What power is in you, who are so well known?" Vayu replied: "I can carry off all—whatever there is on earth." Brahman put a straw before him and said: "Carry this." He rushed toward it with all his ardour but could not move it. Then he returned from the Spirit and said to the gods: "I could not find out who this Spirit is."

11—12) Then the gods said to Indra: "O Maghavan! Find out who this great Spirit is." "Yes," he said and hastened to It. But the Spirit disappeared from him.

Then Indra beheld in that very region of the sky a Woman highly adorned. She was Uma, the daughter of the Himalayas. He approached Her and said: "Who is this great Spirit?" (Nikhilananda 2003, 100–101)

Though pride may look like strength, it is actually weakness garishly disguised, for it is an expression, plain and simple, of our clinging, and hence of our dependence. It is only by letting go of what we desire that we can properly enjoy it; only in being free and open can we be independent and strong; it is only by relinquishing who we think we are that we can genuinely be.

The peel of an unripe banana will be tough and resistant. It will tear if we try to remove it. A scab may itch, but if we detach it prematurely, we will only expose the wound, the scab will grow back, and the process of healing, thus interrupted, will have to proceed anew. Enlightenment, like healing or ripening, is a natural process. It only reveals more ego to pretend we don't have one—real or imagined. Once we are fully established in our ultimate nature as spiritual beings, the scab of ego will drop off, the peel of what is extraneous (i.e., pride) will easily pull away. Until then, the fact that we have an ego shouldn't concern us. That is Nature's business, not ours. Our task is to proceed forever in the right direction, however long it takes to reach our journey's end.

NOTES

1. This is a line derived from a Zen koan, "Show me your original face before you were born."

2. As Goldstein describes it, "When there is no self, there is no other. That duality is created by the idea of self, of I, of ego. Where there's no self, there is a unity, a communion. And without the thought of 'I'm loving someone,' love becomes the natural expression of that oneness." (Goldstein, The Experience of Insight 1983, 38)

Chapter 9

Id, Superego, and Soul

When we respond from the standpoint of ego, our actions are unbalanced and false. One moment, we are excited, and the next, forlorn. We "love" someone, then loathe them again in short order (typically due to our not having obtained what we wanted from them to begin with). We exalt ourselves with undue pride, then condemn ourselves with undue harshness. These precarious and unbalanced extremes are all indicators of a mind that dwells among rather than above the dualities of the relative world, a mind whipsawed by the hurricane of matter. Such mind states may seem opposite, but they always coexist, like the dual halves of the Yin Yang symbol. Like the flip sides of a coin, they are complementary in nature. Wildly oscillating between them is the tell-tale sign of a disharmonious mind. Like the Id and Superego in Freud's psychological scheme, both draw from the same energy, the energy of the material mind. As recorded in Evans-Wenz's Tibetan Yoga and Secret Doctrines, "An excellent man, like precious metal, / Is in every way invariable; / A villain, like the beams of a balance is always varying, upwards and downwards." (Evans-Wentz, Tibetan Yoga and Secret Doctrines 1967, 61)

Neither Id nor Superego is based on conscience or truth, though the Superego pridefully masquerades as such. One embraces the straightforward pursuit of pleasure, and the other, that pursuit in reverse, in the avoidance and fear of pain. Both have physicality and the senses as their touchstone. It is only in the upper reaches of the mind, in the domain of the soul—the True Self—where our joy and the joy of others are one, that true morality pertains. Thus, there exists the obstacle of misidentifying conscience with the Superego function, with the draconian and divisive demands of the "internal parent."

Quite often what we stubbornly avoid we are curiously drawn to later, as the pendulum of unbalanced action reverses; someone suggests a new idea or situation to us, and we instinctively reject it; later we feel bad that we did and try to assuage our guilt by pursuing the original suggestion uncritically. All this is very unskillful. As the Dhammapada states, "Let a man but keep these three roads of action clear, and he will achieve the way which is taught by the wise." (Muller 2009, 68) "Clear of what?," you might ask—of attachment and aversion, of that which resists the underlying Flow of Life.

A good way of countering the unnatural inversion of self-interest, associated with a hyperactive Superego, is through what I call "the third person technique." This method can help you to keep your needs and others' needs in their proper perspective. If, for example, your name is Tom Smith, ask yourself about Tom Smith and what he needs today. How is he feeling? What are his aspirations and goals. If you tend to be particularly unkind to yourself, while prostrating routinely as an unconscious martyr before others, this technique would allow you to respect yourself and your personal needs, while you attend to any obligations you may have toward the rest of Life.

The universe and its laws are all founded upon Truth, the truth of their own nature. Attachment and aversion are essentially ways of being "untrue," of denying the factual reality of existence; but denying it won't make it go away; it will only serve to render our resulting circumstances less favorable. When we bat the world away, we are violently repulsing Life. We are denying the factual reality of the moment, for which Life must then exact its evenly-calculated payment for that living denial of truth. This is what is meant by Karmic law, the law that restores the balance.

There are two unwholesome extremes we find in the world and in reference to the spiritual life. The first, as previously alluded to, is the wayward thirst for pleasure. It as a common and lowly obsession, one that neglects the consequences to oneself and to others of an unbridled pursuit of limited material objectives. Those who follow that course to its natural end, find pleasure but not happiness, and ultimately, neither one. The other extreme thinks that to suffer and to be spiritual are interchangeable conditions. It shouldn't surprise us that a compassionate God should want us to be happy; yet we often torment ourselves needlessly on His behalf.

The Buddha said that truth and enlightenment are to be found along the Middle Way, the way between self-indulgence and self-torture. Why emphasize the latter? Because our greatest happiness, and particularly for those on a spiritual path, comes from growth and because growth is often—though not necessarily—accompanied by pain. And just as we tend to confuse one thing for another, the happiness that comes from within as localized in external objects and people, so spiritual enthusiasts tend to confuse the symptom with the source and to actually, at times, become unconscious masochists. This is apparently what caused Thomas Moore, one of the most enlightened individuals of his time, to wear a hair shirt—as if, in a world of pain, we need to be reminded that pain exists! It is a definite obstacle.

Those on a high-growth path ravenously devour new learning. The loftiest climb leads at once to the greatest bliss and to the most intense initial suffering. That great beings who endure heavy trials on earth are said, in the Eastern view, to spend many years afterwards enjoying happiness in a heavenly realm is a reminder that the end is not about pain; it is still about growth, and growth is, in the end, about happiness. It is our failure to realize this that causes us at times when we are bored, frustrated, or thwarted in our efforts to quickly progress, to topple our own apple carts. We cling to the sources of our earlier frustrations, as if renewing them will hasten us forward. But the old challenges are never the ones we need. The trials and obstacles we have already surmounted are but a tree notch on the trail of progress. This is only us perversely clinging to our comfort zones. What we need is the new learning that will lead to even greater happiness. To be happy you must lose the hair shirt!

Once we do become one with the Flow, we are carried through calmer and clearer waters to where the river empties expansively into the sea. We realize, in reducing the falseness of our egos to nothing, that we are in truth one with everything. At the highest level, a Master is one who can feel the sap flowing through the trees as if it were the blood coursing through his veins. That wondrous state, that inseparable oneness with everything is a higher beatitude, a loftier destination, than to have endless incomplete and limited experiences splash over and through our separate selves for all eternity, the way they do in our physical existence here on earth, and in the similar, more limited way, that Heaven itself, by some, has been childishly envisioned.

It is an affirmation of life's essential goodness that after our Herculean trek through trials and difficulties is done, we will reach a point where we will be able to say definitively that we have done what we needed to do. We will then cease to hurl our punches midair against the stomachs of enemies who have already been defeated. It is then that we shall attest with our lives and souls to the Biblical truth that "surely goodness and mercy shall follow me, all the days of my life, and I will dwell in the house of the LORD forever." (Bible Hub, n.d., King James Bible, Psalm 23:6) The cool down after the workout will have begun. All critical trials left behind, we shall survey the results of our former struggles from a higher level of attainment; our lives, no longer dangling precariously over an abyss in strain and uncertainty, shall rest secure in that bounty and attainment implied in the Buddhist notion of an "unshakable deliverance of mind." The struggles that went before, as with Kabballah's "bread of shame" will then only add to the sweetness of the prize. When the fullness of wisdom dawns, the depths of compassion will be realized as well, with the labor yet to be performed related more to helping others through their struggles in a way that is not egotistically driven, but fully in tune with the overarching needs of Life.

Chapter 10

Moving Forward

Once you rise above attachment and aversion, you arrive at a new standard, one that may best be termed energetic. As the mind grows accustomed to being calm, clear, and mindful, it also becomes more sensitive to the vibrational quality of its environment. You become sharply aligned with the energy of your purpose—or purposes—if there happen to be more than one. By means of energetic perception you penetrate to the core of what's true and real. You transcend all uncharitable sectarianism by discerning the essence of truth beneath the bewildering number of conceptual garbs it wears.

Many a pilgrim has journeyed to Bodh Gaya, to the Ganges, or to Nazareth, to be uplifted by the presence of the holy vibrations that cling to these divine places. Such vibrations are not specifically Buddhist, Hindu, or Christian, but Spiritual. But for those who remain at the sensory level only, there is no energetic standard and thus no reconciling separate forms of worship; the oppressive energy of that low-level conflict never reaches anywhere near to the throne of God; it instead invisibly encapsulates the dark forces of isolation, incompleteness, fear, and hate. As the Gita notes:

> When thou shalt rise above the plane of illusion, then shalt thou cease to disturb thyself regarding doctrines, theology, disputations concerning rites or ceremonies, and other useless trimmings upon the cloth of spiritual thought. Then shalt thou be liberated from attachments to sacred books, to writings of learned theologians, or to those who would interpret that which they fail themselves to understand; but instead, shalt thou fix thy mind in earnest contemplation of the Spirit, and thus reach the harmony with thy Real Self, which underlies all. (Yogi Ramacharaka 1930, 87)

With reference to our thoughts, they too become "spiritualized" and creative, they too become divine—or demonic—as a result of the energy behind them. We manifest better what we feel most strongly about. If we have a keen interest in backgammon, we are likely to draw into our lives, people who share that interest, and perhaps in venues, such as the work environment, that have nothing ostensibly to do with backgammon at all. We will also attract people for whom we have a strong aversion. That is why hatred is such a "losing throw."[1] Through it, we are investing energy, energy with the power to manifest precisely what we don't want. The act of balancing karma consists, in essence, of cultivating an energetically neutral attitude towards what we especially dislike. Outwardly, that involves transforming hatred into acceptance. We may not particularly like stupid people, know-it-alls, Muslims, Buddhists, born-again Christians, Blacks, Whites, or Orientals, brutally aggressive women or openly chauvinistic men. But to the extent that we hate them, we will have them. By contrast, once we develop an energetically neutral attitude towards them, and wisely acknowledge their right to exist, we will find fewer situations arising in which they are likely to loop around our corner, situations that lawfully reflect our negative energy, demanding that it be balanced.

NOTE

1. See (Babbitt 2012, location 411, verse 202).

Chapter 11

The Principle of the Vacuum

The Principle of Flow relates directly to what may be termed the Principle of the Vacuum. In both the physical and the metaphysical realms, the universe operates according to law. Jump off a cliff, and you will be injured. Lean on a hot stove, and you will be burned. This is not the universe being harsh, but the person being ignorant of its laws. Take from the world, and it will take from you; push it, and it will push back. Each act of giving intensifies the vacuum of exchange that the universe must ultimately fill. Every act of acceptance makes the world more your home. The Principle of the Vacuum states that what we hope to receive we must first be willing to give. We must love if we wish to be loved. We must be generous to be the recipients of material good fortune.[1]

The Principle of the Vacuum thus also demands faith, for it implies a willingness to let go and to give to others that which we most desperately seek for ourselves, knowing in our hearts that this is the very best way, ultimately, of obtaining it. Through acknowledging and cherishing our oneness with others, we inexorably arrive at the goodness we individually seek.

Both the Bible and the Tao Te Ching contain numerous paradoxes that pay homage to the Principle of the Vacuum by suggesting that what we seek for ourselves can only, in truth, be obtained by indirection. Jesus proclaimed that ". . . the last shall be first and the first last," (Bible Hub, n.d., King James Bible, Matt. 20:16) and "If you cling to your life, you will lose it; but if you give up your life for me, you will find it." (Bible Hub, n.d., Boolean Study Bible, Matt. 10:39) We receive on the road to giving; what we gain, we gain enduringly, not by force or by violence, but by law, bestowed harmoniously by the hand of selfless service.

Yet we are often so driven by a narrow and selfish definition of our own good that we don't see how this process is already working for us. Many of us, for example, if asked where we get the money to pay our bills would say "from the paycheck I receive from my employer." But this paycheck is just an effect of services rendered; and if the services weren't there, the paycheck wouldn't be either.

This acknowledgment of the ultimate Source of our good resembles an exam question in which no answer is entirely false, but only one is completely true in being more correct than the others. "What do I drive?" for example, a) a car, b) a Hyundai, or c) a 2019 Hyundai Sonata. The last answer is correct in being the most descriptive. Taking by violence, as the harsh history of the world reveals, is still of course possible, but what is left, as a result, is but a residual effect, a shadow, if you will, of the happiness sought, while through the Law of Cause and Effect, every act of violence sets into motion the reverse swing of the pendulum by which, in Biblical terms, those who live by the sword will at one point or another die by it. The violent will draw the violent, and together they will suffer.

As described by Hindu Master, Swami Sri Yukteswar Giri, "The balanced rhythm of the universe is rooted in reciprocity." (Yogananda 2003, 188) It is upon reciprocity that the Great Law of Karma itself is based. This principle is ideally illustrated by the Christian "Parable of the Long Spoons." As that parable goes:

> One day a man said to God, "God, I would like to know what Heaven and Hell are like."
>
> God showed the man two doors. Inside the first one, in the middle of the room, was a large round table with a large pot of stew. It smelled delicious and made the man's mouth water, but the people sitting around the table were thin and sickly. They appeared to be famished. They were holding spoons with very long handles and each found it possible to reach into the pot of stew and take a spoonful, but because the handle was longer than their arms, they could not get the spoons back into their mouths.
>
> The man shuddered at the sight of their misery and suffering. God said, "You have seen Hell."
>
> Behind the second door, the room appeared exactly the same. There was the large round table with the large pot of wonderful stew that made the man's mouth water. The people had the same long-handled spoons, but they were well nourished and plump, laughing and talking.
>
> The man said, "I don't understand."
>
> God smiled. It is simple, he said, Love only requires one skill. These people learned early on to share and feed one another. While the greedy only think of themselves . . . [Author unknown] (Archon n.d.)

By the Law of the Vacuum and the Principle of the Long Spoons, the ideal life proceeds as a continuous act of service, where each favorable demonstration invites a return benefit, where happiness follows "like a shadow that never leaves . . ."[2] This doesn't mean that we will then live lives without obstacles, for the obstacles are meant to be there, and are an important benefit too! When life is led continuously this way, our will becomes harmonized with the greater will of God or Way of the Tao. It then conforms to the very definition of Flow, and one's physical existence, though no less a wasting asset, becomes a genuine blessing. Here the Tao Te Ching compares "those of the Way to torrents that flow into river and sea." (p. 100) As for our individual needs, they are reliably met through the Law of Cause and Effect; as the Gita states, "Those who enjoy what remains of the sacrifice go unto Brahman." (Mascaro 1974, 64) Contribute a little, and you will receive but a little. Contribute a lot, and your life is ultimately and inevitably filled with abundance. Give all, when it is called for, and you are ultimately glorified as Christ, Himself, was. Effectively relinquishing the self, we realize the infinitely greater and more satisfying Self. In becoming nothing, you become everything; in non-ego, shines the Light of the Eternal Mind.

The "Parable of the Long Spoons" should not be seen either as something strictly otherworldly, pertaining only to a distant heaven or separate sort of Earth, yet to be realized, for it suggests, in the sense implied in "Genesis," that we have somehow, to some degree, and by some tragic means, somewhere along the line, lost our way. Rather than living by the true method of giving and serving, as the means of ensuring our enduring success and prosperity, we began to act beneath our station in a purely animalistic way. We began to falsely reverse the polarity of the Law by thinking that grasping and greed were the ways to achieve our ends. The entire modern field of Economics has been consequently dubbed "the dismal science," with whole civilizations now operating according to this erroneous "greed leads to good" methodology, civilizations that, to whatever degree they may be living in peace right now, are teetering invisibly on the edge of an abyss. As the *Hua Hu Ching* prophetically warns:

> When a society misuses partial intelligence and ignores holistic wisdom, its people forget the benefits of a plain and natural life. Seduced by their desires, emotions, and egos, they become slaves to bodily demands, to luxuries, to power and unbalanced religion and psychological excuses. Then the reign of calamity and confusion begins.
>
> Nonetheless, superior people can awaken during times of turmoil to lead others out of the mire. (Walker 1992, 98)

To have knowledge with wisdom is best; it allows for the full range of accomplishments. To have wisdom without knowledge is still okay, for it limits the harm we can do. But to have knowledge without wisdom is a recipe for disaster. That is where our world is now. In fact, we know so much, in terms of material understanding, that we think it makes us wise. It doesn't, it can't, and it won't.

And even more than that, our society's ubiquitous emphasis on commerce and acquisitive ends, routinely turns normal, friendly and open-hearted people into manipulative weasels and monsters, artificially insensitive, coldly and fearfully distanced from one another, and confused and alienated from themselves. It mass produces such people in the same way, by the same process, and for the same acquisitive end as the consumer goods whose production and distribution they serve. Such is the inevitable consequence of turning life on its head, of giving precedence to the wrong goals, of seeking "all else" before "the kingdom of God." Instead of using our resources to aid each other, we use each other to savagely acquire them. What we secure in the process turns to ashes in our hands; thus scarred, and burned, we scramble off again to ignorantly acquire more.

As the Tao Te Ching states, "The highest goodness, water-like,/Does good to everything and goes/Unmurmuring to places men despise;/But so, is close in nature to the Way." (Tzu 1983, 67) What is it that men despise? Work for one. Service and giving for another. Having to wake up early in the morning to go to the gym. All those things that the Gita identifies as "what seems at first a cup of sorrow (but is) in the end immortal wine." (Mascaro 1974, 87)

The double reward is that when you do find joy in such things, no one will think to challenge you. Who, in his right mind, would complain that you would want to work harder or operate more efficiently? Who would complain that you would want to share your knowledge or resources with them? Maybe some would, just to be difficult, but certainly not many. To extract joy from the obstacles. To benefit from the disadvantages. To derive happiness from the treasures that others neglect and deride—that is the highest and most skillful way to live.

As for the results of our actions, probably the best thing about the Law of Karma, for those yearning for a map on their spiritual journey, is that it is reliable, and predictable in its effects. You have the assurance of knowing that "whatever a man shall sow, that also shall he reap." (Bible Hub, n.d., Darby Bible Translation, Galatians 6:7) By patterning our lives in accordance with this law of balance and reciprocity, we begin to consciously mold our futures.

Additionally, as Sri Yukteswar noted, though by no means in a condemnatory but rather in a gentle, forgiving way, "the vanished lives of all men are dark with many shames." (Yogananda 2003, 138) We cannot tell what we are trailing behind us, good, bad, or otherwise. We cannot tell what future harm our past ignorance may yet cause. But we can begin now to put the reins into our own hands, and with the limited faith required to believe that this life is not the end, and that a cause will produce an effect corresponding to its nature, begin to build a better future now. This is a tremendous source of empowerment, one that no pauper would fail to access, and which no king could successfully evade. As the Dhammapada states, "Not in the sky, not in the midst of the sea, not if one enters into the clefts of the mountains, is there known a spot in the whole world, where if a man abide, he might be freed from an evil deed." (Babbitt 2012, verse 127, location 287)

If we don't like being pinned to the earth, we can at least rest assured that the Law of Gravity is reliable. We can feel confident that we won't exit our front doors and be propelled helplessly into thin air. In Buddhism, one of the three refuges is the Dharma, the Law. It is something we can place our confidence in with the highest level of assurance. It doesn't work for us sometimes and fail us at others. Like gravity, it is perfectly consistent.

It is said that the Buddhas are overwhelmed with compassion when they see how, driven by their desire for happiness, beings generate causes that lead to their contrary unhappiness. They get the very opposite of what they so desperately seek. The causes that lead to unhappiness are those that are narrowly selfish. They are the ones that ignore the good of others in the stifling pursuit of one's own. They are the ones that conflict with the Law of Reciprocity. They are the ones that conceive of happiness inaccurately as something to be held, rather than something to be shared openly, and thus multiplied, through the "loaves and fishes" Principle of the Vacuum. The worst of such twisted methodologies actually inflicts harm en route to achieving one's selfish ends. Here genuine prosperity is revealed to be a boon that, within the framework of contemporary commerce, is rarely seen as it is (i.e., as a substantive joy, to be obtained indirectly through the Law of Cause and Effect).

NOTES

1. The "Principle of the Vacuum" is nothing new. It is common in New Thought Literature. One example of its use is by Cindi Sansone-Braff. (Braff 2009, 26)

2. The full quote from verse 2 of the Dhammapada is "If a man speaks or acts with a pure thought, happiness follows him, like a shadow that never leaves him." (Babbitt 2012, 10)

Chapter 12

The Principle of Balance

It is important to achieve balance in all areas of your life, for the one you neglect is the one that will wreak havoc on those you have focused on inordinately. You may say, "I have too much to do at home or at work to go to the gym." Well, do you have sufficient time for a heart attack?!

Deprive the body of exercise, and the mind will become unmanageable. Let your mind go its own way, and your negative thinking will wreak havoc with your physical health and relationships. Neglect the needs of your soul, and the spiritual center of your life will be tragically lost, casting your entire existence into chaos. You also have responsibilities to the larger world, to those who have been entrusted to your care. Neglect those and you will—no doubt—be painfully reminded!

These four sets of duties, physical, mental, spiritual, and worldly are like the balanced legs of a four-legged stool. Eliminate any one leg, and the stool will topple over, ceasing to serve as an effective support. Maintain them all, and your life will have all the support it needs to stay balanced.

Chapter 13

The Pivotal Role of Meditation

When you harmonize your mind through meditation, you are in a continuous state of flow, and that state of flow is a state of giving. You are then optimally situated, in keeping with the Principle of the Vacuum, to attract the best things that life has to offer, including a fair smattering of those ostensibly negative experiences that you most need to grow. Through the practice of meditation, one is, in every moment, offering one's entire self into Life, with Life, in turn, giving back. As Lao Tsu states, "In this world,/ Compare those of the Way/ To torrents that flow/Into river and sea." (Tzu 1983, 100)

The end result, the ideal state, is to be in perfect harmony with the way things are. This is the optimal way to live. It manifests as a course in which even the smallest actions are rendered with an astonishing degree of precision out of that ineffable harmony and oneness by which we are seamlessly linked to All Life. What are described as miracles, what in modern parlance have been interpreted as synchronicities may then occur; but as Augustine argued, "miracles are not contrary to nature but only contrary to what we know about nature." The miraculous, like everything else true, is just an expression of harmony and law. When we are attuned to the larger universe, that universe will then express itself through us and to us through everything around us. To those who don't sense the linkages, this effect will appear "miraculous;" but the fact remains that not a sparrow falls of which God is unaware; it is, to the enlightened, no big deal. To the uncomprehending, synchronous events appear astonishing because such individuals don't see or are incapable of recognizing the connections that have been there all along.

To master a language, or a game like chess, is truly a great accomplishment, one that will help you to develop your mind. Yet meditation furnishes the means of advancing to a higher level, a different functional modality entirely. Thus Charles Evanz-Wenz refers to yoga as "the shortest path to the higher evolution of man." (Evans-Wentz, Tibetan Yoga and Secret Doctrines 1967, 23) As such it represents a unique—and uniquely beneficial—category of activity. While the outcomes of science can be positive or negative, giving us both nuclear bombs and nuclear medicine, Dharma practice directs us to deliberately cultivate that which is most and entirely beneficial, that which is specifically geared toward what we are looking for in the midst of all of our pursuits, the essential boon of happiness.

As Christopher Vogler observes, "You are never more alive than when you are looking death in the face." (Vogler 2007, 16) The individual who confronts impermanence through mindfulness faces death in every waking moment; he or she, to borrow Vogler's analogy, is forever living in the electrifying downward swing of the roller coaster.[1]

NOTE

1. Quoting, in context, from *The Writer's Journey*, "The designers of amusement park thrill rides know how to use this principle. Roller coasters make their passengers feel as if they're going to die, and there's a great thrill that comes from brushing up against death and surviving it. You're never more alive than when you're looking death in the face."

Chapter 14

Courage

One of the perils and pitfalls of the spiritual life, and a truly great obstacle, is the thought that it reprieves us from living rich, full lives in the here and now. We may feel that because Jesus or Buddha have done their part, we don't need to do ours. This is a hideous misconception, an obstacle of the greatest magnitude, and quite simply false. They have accomplished fully, and we must do the same. Even if our role is small by comparison, it is a role that we must play to the best of our ability.

All the great religions we have considered speak of obstacles to be overcome, and of the need for courage and commitment. The scenario of "the bread of shame" accentuates the demand for the utmost striving. Even if life is a game, it is a game played for the highest of stakes, and not to be taken lightly. Yet, like Arjuna on the Kurukshetra battlefield, we are often reluctant to engage with life. We are concerned about what we might lose. We may simply be afraid. It is better, we speciously reason, to avoid potential embarrassment, than to get up on stage and perform, to offer our opinion at meetings, to submit our manuscript to a publisher, to present our art on exhibit, to ask that interesting person out on a date, to run for public office, or to otherwise let our voice and views be heard. What if they hate us? What if someone laughs? What if we trip and fall? Yet it is clear that in such situations, if we don't step up—tripping or not—if we don't engage fully and courageously with life, we will have lost our chance already. If we are as prepared as we will ever be, we really have nothing to lose. It is that same detrimental force, that false clinging rooted in ignorance that makes us believe in the immortality of our current advantages. Yet in business, as in life, we must see our comfort zones for what they are, an illusion or temporary state. They are as subject to change as the changes that have already occurred. The only full and true rest comes at the end, when we have shed our flesh and our years, and our strivings have come to an end.

Like death itself, which it represents in miniature, change and impermanence are the most terrifying of realities to face; but once they are faced, life becomes truly magical. We finally reach a level where we are able to live life properly, knowing it for what it is. In the ultimate state, at that pivotal point in the circle's center, there is no death because there likewise is no change. Neither is there anything that can be identified there, because there is nothing there to which the reality of Life is opposed. The self ceases to exist, which is no tragedy, because "self" exists only because of "other," through the artificial divide that separates experience from experiencer. "Where is my self?" asks the student. "What would you do with a self?" the teacher responds, and the student gains a heightened understanding in appreciating a basic truth: If you are and always have been everything, then what do you ultimately need, other than to fully and properly realize it?

Chapter 15

Experience

In modern times, our standard approach to faith has become a blind and lazy one. It is a cure that can do little to heal us, if it does nothing to improve us. To truly venerate the great ones, we must become more like them. As Thomas A Kempis attempted to do with his renowned Imitation of Christ, we need to become great emulators, and in the process, to uncover our own unique brands, the signatures of our souls. It befits only a nation of followers to believe and not to become.

Experience in every realm amply attests to the fact that we are the result of what we think and do. As with "the bread of shame," even if what we are called upon to do is done for us, it is ultimately less valuable and significant than what we proactively do for ourselves through our own strenuous strivings. We are here to do more than mark time before the Great Light appears again in the flesh, and while we don't accomplish alone, we don't accomplish apart from our own efforts either. As the Buddha proclaimed, "By oneself the evil is done, by oneself one suffers; by oneself evil is left undone, by oneself one is purified. Purity and impurity belong to oneself, no one can purify another." (Babbitt 2012, location 351, verse 165)

Why do you think that—for the most part—we no longer experience miracles as they did in Biblical times, as they did in the time of the Buddha and of the other Great Masters? Well, there are varying opinions. One is simply that we are now more intellectually mature. We don't see miracles now, as there were none to see to begin with. But I think it is really because we no longer—or only rarely—rise to that higher plane where miracles naturally dwell. Once we do, we will see the miraculous appear in our lives once again.

In terms of what we can hopefully observe ourselves, the Dhammapada states directly, "If a man speaks or acts with an evil thought, pain follows him, as the wheel follows the foot of the ox that draws the wagon . . . If a man speaks or acts with a pure thought, happiness follows him, like a shadow that never leaves him." (Babbitt 2012, location 74–76, verses 1–2) This is not a casual statement to be lightly accepted on faith, but part of a fully observable process, one that accords with the Principle of Flow. That we do not recognize this already indicates just how far we have distanced ourselves from our experiences, from the simple act of being present with our thoughts and feelings in the moment.

As previously noted, all that we experience as good and evil can be traced back to our harmonizing with or opposing the Flow as the central truth of life's underlying reality. Annoyance and irritation tap lightly on the brakes of negativity. Anger and hatred, in their strong aversive resistance, are like burning out the brake linings. Lust is problematic as it hazes over the clarified mind, causing us to view, in service to Nature's reproductive end, our shifting sensory reality as solid. Thus, it reinforces directly the unskillful acts of attachment and aversion. Lying is a blunt denial of truth. It resists where the flow of events has factually placed us. All of the above combined constitute a harsh and heavy opposition to the flow of life and to the factual reality of events. Where pain is a natural occurrence, attachment transforms it into suffering, into the screaming agony of resistance as we deny through aversion the truth of what is actually happening.

The denial of life's flow is attended by an immediate sting of pain, as well—one that should serve as a palpable reminder that we are responding incorrectly. In each such instance, it is not the events themselves that are responsible for the greater part of our torment, but our unskillful actions in relation to them. All of this can be directly observed through a calm and clarified mind.

As a dramatic example, let's say that at 4 p.m. an airliner crashes. At 5:00 p.m. you are together with friends, celebrating a recent promotion. Your spirits are high, and your mood is festive and joyous. At 5:30 p.m., a frantic relative reports that the flight your mother was on may have crashed. Suddenly and dramatically your mood changes from joy to extreme fear and panic. At 5:45 p.m., your relative calls back. The plane that crashed was indeed your mother's flight. Now you feel as if the bottom has dropped out from under your world. You experience the deepest amount of emotional pain imaginable. At 6:15 p.m., your relative calls again; while your mother was scheduled to be on the ill-fated flight, there was a traffic jam on the road leading to the airport, and she had to take another plane. Suddenly you feel as if you are on another plane, overwhelmed with the positive emotions of joy, gratitude and relief. At 9:00 p.m. your emotions level off, as your normal mood returns. So, between 4:00 p.m. and 9:00 p.m., what, factually, has changed? Well, factually—nothing. The airplane crashed at 4:00 p.m. with the outcome of that event already determined. It is only your mood that shifted in response to the information that subsequently came in, modified by your attachment to the result.

This example is not cited to suggest that we should react to what we hear in a stoic or unresponsive fashion. In fact, a whole subdomain of Buddhism is devoted to right speech in recognition of the fact that what we say to ourselves and to others is so tremendously impactful. Yet it does emphasize how our moods are determined by our thoughts about what we perceive, and not by the events themselves. In situations less dramatic, where both positive and negative elements coexist, we can hope to emphasize the positive while attenuating the negative, thus coaxing more of the positive into our lives. One of the best ways to do this is to take stock of the many things for which we are—or should be—genuinely grateful.

There were times (thankfully few) in my youth and adolescence when I behaved toward others in a cruel and thoughtless manner. In high school, for example, I sometimes went looking for fights to demonstrate my adolescent machismo. To this day, such events, though limited in number, are extremely painful to recall. I had hurt someone inconsiderately, and now the pain of that guilt is mine to bear for life. But I not only recall such incidents painfully, I experienced them as painful at the time. I simply chose to ignore the internal alarm of empathetic suffering, a feeling that was shouting at me urgently from the sidelines of my rampant cruelty and ignorance.

Conversely, there were other times, later in life when, subject to a verbal attack, I would find myself asking why I felt so good amidst a happening so ostensibly negative. I then realized that it was because I was being patient, and that the energy of patience is very powerful and uplifting. It was happiness following "like a shadow," a shadow that didn't leave, one that didn't have to leave despite whatever else was going on. This more stable happiness had nothing to do with other people's actions, but with how I chose to respond. And it was all there for me to experience. There was nothing to be taken for granted, on belief or unobserved. As the Abraham writings assert, while we are not equipped with a blueprint for this life, we have been supplied with something even better, an emotional guidance system. Should we clear the way for its directives, it will show us what to do. (Hicks 2006, 40–41)

In further reference to our emotions, when we choose to interact angrily, we effectively enter into a contract with others binding us to our mutual destruction. When people get angry with us, there is always a pull to react, like a TCP/IP handshake in the world of computer networking, one we can reply to—or not. If we resist the demand to respond in kind, we will build our spiritual strength against the resistance that invitation presents. We thus help to ensure that the next time around we will be prepared to respond as serenely. Give in to anger, and we are more likely to respond with anger again. While most people who adopt an Eastern (Hindu/Buddhist) approach, don't believe in an eternal hell, but rather that even the deepest hole is one we will eventually climb out of, though it may take eons of time and a colossal amount of suffering, the closest thing to that notion can be found in the realm of habit. We become so inured to doing something one way, that it ultimately requires a superhuman effort to ever do it differently.

In every moment, through every thought and action, we are either going with the Flow or clinging to the shore. We are either giving and serving, naturally receiving what we need along the way, like a marathon runner who grabs a cup of water from the sidelines of his focused effort, or we are lodged in the delusion of separate selfhood, attempting, in isolation, to get "what is ours."

Since the clinging is delusive anyway, since it is opposed to the Truth of Life's Flow, each time we cling we incur a karmic demerit, one that we can feel registered like a wound on our astral bodies. It is there to be experienced within the quiet mind, not merely believed, or taken for granted. When we attempt to achieve happiness by taking something away from Life, Life is then poised, like a coiled spring, to snap it back from us. We incur a debit that we must subsequently repay. We head further away from the suppleness and joy associated with the higher energies; we move further and further away from the Light. It is a way of mortgaging our futures.

Sunk into the realm of the lower chakras. we are literally and habitually pulled toward matter the way Ulysses, tied to the mast, was drawn to the call of the Sirens. When suffering and obstacles cause us to relinquish our hold, if only for a moment, a movement away from our material addictions and toward the dominance of the upper chakras occurs. Thus, Ram Das referred to suffering as grace; here our obstacles serve us well, and in a way that nothing else can, for it is what is undesirable in life that causes us to let go. (Das, Grist for the Mill 1987, 29)

Once we are centered at that point where consciousness becomes internalized, the point where we survey Samsara's badlands from the cool terrain of Nirvana's shimmering peaks, the swirl of matter from the spiritual eye of the storm, we are ideally poised to receive a never-ending flow of blessings. Then our every thought and action naturally become an act of giving, and by Karmic Law, the Great Life gives back. When we are governed instead by our clinging, greedy, animal side, the domain of the lower chakras, we are prepared only to take, and therefore, by the Law of Karma, have to return what was taken to restore the balance.

Through mindfulness and its attendant clarity, we are able to reconnect with our innate emotional guidance. We thereby harmonize reliably with the Flow of Life. Then, as we begin, through meditation, to clear epic amounts of debris from the building site of character, a fascinating and legitimate question inevitably arises: how can we even begin to be spiritual, in the way that the Bible, or the other great spiritual books, describes, without meditation? Before the mind is tamed, there is just too much feral badland. Giving into the kleshas (i.e., disturbing emotions), one's subsequent actions are tainted. The individual to the extent to which he has succumbed to lust, wrath, or greed, is now more prone to negative responses. He is more likely to respond with anger and irritation to the same situation that someone with a trained mind would accept with calmness. The benefits of mindfulness and meditative stability are not entirely—or even mostly—a matter of faith, but of demonstrating the willpower necessary to render our actions skillful, and with the cleansing effect that mediation has on the mind. As noted in *Autobiography of A Yogi*:

> The human mind, bared to a centuried slime, is teeming with the repulsive life of countless world-delusions. Struggles on the battlefield pale into insignificance here, where man first contends with inner enemies! No mortal foes these, to be overcome by a harrowing array of might! Omnipresent, unrestingly, pursuing man even in sleep, subtly equipped with miasmic weapons, these soldiers of ignorant lusts seek to slay us all. (Yogananda 2003, 51–52)

Through meditation, we reclaim that "visionary gleam," whose loss Wordsworth elegantly lamented as forever vanished since childhood, for it is not an aspect of youth per se, but of a calm and purified mind. Through meditative clarity, colors begin to vividly leap out at you; even drab and dreary days appear, in their own way, fresh. While circumstances may remain very much the same, meditation changes the way you experience them. It enhances your ability to deal with everyday problems, and to simultaneously appreciate all the good things in life. All of this is within the realm of discovery, and not the subject of belief alone.

The traditional Western answer to our paradoxical dilemma, to Christ's demand for morality, while we possess afflicted minds, has been to give up entirely on the idea of being spiritual. It has been to see human beings as irredeemably corrupt, with all goodness attributed to the guiding Will of God. While God is truly the source of all goodness, we can embody that goodness too, while not claiming its virtue to be exclusively our own. Meditation is a proven way to get there.

And it does something more as well. It is a gateway to our highest potential, to all those supernal abilities the ancient world saw as miraculous, and the modern age dismisses—perhaps too lightly—as simply unreal. The historical account of varied cultures attests to the reality of such miracles, miracles which, as Saint Augustine argues, "are not contrary to nature but only contrary to what we know about nature."

As we access the road that leads to our Higher Selves, we initiate a journey that proceeds through many obstacles. We face the hidden terrors, waiting for us within; we grapple with those ugly aspects of ourselves that we prefer to believe don't exist. And in the process, abilities that we once thought could only be imagined and never actualized begin to present themselves. They dramatically unfold as our energies are progressively refined. Those energies, energies that had been dedicated to repressing so much cathected material are now released for higher and better purposes. Telepathy and astral projection, superhuman strength, levitation, and wingless flight. These and more have been cataloged as real by both ancient and modern adepts, forthright representatives of religious cultures whose faithful adherents simply don't lie. Such abilities are also the stuff of modern heroic myths, as encapsulated in the comic strip legends of Western culture. The basic characteristics are identical. Yet, as with so much else in our society, we see the road to this intriguing end only in the outward domination of Nature and in the precarious manipulation of the gene, leading potentially to the creation of super viruses and monsters. We are too spiritually blind, in our modern arrogance, to realize that much the same objective has been and can be harmoniously realized within the laws and structures of Nature, and not properly through the control or violation of them.

As we set foot on the spiritual path, we undertake "the hero's journey," and when we accept that journey, we test the boundaries our personal obstacles impose, boundaries that divide us from the realization of our greater potential and Higher Selves. What we commit to, in response, is a courageous and meaningful quest into the larger and more wondrous unknown. The opportunity thus presented represents the greatest and noblest that human existence, that shimmering snowflake of a wasting asset, has ever had to offer.

Chapter 16

The Realities of Change and Suffering

The Buddha's first "noble truth" is that life is "dukkha," where dukkha is commonly, yet misleadingly, translated as "suffering." For clearly, we are not suffering when we are receiving an award, dining at the Ritz, or vacationing in Aruba, at least not by any definition of suffering with which we are commonly familiar. Dukkha's precise meaning has been captured, in relation to its etymological roots, more accurately and adequately by Huston Smith. (p. 101) As Smith elaborates in the World's Religions:

> The word's constructive implications come to light when we discover that it was used in Pali to refer to wheels whose axles were off-center, or bones that had slipped from their sockets. (A modern metaphor might be a shopping cart we try to steer from the wrong end.) The exact meaning of the First Noble Truth is this: Life (in the condition it has got itself into) is dislocated. Something has gone wrong. It is out of joint. As its pivot is not true, friction (interpersonal conflict) is excessive, movement (creativity) is blocked, and it hurts.

It is also, in a similarly better way, translated as life, as it is ordinarily lived is dissatisfying. So long as we remain oblivious to our spiritual natures, so long as we are falsely and delusively reading permanence into impermanence and trying to grasp Life's flow in its ongoing passage, we can't hope to be truly happy.

Moreover, if we say that "existence is suffering," then this would logically and inevitably lead to a desire for non-existence as an immediate—and seemingly decisive—solution to the problem. Yet this "desire for non-existence" is specifically identified in the Second of the Four Noble Truths, as an extreme to be avoided. With dukkha thus mistranslated, and with that mistranslation interpreted literally, the only drawback to suicide would be that it doesn't work. To say, in keeping with the original Pali meaning, that "the world is out of joint," leads naturally to a desire to raise it up on the mechanic's hoist and

69

fix it. This alternative—and better—definition is also in keeping with exactly what we must do, which is to make the required adjustments; by analogy, it illustrates this perfectly. We need to stop being obsessed with material things and start being centered in spiritual ones; then, since the spiritual is the true and proper center of each of our activities anyway, all of them will fall neatly into place.

The proper meaning of dukkha can best be demonstrated by example. Let's say you own a home. It had been your wish to own a home for a very long time, and now that desired home is yours. But suddenly, because it means so much to you, because you have made it so important, you begin to fear its loss. Suddenly, what had been a source of joy, becomes the root of a novel fear, and perhaps, even of torment. Maybe your boss tells you, "you'd better shape up, or you'll be out!" While such a pronouncement may well have concerned you before, it now spawns a nerve-searing terror. Every fiber of your being is on edge, as you succumb to a nagging and persistent torment: "Will I now lose the home that I value so much?" Fear of loss may then cause you to abandon your integrity, to operate against the Laws of Life, as you connive and scheme to keep what is yours.

Another example of dukkha is when we pursue an objective that seems to be entirely positive and morally good; then someone or something stands in our way. At that point, and over this seemingly very good thing, our frustrated minds turn to hatred—and often a very intense hatred. Perhaps we hoped to build a shrine to a fallen comrade, and a "greedy" corporation claims eminent domain over the memorial spot. Or we find an ideal job, and everyone seems pleased with our work, everyone that is, except the guy who is preparing our reviews and signing our paychecks, a circumstance that places that ideal job in jeopardy. In such instances, as in numerous others like them, we normally become sad and frustrated. That frustration and despair makes us loathe the people and situations that are sparking our grief. When we wander away from our centers, when we refuse to relinquish outcomes that are in God's hands alone, we lose the good in the otherwise good things we happen to be experiencing; and dukkha is the inevitable result. What is not all-important, in our own minds becomes so, and our excessive attachment tears us apart.

The Dhammapada states that, "Not to see what is pleasant is pain, and it is pain to see what is unpleasant." (Babbitt 2012, location 426, verse 211) This is life's essential dilemma, that we seek one thing be it wealth, status, or possessions, something that we think will ensure our happiness, and something else—and undesired—comes along instead.

This was supremely exemplified in what is perhaps the greatest historical loss on record, Napoleon's defeat at Waterloo. Locked in a battle that could have gone either way, each side, French and British, was awaiting the arrival of critical reinforcements. Peering out into the distance, Napoleon could see the obscure shape of troops on the march. He was thinking and hoping that this was the brigade of one of his marshals, Emmanuel de Grouchy, fast approaching. Instead, to his dismay, he discerned as it drew near, the flag of the Prussian army led by Gebhard Leberecht von Blucher, heralding the arrival of enemy soldiers, coming to the aid of the beleaguered British. Faced with the prospect of immanent defeat, the hapless French were summarily routed.

How many times have we experienced, in a less dramatic way, the arrival of disappointment in our lives? How often have we longed for Grouchy, only to find Blucher headed our way? Longing for a promotion, how often have we received a reprimand instead? Yearning for love, how often have we experienced instead a scathing rejection? "Joined to the unloved; separated from the loved," (Humphreys 1962, 28) wildly orbiting the periphery of a perpetual wheel of change, we act in a way that fits a common definition of insanity, which is to do the same thing repeatedly, (i.e., clinging to changeable matter, in one form or another), while expecting a different result, (that the pleasure we currently enjoy will never have to end). We thus mislead ourselves continually, until we realize, typically through the shock of a beneficent harshness and through obstacles, just how temporary all these transient states of mind and existence are and will always be.

When we do eventually get what we want, we are often surprised to experience something else, an alternate form of dissatisfaction—satiation. Because the experience is dualistic, because it is incomplete, the level of satisfaction it delivers can only be incomplete as well. You could be eating the best pizza in the world, and be momentarily immersed in pizza heaven. What the Tibetans would say at that point is, "eat more." The truth of satiation would then become clear. Understanding the truth of pain requires little subtlety; it is evident enough; that of satiation in pleasure is more difficult to discern. It takes an ample measure of spiritual maturity and self-honesty to grasp it appropriately and realistically.

To summarize, the good things in life, apart from those that are spiritual or that point toward the spiritual, are dual in nature, like the two sides of the Yin Yang symbol. Nowhere is this more apparent than in Nature, Herself. In Nature, there is so much beauty. There is a plethora of breathtaking vistas adorned with glistening mountains, azure skies, and emerald seas. Yet nowhere is there more savagery, cruelty, and cataclysm, "nature red in tooth and claw." Even when we have time to appreciate the view, to live for it, as for the next vacation, the day after, we must go back to the office and its drudgery, making it all seem that much worse.

The implicit irony is that only those who have transcended the world can properly appreciate it. This further suggests that our transcendent center is where we, as spiritual beings, properly belong. The wonders of duality do not captivate the rest; they are writhing in its jaws. They are continually self-driven to obtain a separate peace, a private happiness, something which ultimately doesn't work, and which life cannot offer the selfish aspirant. For duality eventually asserts itself; the cataclysms finally catch up. As the Dhammapada notes, "Few are there among men who arrive at the other shore (become Arhats); the other people here run up and down this shore." (Babbitt 2012, location 261, verse 86) The Tao Te Ching states, ". . . the man who knows/ On land how best to be at peace/ Will never meet a tiger or a buffalo; In battle, weapons do not touch his skin./ There is no place the tiger's claws can grip;/ Or with his horn, the buffalo can jab;/ Or where the soldier can insert his sword./ Why so?/ In him there is no place of death." (Tzu 1983, 121)

Yet, if we are all gods, as the Bible proclaims, then why all this misery? Why does the sword still pierce, the horn still jab? The answer is that we haven't yet transcended. Through obstacles, the dualities of life "beat us" into a state ultimately beyond their reach, and it is beyond their reach alone that life's inherent perfection can be perceived and declared. Until we reach that august plateau, we can't rightfully clam victory, for until then, our enemies on the battlefield of life will continue to harass us with a greater or lesser degree of effectiveness.

To summarize, the painful things in life are patently aversive. They reveal their true face unmistakably. The good things are knottier, for when the bad ones are gone, we do not miss them; yet when the good things depart, their absence torments our hearts. This is particularly clear in matters of love.

As the Buddha stated, in the Dhammapada, "Follow not after vanity, nor after the enjoyment of love and lust. He who is earnest and meditative obtains ample joy" (Babbitt 2012, location 118, verse 27). We are likely already clear on the lust part of it. No matter how much salt water we drink, it won't quench our thirst. But love? Isn't love all you need, as the both the Beatles and our more traditional mentors have told us? Well, yes and no: certainly Love is, but love, maybe not.

Let's just say you find an unimaginably fine and beautiful person, someone who not only looks good to you physically, but who shares your interests, values, and goals. This person cares about you as much as you care about him or her. Your relationship appears ideal, and you are resonating with energy and happiness, states you carry with you throughout the day as you muse on your beloved. Your love is, moreover, a refined and exalted one; you do not desire to simply leap into bed, but look for any opportunity you can find to help and serve the one you love. Suddenly, he or she leaves to take a job in a distant town. Maybe they no longer keep in touch, and you find yourself on your own again. Or, more devastatingly, they decide they want to spend their lives with someone else.

While you enjoyed the experience of being with them too much to ever regret it, this condition of love and loss seems, in a sense, even worse than being continuously alone, and you must strenuously resist the urge to be morbidly pessimistic. You were shown enough to experience what you have always wanted, just enough to see that it actually did exist as a sublime and genuine feeling, that it was indeed more than an imaginary hope. And then amid that recognition, the love you had always sought was painfully and abruptly torn away. What you hoped would be the love of your life has departed, while all the annoying people and circumstances you thought you had, at last, found some timely relief from, are all still there, swarming around you menacingly. You see others enjoying the type of relationship bliss you had, until recently, savored, and you find it hard not to be envious. As the pain of your loss is virtually unbearable, you fall back hard on all of your bad habits, on all of your customary addictions and dependencies; they, whatever they may be, return anew, with an almost irresistible and seemingly sadistic force.

So, what has happened here? What happened is that you depended on love in your broader quest for Love; in a contrary move, you made your spiritual state of bliss and independence dependent on a particular dualistic experience. You made having a certain someone around the precondition for loving anyone or anything at all. Thinking you had reached the apex of joy, you ended up instead only skewered once again on the prongs of a dissatisfying duality. The Buddha had as perfect a wife as any on earth had ever been. His conclusion, as couched in the poetic language of *The Light of Asia*: "if love lasted, there were joy in this; / But life's way is the wind's way, all these things/ Are but brief voices breathed on shifting strings." (Arnold, The Light of Asia 2012, 63) The reverse obstacle, once we realize this, is to go to the opposite extreme, to avoid all relationships because we know they may cause us pain, to disengage with life entirely, to become a stoic or cynic. But that is not the way to be either; we must still have the courage to live and to emerge happy and victorious. Such are the two egoistic extremes of attachment and aversion, the enemies on our path. Through them we either cling to a life that can't be held, or petulantly condemn it for its intractable deficiencies.

We grow most through our primary relationships—particularly our love relationships. They are the ones that cause us the greatest joy, and also the deepest pain. When a person is sufficiently advanced to realize that permanent happiness is not to be found among the perpetual ups and downs of life, yet not enough to seek it through its Source alone, he looks for it within the context of human love. Convinced he is rocketing into the stratosphere, he hasn't in fact left the ground. Not even those involved in the most successful relationships have cause to say that those meaningful associations are nothing but a joyride. What they experience instead is the totality of life, and after both joy and disillusionment, typically with the other person and with the image they had of them, they arrive at a higher level of love and understanding. But the unavoidable duality is still there.

Twin Soul relationships, relationships between individuals who are a perfect vibrational match at the level of Spirit, have been described, in this context, as "growth on steroids."[1] This type of relationship, matching the duality inherent in material life itself, is often the most frustrating and blissful at once.

The essential problem with this Love versus love scenario is that it ties what is permanent, and thus fully satisfying, to what is changing and unreliable. At least with an inanimate object that we are attached to, it is likely to remain on the shelf where we left it; but with people, you can never know or control who they are, or what they may decide to do; nor could a meaningful relationship ever develop from so doing. The problem here is in not seeking Love first on its own ground, before experiencing and appreciating it elsewhere. Adopting this broader view doesn't involve our becoming unaffectionate, cold, and callous or of never forming deep, full relationships, but of avoiding what is the essential issue with all things or persons to which we become attached, confusing the scenery along the way with the journey's end, and focusing on the part as if it were the whole.

In Buddhist lore and cosmology, and among sentient beings, the highest happiness is said to be enjoyed by the long-lived gods. They are purported to dwell in exalted realms of intensified bliss for many thousands of years. It is also said that when their end is near, their suffering is greater than that of the hell-beings. Greater!! There is a lesson here for us. About how to view, in perspective, the ostensibly "good" and "bad" that happens to us. Absorbing this lesson should place a rational cap on the amount of suffering we might reasonably expect from not getting what we want, knowing that the pleasure we receive through the mundane objects of our desire, as great as it may be, is finite, that there is pain associated with to its absence, both before and afterwards, and that we must first seek the highest happiness, where it is to be reliably found—within. It also advises us to enjoy change ideally from a vantage point that is permanent. Once immersed in the ocean you no longer will be devastated when a tributary dries up.

A good way to get beyond the stranglehold that our attachments have over us, and to maintain a sound and valid perspective on life, is through the following exercise. When something bad occurs, immediately see how it could well have been worse—and usually much worse. For example, we may find ourselves annoyed by a traffic jam, in the wake of accident, a veritable snarl that is preventing us from getting to work on time. Yet at least we weren't part of the accident! If we were involved in the accident and our car is wrecked, but we are okay, we can derive much solace from that understanding. If we are injured but the injuries can heal, this can encourage us too.

On the flip side, when something good appears, we should appreciate that it is only one of many possible good things, and that this particular good thing can be potentially even better. We may have a good job, but there could well be better ones out there that will likely, in time and as we gain experience, make themselves available to us. We may have many positive relationships; yet the best person we are destined to know may be one we haven't yet met. We may live in a good neighborhood, but our finest dwelling yet, may be in a different region, one we haven't yet seen.

Unwarranted clinging to the good things in life is the sign of a poverty consciousness; it keeps even better ones from arriving as soon as they otherwise would. Life often has to clear our plates to make room for better offerings.[2] If the time has come to let go and we don't, we are destined to suffer hideously. This isn't to suggest that we take for granted what we already have. We should never cast our fortunes to the winds without considering the greater consequences, or suddenly become cold and indifferent. What it does mean is that we recognize 1) that life is continuously changing, 2) that clinging is a delusion, and 3) that if not now, then eventually, we are all destined to move on. These conclusions, all of which can be amply corroborated by experience, should enable us to proceed through life and love with courage and hope, and to demonstrate a lighter touch.

NOTES

1. This expression was used on the Twin Flame Connections website, though the author disagrees that it accurately applies to the Twin Flame relationship. (Twin Flame Connection: Twin Flame guidance and Insights with Twin Flame Psychics n.d.)

2. I once stated this idea similarly, when I wrote in *Guideposts to the Heart*, "Sometimes, life must clear our table, so to speak, to make room for better entrees. This becomes a problem only when the person then thinks that he has nothing better to do than starve." (G. Hallett 2011, 30)

Chapter 17

The Gardener

Voltaire, at the end of his tragi-comic masterpiece, *Candide*, in which his awkwardly naïve, yet optimistic protagonist runs, literally and figuratively, a gauntlet through life, concludes that one should go and cultivate his garden, to in effect retreat to his own corner of existence and till away at what joy and productive interests he can scavenge there. James Allen, by contrast, employs the analogy of the gardener in a more upbeat, social, optimistic, and expansive way.

A good gardener tends his growing area well, extracting the weeds, and encouraging the useful plants to thrive. We know that the weeds, once pulled, don't stay submerged forever, but tend to annoyingly resurface; yet with constant and routine elimination, they gradually and permanently wither. The gardening Allen refers to takes place in the soil of the mind.

The type of tilling, literal or figurative, to which we give precedence, reveals our personal priorities. Middle class suburbanites are constantly mowing their lawns and trimming their trees. They look askance at anyone in their proximate vicinity who neglects to do the same. Yet they will heedlessly allow the weeds of ignorance, ill-will, anger, and negativity to tear rampant through their mental gardens.

Many business people, comparably, will dress as if they were posing for a fashion issue, while pursuing a less than morally-tidy cutthroat agenda. Those who conform to this pattern, are typically as clean on the outside as they are dirty on the inside.

As a society replete with external objects of interest, our focus tends likewise, to be outward, not inward. We tend to care more about style than about substance, more about how people look than about who they are, the impression we make rather than the values we espouse. Yet while styles change and are as variable as the tides, substance remains constant and enduring. Someday we will leave—not just our homes—but the very carapace of flesh with which we are so intimately identified. Our worldly gardens, then, will be abandoned, to lie in stasis, to be overrun, or to be managed, perhaps, by someone else; but the effects of the gardening we have done within will carry forward with us. So, which is truly more important? And which, ultimately, can give us hope, for here, from within the modest domain of our peaceful walks and cathartic meditations, we can stage a triumphant and compassionate return to Life from Voltaire's harsher and more pessimistic viewpoint. We can cultivate "in our own gardens" those values that may quietly and unobtrusively remake the world.

Chapter 18

Independence

"Ye are all gods."

The Biblical injunction to "seek first the kingdom of God and his righteousness, and all these things (all else that you need) will be added unto you," (Bible Hub, n.d., Berean Study Bible, Matt. 6:33) implies essentially two things; that there is a natural order of priorities in which the spiritual takes precedence over the material; and that what exists apart from the spiritual has value for us too. We will naturally prefer a dulcet harmony over a grating cacophony, a Mozart concerto to a toilet flush, success over failure, beauty over ugliness, in whatever form they may happen to take. If we didn't, we'd be no more sentient than hunks of wood or blocks of stone, and should probably have our heads examined. So how then do we reconcile the apparent contradiction between having preferences and staying balanced between extremes? The answer is that we can align ourselves between them, when the glory of our attainment is beyond them. The waves may pulverize the ships on the water's surface, but the ocean depths remain undisturbed. By comparison, we can hope to dwell safely amidst the pleasures of the world, knowing that a joy that transcends them is continuously available.

A man may covet his neighbor's Chevy so long as he has nothing else to drive, but can view it with relative equanimity—perhaps even with pride and satisfaction—if he, himself has a Mercedes. That is why many retreat from the pleasures of the world in a strenuous effort to be spiritual, not because pleasure is inherently evil—it isn't—but because in knowing nothing better or higher, what is worse and lower would invariably tend to distract.

This would seem to be why in the domain of sin, sexuality frequently takes top billing over murder or larceny, not because its offenses are more heinous—they are not—but because its lures are more provocative. They also, by increasing our susceptibility to anger and delusion, pave the way for other, more serious transgressions. As most people are not irresistibly drawn to kill or steal, but are more generally enticed by "the pleasures of the flesh," knowing that "something higher" becomes our key to victory. We then become like the man who, having found the kingdom of heaven, sold all he owned to attain it, where no more-limited loss could affect that greater gain.

I remember reading a news blurb about an amusing event that happened shortly after the Berlin Wall came down. A man from West Berlin visited East Berlin. He happened to have his boxed lunch with him, which included a banana for dessert. A citizen of East Berlin who had never seen a banana before asked if he could try it. To the other's amazement, the Westerner's new acquaintance ate the banana, peel and all, pronouncing it delicious.

Well imagine a similar scenario in which you are an exchange student from a foreign country, East Total Ignoramia, who has never had a pizza before. When you arrive home from your evening class, you discover an empty pizza box with traces of mozzarella and sauce on it. Delighted with this discovery, you devour the remains, cardboard, and all. Like the man who ate the banana, you likewise pronounce it delicious, and look forward to repeating that culinary experience again in the near future.

Later your housemates come home. They discover after the second or third week that this is what you have been doing and decide that this preposterous routine simply can't continue. After all, if you keep eating all that cardboard, you will eventually make yourself sick! So, one day, as usual, you return home from class, expecting to find the much-desired pizza box, only to find it gone—thoroughly disposed of! You know that it was there from the pile of plates in the sink, and from the heavenly aroma of mozzarella and sauce that still hangs redolent in the air—but no box!

Your first thought is one of outrage. How could they do this to you, and why? "It is unjust! It is wrong!! I was really enjoying that food-coated cardboard." So, with that chip planted firmly on your shoulder, you come home early the following week, intending to confront your housemates in anger over the issue, only to find them waiting for you with a full uneaten pizza, welcoming you in to enjoy it.

It is almost certain that what is valued too high will cost us too dear. It may cost us in terms of dollars. It will certainly cost us, ultimately, in peace of mind. And should we see any one person, or any one thing, as being the only option available, it is a clear sign that we are too-heavily invested.

One time, between graduate semesters, I went looking for some temporary employment. I responded to a want ad for a telemarketer to work at a furniture store in Bridgeport, CT. The store was located in a questionable area, flanked by two erotic bars. The front office, in which I interviewed, appeared cluttered, cramped, and dingy. I thought to myself, even as I was applying for it, that it wouldn't bother me too much if I didn't get this job. So, when the manager said the position paid between nine and twelve dollars per hour (numbers that would be much higher today with inflation factored in), I said, "I would have to have to take the 12." After consulting privately with his assistant, he agreed to pay me what I asked. He then led me from the dusty front office to a showcase area in back, one which was beautifully furnished and, during the course of that swelteringly hot summer, blissfully air-conditioned. I would sit peacefully and alone at an ornately-adorned desk and make outbound calls. The manager even brought me a cup of coffee every evening, taking a few minutes each time to stop and chat. Had I known initially how easy and pleasant this little job would be, I might have cheated myself out of the higher rate of pay. In not wanting it too badly, in not seeing it as the only option available, I ended up receiving more.

Since "the world is won by those who let it go," (Tzu 1983, 119) the very best way to get something, or so it would seem, would be to not want it at all. As in the pursuit of the lover's quarry, chase the world and it runs away; ignore it, and it pursues us. This fickle attitude on the part of Life can lead to an immediate cynicism, prompting us to declare along with Solomon, that "all (is) vanity and vexation of spirit," (Bible Hub, n.d., Jubilee Bible 2000, Ecclesiastes 2:11) that all the world's joys are, from the outset, nothing but cheats. Yet here, as elsewhere, the kindness of God lies hidden within the cruelty of our immediate experience. For this scenario begs the larger question of what it is we want, and the way in which we should want it.

"Seek first the Kingdom of God." "Aim first for the highest happiness," as Joseph Goldstein states, affirming this Christian ideal from a Buddhist perspective, "and all other types of happiness come." (Goldstein, The Experience of Insight 1983, 113) The things of the world become burdensome, only when we experience them out of context and out of place in relation to our legitimate center. We realize this, finally, in fully understanding that the feverish swirl of activity we have been fearfully making our way through is but an infinitesimal part of life, and who we think we are, but a shadow of our genuine selves.

In the Gita, Krishna tells Arjuna, prior to appearing to him as God in His infinite form, that "What I have spoken here to thee is only a small part of my Infinity." (Mascaro 1974, 87) The Kabbalah similarly refers to the ninety-nine percent world where what we are so preoccupied with and take to be the All is only a measly one percent of Life. The world of the senses, one that wondrously encompasses what can be catalogued within the vastness of space and in the broad visible immediacy of the sun and stars, is still, finally, only that limited one percent. How little we know compared to what we don't know! (Y. Berg 2004, 14–15) It is like climbing a peak only to discover the horizon we can progressively observe stretching expansively into the distance.

In Buddhism, the supreme obstacle has been labeled, without any direct translation, "tanha." It has been described by E.A. Burtt as, "the blind

demandingness . . . in our nature which leads us to ask of the universe . . .
more than it is ready or even able to give." (Burtt 1955, 28) It is what the
exchange student exhibited when he couldn't eat his cardboard. Tanha makes
one great, false, and ultimately disastrous assumption—that we know more
than God or our spiritual guides about what we need to do to reach our
proper ends.

At first, we are stumbling around in the dark, before intuition's light is
successfully ignited; until then, we have not the means of accurately discerning what we should do and where we should go. That is why, in the East, the
initial surrender to a guru is so strongly emphasized. At the outset, we are like
Odysseus tied to the mast; we think we can listen to the siren call of our old
material desires, and not be pathetically sucked in.

Also, in not seeing all, we don't always understand our own good. Each
of us is, at first, like a child who insists sticking his hand into an electrical
socket.[1] We demand our own way with things that can't, from the outset,
bring any sort of enduring satisfaction, but which will, more likely than not,
cause us harm. This is the realm that tanha surveys.

NOTE

1. This is an analogy I used in an earlier book, *Guideposts to the Heart*. (G. Hallett
2011)

Chapter 19

Change, Independence, and "The Powers That Be"

Americans are addicted to progress; progress, implies change. Americans are okay with change, so long as it serves to enhance their lives rather than to disrupt them. Cars and cell phones are as radical in their own way as the *Communist Manifesto*, the difference being that they connect families through travel and the airwaves, rather than abolishing the family altogether as a presumed bourgeois myth, with the first being acceptable to most Americans and the second not.

The Democratic Convention of 1968, represented the high-water mark of American Liberalism; it featured militant Yippies violently protesting, amidst ongoing confrontations with police, in the streets outside the convention hall. The American mainstream determined, then and there, that enough was finally enough. It opted for stability over change in the presidential election that followed. It continued to do so in many of the years to come. The tide had begun to turn. Richard Nixon won.

"The Powers That Be" are well aware of how this works, and so, are quick to associate undesirable change with an abrupt toppling of the apple cart. For example, Ram Das has certainly been an intelligent and articulate spokesman for Eastern spirituality. But I am sure he is more palatable to the mainstream establishment, more acceptable in his role as cultural rebel, in having been kicked out of Harvard for his lifestyle choice of massive LSD consumption. Shirley McClain became more acceptable in titling her book Out on a Limb, as "out on a limb" is where most Americans clearly don't want to be. The overwhelming response of the American majority to the idea of leaving their safe suburban homes to cavort recklessly through the Peruvian Andes in search of aliens, in cars that drive themselves, would be a sharp and definitive "no." 1968 revisited. "The Powers That Be" thus encourage us to, in effect, cast out the baby of change by polluting the surrounding bathwater.

Communism long stood as a clear and explicit challenge to American capitalism, plotting deliberately for its overthrow. There the threat was obvious. Yet what could the dominant capitalist culture have against the mysticism of the East? After all, from one angle at least, and as Marx wryly observed, religion often serves as "the opiate of the people." It can make us more tolerant, perhaps of what we should not be tolerant of to begin with.

Perhaps if worker A goes home to meditate after his shift, he will endure with spiritually-cultivated patience the unreasonable demands and irascible temper of his boss, not to mention the undercutting of his salary and the curtailment of his ambitions, whereas worker B, who doesn't meditate, would likely choose instead to go on strike, to join a union, or to embark on a vindictive rampage. Veteran meditators may be expected to instead tune out, thereby rendering themselves pitifully irrelevant, and thus less likely as a result to be positioned up on the roof of corporate headquarters with an AK-47.

Yet from a broader perspective, the meditative lifestyle does represent a challenge, for it bluntly contends that the headlong pursuit of outward material enjoyments, the bedrock of our consumer culture, is not and should not be the end-all and be-all of Being, and that it may, in the final analysis, be nothing but a sham, delusive to the mind and hazardous to the soul. Less bound by material goods and goals, such people would be less enslaved to their jobs and their bosses. In attaching less value to standard material rewards and more to spiritual ones, over which the entrenched establishment has no real control, might be expected, ultimately, to render the spiritual person less materially ambitious and less socially compliant.

Yet despite all caricatures and negative associations as harbingers of questionable change, yoga and meditation have stuck around since their 60s heyday, and are commonly practiced now, even in corporate rec rooms. The reason is, at least partially, that they satisfy a glaring need. They fill a gaping hole in the center of our presumed happiness that no amount of religious ritual or material consumption alone can fill. The American Dream, popularly defined, as based solely on a rampart and unquestioned consumerism, is so flawed, that it has become for many a form of diurnal nightmare. In the midst of its circular activity and emotional carnage stands revealed a genuine need for the spiritual to balance the material in our personal declaration of independence and individual pursuit of happiness. The same sense of "quiet desperation" which once sent Thoreau tramping off to the woods near Walden Pond, now directs many of us to a quiet room in our suburban homes to meditate. Meditation, thus practiced, allows us to both adhere efficiently to our daily routines and to manage them more effectively.

At both a spiritually higher and at a pragmatically productive level, the character traits developed through meditation help us to cope without caving in, to develop as good team players without abandoning our personal ethics or values. It makes us good and thoughtful citizens and participants. It makes for excellence in our creative endeavors and work. Of course, the main marketplace has its own brand of spirituality, one which, in its dominant form and impetus reflects our overarching materialistic ethic and agenda. Either we can be properly spiritual only by following some external voice and outward ritual (the Catholic bias), or we are alternatively regarded from the outset as nothing but "puny worms crawling in the dirt," (the Protestant extreme) with each variant, at the end of the day, leading to the same conclusion: that we cannot trust in or rely on ourselves, and must remain helplessly subservient and mindlessly acquiescent to authority; this is something that those who would keep us docile and controlled would naturally want us to be. This is not to say that there is some form of systematic conspiracy designed to keep us down, or that organized religion itself has no value, but that for those who are willing to be drawn in by shallow pursuits, canned answers, and limited dreams there are—and will always be—swindlers and enablers to match. To reemphasize what PT Barnum observed, "there is a sucker born every minute." Those willing to be deceived and those willing to deceive, now, as fully as in Barnum's time, form a matching pair.

Chapter 20

The Three Dark Doors

As the Gita states, "Hell has three doors: lust, rage and greed. These lead to man's ruin . . . He who passes by these three dark doors has achieved his own salvation." (Isherwood 1972, 116) Lust for sex can be best understood as analogous to greed for food. Both pertain to legitimate physical requirements. Both have an appropriate role and measure. Both are satisfied not merely to meet a physical need but—and let's face it—for the genuine pleasure they give. Both can be extremely destructive if indulged in excessively. Both are the focus of known and problematic addictions.

Greed is the extreme of attachment, as anger (wrath) is the extreme of aversion. The point to remember about all of these extremes is that we only pursue material things excessively and obsessively when the joy of our spiritual center, our sustaining connection to our Source is lost. When we have the pizza, we won't want or need to eat the box.

That being said, there are ways in which the demands for food and sex do differ; while the absence of food leads inexorably to starvation and death, the ability to abstain from sex can lead, when intelligently undertaken, to the salubrious conservation of energy. But this is only if the drive itself is not repressed but expressed at a higher level.

During the World War II siege of Leningrad, the city's inhabitants were being starved into submission by the surrounding Germans. They ate bread made from sawdust, and were known to consume rats, pets, and presumably even the corpses of the dead to survive.[1] Deprived of proper nutriment, their hunger took an unnatural turn. Much the same can be said for members of the clergy who, having entered what may, for many, be an unnatural life of celibacy, turn to pedophilia, and to other unnatural acts as a warped means of expressing their bottled-up drives. This is not to suggest that celibacy, correctly practiced, doesn't have its notable benefits, but only if it is based on the individual's recognized needs and true spiritual condition.

NOTE

1. For more on this topic, see *The 900 Days: The Siege of Leningrad.* (Salisbury 1970)

Chapter 21

Sex and Spirituality

Sex is a complicated subject, virtually as complicated as life itself. Most who claim to thoroughly understand it, don't understand it much at all. Sexual energy is like gasoline (i.e., a substance that can be used to run a car, or by an arsonist to torch a building). Its value depends on its use. To condemn sex for its abuses is like banning speech because some people use obscenities.

Our prevailing attitude toward sex reveals less about sex and more about our ignorance of it, for we would not condemn it if we saw how positive some of its spiritual (yes, spiritual!) outcomes could be. Enlightenment itself is a creative process and one can easily argue that without the creative energy of sex, in its exalted and sublimated form, one cannot become enlightened!

The negative societal attitude toward sex is based on an appreciation that at its rudimentary level it is tied in with the most out-of-control forms of aggression on the competitive plane of physical reproduction. For example, men who find their wives sleeping with other men might throw reason to the wind and commit crimes of passion, perhaps even murder. It is because of the potential of sex at this raw and rudimentary level to lightly tear asunder the delicate fabric of society that it has been so heavily regulated. The Ten Commandments, which include prohibitions against sexual coveting and adultery, are, in this sense, not simply the basis of an objective morality, but of social cohesion itself.

The fact remains that Western society sees sexuality only in terms of its basest forms, while remaining oblivious to its fuller and higher expressions, expressions associated with health, creativity, ethereal (and not merely carnal) love, and enlightenment. As Da Liu states in T'ai Chi Ch'uan & Meditation:

> Meditation consists of using the mind to direct the breath so that all elements in the body are gathered up, heated, and transformed into an elixir. This elixir is called "the golden pill" or "the golden flower" by Taoists. In modern scientific terms, the elixir is actually sexual energy. The presence or absence of sexual energy is very important to the health and well-being of the body. When sexual

energy is at a high level, the body will be healthy; when it is exhausted, the body
will die. (Liu 1991, 150)

At the spiritual level, harmony, unity, and love, exist. At the material level,
duality and conflict predominate. When a couple operates primarily on the
spiritual level, their relationship reflects the preponderance of the higher,
more spiritual energies. But when it is defined overwhelmingly at the physical level, it reflects instead the duality and conflict associated with material
existence itself.

At that baser level, men and women are found to have fundamentally
competing interests. Women there see men predominantly as "pigs" who
only want to have sex with as many female partners as possible, while men
view women as "gold diggers" who would coarsely place a price tag on love,
seeking security at the expense of intimacy. And at the material level, should
a couple rise no higher, both would be correct. Only a fundamentally spiritual
relationship based upon love, respect, and mutual service, expanded into the
broader service of others, can be a happy and harmonious one; only a relationship grounded in eternity can hope to endure through time.

Sexual energy, as it is recognized in the East, is a concentrated form of
prana, the root energy of Life. When conserved and channeled upward, rather
than being allowed to outwardly dissipate, it revitalizes and awakens the system of nadis and chakras which, in combination are known as kundalini. The
ancient symbol of the caduceus is none other than a thinly-veiled representation of this kundalini, directly associating its functioning with the mainte-
nance of physiological well-being, with our routine good health and longevity
tied, to a far greater extent than Western medicine currently acknowledges, to
intelligently conserving and channeling this energy. This transcultural symbol
of the caduceus been staring the Occident's medical profession in the face for
years; it nonetheless looks outward rather than inward for the primary means
of restoring good health.

Still, if this kundalini system, with its intricate network of nadis and
chakras really does exist, as those who have experienced it unequivocally
claim, then how could an entire civilization, including its esteemed medical
experts, be so persistently ignorant of it? Part of the answer has to do with our
excessively material orientation.

If we wish to view water as steam, we will do so only if the temperature in
an area rises to the evaporation point. Below that, water will remain as liquid
or solidly as ice. Similarly, if the dominating thoughts of an individual remain
outwardly-directed and material, his energies will be predominantly dark
and dense as well, and it will be, for that individual, as if this subtle energy
system never even existed. Secondly, even among spiritual people, and in
regions where it is more widely known, the awakening of the kundalini force

remains a relatively rare event, though in the current age, it is happening more often. Where it occurs spontaneously, particularly in environments ignorant of its workings, in societies, like ours, where material norms predominate, and where the individual has not let go of his inharmonious and grasping tendencies, the inevitable result is a heightened level of creativity, coupled with emotional imbalance. Hence it has been said that "there is a fine line separating genius from madness." Such madness is the ethereal level of thought as yet incompletely decoupled from the downward pull of matter. It has been speculated, by Gopi Krishna and others, that certain optimally-inspired individuals (one immediately thinks of van Gogh) were both highly creative and insane based on the spontaneous, premature, and unregulated rise of this force, an event that can have unpredictable consequences.

When the kundalini force is activated, as all who have experienced it would readily attest, it becomes essential for the affected individual to live in an increasingly regulated way. Exercise becomes not only beneficial, but indispensable, with specific asanas (postures) emphasized to open channels for the upward flow of energy, and to prevent troubling blockages. No longer is it possible to do just anything, to think just anything, to eat just anything, or to live in a random and reckless way; and although the rewards more than compensate for these constraints, the penalty for failing to live a regulated and disciplined life for a person who has undergone this atypical transformation is to a greater or lesser degree, a loss of mental balance; and in a society that doesn't even begin to acknowledge the underlying cause, the results can be personally catastrophic.

Still, it should be recognized that this is all part of an evolutionary process, one that kundalini itself initiates. Those who have been blessed—or some might say cursed (though it ultimately is a blessing)—with this unusual transformation will go where few have gone before. They may even acquire some supernormal abilities along the way, known in the East as siddhis. Lest that make them feel too proud or godlike, they will also know humiliation, embarrassment, and shame as they have never experienced them before. As Christmas Humphreys states, "He who takes his future in his hands, and molds his life accordingly, may be called on to pay (his) debts more quickly, that he may be free. He who is thus privileged will the sooner learn first-hand of that 'sea of sorrow formed of the tears of men'" (Humphreys 1962, 158–59), and this as the energies of kundalini's personal cataclysm transform him from a helpless embryo of sorts to an enhanced mode of life.

The end result of properly governing your sex life without repression, is that in ceasing to be enslaved by the desires of your lower nature, you achieve an inner harmony by which you come to realize progressively the purposes of your Higher Self; by pursuing your highest purpose, you come to be aligned with the still greater Will of God. In alignment with the Will of God, you harness the ability to satisfy all valid desires (including those associated, in the broadest sense, with sexuality), fulfill all worthy intentions and achieve the larger and more encompassing end of happiness.

At the opposite extreme, for an individual on the road to enlightenment, the expression of sex at a lower level means generating denser energies which can clog the psychic nerves. The purge of these lower energies from the higher functioning system is achieved by burning them off in a process that, when it occurs, is by no means pleasant.

I, for one, have never, ever had a dissipative sexual experience, one entirely physical, without love involved, where I have ever felt energetically better afterwards; relieved perhaps, but not better. And this is, once again, because pleasure at the sensory level and satisfaction at the spiritual level, at the level of our inner being, are two different things. What leads to one doesn't necessarily lead to the other, and may in fact take you in a separate direction entirely. Secondly, and more critically, with the physical orgasm itself, there is a burst of energy at the denser material level which for a spiritual person, dwelling most of the time, at the level of elevated energy, clogs the system, sticks to the nadis like glue, and activates the animal nature disturbingly. These are the "snares and poisons" the Buddha spoke about.[1] For a spiritually advanced individual, in part due to the friction caused by all this internal clogging, and the pulling toward the material and spiritual centers of gravity simultaneously, a very unpleasant amount of heat is generated; it can even be felt by others as a negative vibration or energy; as one Master expressed it "lust fries the brain."

Finally, the spiritual person undergoes trials from which the sensory world is the source. Indulging in sex, excessively (once again without love—and with dissipation) will literally pull him out of his spiritual center and into the material whirlwind that threatens to engulf him. Hence the Dhammapada states, ". . . so, a man's wickedness, when it is very great, brings him to that state where his enemy wishes him to be." (Babbitt 2012, location 347, verse 163)

As further elaborated by Brian Walker, in his translation of the *Hua Hu Ching*:

A person's approach to sexuality is a sign of his level of evolution. Unevolved persons practice ordinary sexual intercourse. Placing all emphasis upon the sexual organs they neglect the body's other organs and systems. Whatever physical energy is accumulated is summarily discharged, and the subtle energies are similarly dissipated and disordered. It is a great backward leap.

For those who aspire to the higher realms of living, there is angelic dual cultivation. Because every portion of the body, mind, and spirit yearns for the integration of yin and yang, angelic intercourse is led by the spirit rather than the sexual organs.

Where ordinary intercourse is effortful, angelic cultivation is calm, relaxed, quiet, and natural. Where ordinary intercourse unites sex organs with sex organs, angelic cultivation unites spirit with spirit, mind with mind, and every cell of one body with every cell of the other body. Culminating not in dissolution but in integration, it is an opportunity for a man and woman to mutually transform and uplift each other into the realm of bliss and wholeness. (Walker 1992, 88)

There are two outlets for sex that are particularly problematic to the point of being unwholesome: sex (or strip) clubs and pornography. In each case, the act of sex is estranged from the expression of love, where the two were originally meant to conjoin. Prostitution, being thoroughly problematic, falls outside of this discussion entirely. Considering it first, pornography deals with elements that are entirely unnatural. The illusion of sex is there, but none of the reality.

In the *Star Trek* episode, "I Borg," engineer Jordi Laforge, constructs a paradox, an insoluble problem, that is designed to take down the Borg, a race of cybernetic beings possessing a collective consciousness, and his Federation's chief enemy; it is intended to do so by excluding certain basic elements that would allow them to arrive at a solution. (Lederman 1992) The comparison with pornography is that there are key elements of the real experience that are troublingly absent; hence no amount of it can ultimately satisfy. As the Dhammapada states, "There is no satisfying lusts even by a shower of gold-pieces; he who knows that lusts have a short taste and bring suffering in their train is wise." (Babbitt 2012, location 387, verse 187); thus, the tendency of lust, both short and long term, and particularly in this form, to foster insatiable desires, much like the Star Trek paradox that created an endless and unsolvable loop.

Real-life sex displays, such as those found in strip clubs, have a slightly different drawback. While often lumped together with pornography under the broader rubric of "fantasy," they are only fantasy if what one is fantasizing about is true love or an enduring relationship. While some people who view such displays may deceive themselves into believing that the person gyrating on the stage really loves him, the majority are not so bluntly deceived.

Still with strip clubs to the extent that sex itself is real, there is certainly someone there. There are also subtle elements of reality, pheromones and the like, which can make the experience, unlike that associated with pornography, temporarily more complete and satisfying. Yet the drawback here, one that pornography lacks, is that it is a communal activity focused essentially on a form of matter worship.

It has been said that, when people meditate or congregate at a temple or church, the positive impact of one's spiritual practice is greatly intensified by the fact that it is communal. With public displays of sexuality designed to stimulate lust among a significant gathering of people, a communal activity is engaged in, focused on something less exalted. While the vibrations in a temple or church can be expected to be highly elevated, those in places where matter is effectively worshiped, can be thick, dark, and disturbing. That being said, it may still be wrong to dismiss any such relative activity as absolutely negative. Repressed sexuality has led to neurotic and even criminal behavior, making deficient outlets arguably still better than none at all, particular for young people at the height of their sexual powers. Whatever the prospective utility, it remains important to remain keenly aware of the deficiencies, also.

If someone were to ask me what the most valuable thing is that I have learned from the practice of yoga, I would say unequivocally, it is the enormous—almost incalculable—value of conserving sexual energy. The benefits that accrue from such a practice, some of which have already been noted, can hardly be overestimated, while the drawbacks of living a dissolute life, even for someone young, can hardly be overstated.

The prevailing wisdom in this society is that sexual health consists of nothing else or more than robust and frequent orgasms. I adhered to this common idea in my early 20s, when the application of sexual moderation, in any form, would have seemed to me to be nothing less than a cruel and unnecessary form of self-torture. During that time, I also felt constantly weak, tired, and agitated. I seemed to get sick very easily. When it was time to sleep, my mind was locked in overdrive, my thoughts racing rapidly. When I woke in the morning, I was invariably enervated to a degree that, over time, became maddening. A classmate of my brother's, who commuted with us to school, would regale me, after he arrived in the morning, with his tormenting, "rise and shine."

Nowadays, at a time when I am significantly older, my mind at night is typically calm and clear. I usually sleep well. I have also discovered that I can often get by just fine, most days, with only five or six hours of sleep. I am rarely ill. It is only when the system has been refined and purified through meditation and other spiritual practices that the positive effect of retaining and sublimating the pranic fuel becomes noticeable. Until then it is like noise upon noise, the activation of rough energies against a backdrop where rough energies predominate.[2]

Sexuality is also the primary thing—the primary thing—which lowers what Hindus term the veil of Maya, the illusion that the fluid, unstable, and shifting elements of Life's 3-D movie are fixed, stable, and real. The haze of lust, the reification of sensual pleasure, the over-conceptualization of our experiences, all combine to cast a delusive shadow, contributing to a heavy egotism.

Nature gives such priority to the procreation of the species that, when the objects of our sexual interest captivate us, they stimulate us to pursue them as if they were the end-all and be-all of life. If we allow ourselves to be too thickly immersed in this fog, it will cast a frightening cloak of darkness over our eyes. This is why *The Voice of the Silence* states, "If thou would'st cross . . . safely, let not thy mind mistake the fires of lust that burn therein for the Sunlight of life." (Blavatsky 2011, 6–7)

It is further to be noted that each of us transmits, through the energy of our thoughts, the signature of who we are out into our larger world. Then by the Law of Attraction we draw resonant persons and conditions. In a concerted way, the conservation of energy adds power to our personal grids, allowing the standard version of the law to function more powerfully and reliably. When our minds are darkened, what we attract into our lives is wrong.

So why do some people continue to engage in questionable sexual activities even after becoming conscious of their drawbacks? Reasons are, that 1) after survival itself, sex is the strongest of instincts and is, as such, extraordinarily alluring; the Buddha, himself, admitted with a touching and self-effacing candor that if there was another instinct like sex, he wouldn't be the Buddha (Smith 1991, 90), and 2) Sex is totally absorbing, making it, like alcohol, a genuine temptation for people who feel the need to distance themselves from issues too seemingly problematic for them to immediately confront.

The Dalai Lama, quoting the ancient sage Nagarjuna, analogized the sex drive in pedestrian terms: "when you have an itch, you scratch, but not to itch at all is better than any amount of itching"; perhaps for someone of his exalted stature, a sexual impulse may be nothing more than an undesirable itch, but for the rest of us, it remains compelling enough. (2008, 225) Yogananda's preceptor, Sri Yukteswar advised, that "even when the flesh is weak, the mind should be constantly resistant. If temptation assails you with cruel force, overcome it by impersonal analysis and indomitable will. Every natural passion can be mastered." (Yogananda 2003, 148) Of course he was speaking at the time to a group of renunciants living in an Ashram.

One bit of advice I found personally helpful is contained in the Thirumandiram of the Tamil Siddhars, which argues that even if desire itself cannot be defeated, through the avoidance of dissipation greatness can still be obtained. From that source directly, "If Bindu stands retained in body/ Life ebbs not; great strength. Energy, intelligence alert, /Tapas, contemplation, and silence/ And siddhis (supernormal powers) enduring, /All these are attained,/ If Bindu be conserved true." (Thirumoolar 1993, 7–56, stanza 1948). If the mind is balanced, focused, and without undue attachment, the inner energy will be channeled upward; it then becomes the atomic bomb (sex) that ignites the thermonuclear bomb (of kundalini).

The Gita states that "when self-control is self-torture . . . then self-control is of darkness . . ." (Mascaro 1974, 113) As Sri Krishna Prem, consistently noted, Origen's self-castration did not make him a true bramacharaya,[3] while

Gopi Krishna's assessment of Kundalini is that the spiritual person has more sexuality not less. (Krishna 1970, 99) What is different is how it is channeled.

We are, and have always been, part of the natural order of things, an order which includes both the material and spiritual realms. Our current "modern" way of defining ourselves takes account of the first way, but not the second. As our approach to happiness is geared primarily toward pumping in pleasure from the outside, our way to health relies similarly and predominantly on external cures which, rather than leading us to harmonize with who we are, with our own inner energies as an integral part of Nature, involve elixirs which themselves fall outside of what we would naturally tend to imbibe. While it is clear that we should make use of whatever efficient means are available for maintaining good health or restoring it, we should continue to recognize the supreme power of mind over body, and of harmonizing our energies at an appropriately elevated level. That power refers to something very real indeed, though, as yet, incompletely understood; it is more than just New Age pabulum. As Doctors Roizen and Oz state in their popular book, *You: Staying Young*:

> When it comes to the human body, we can talk about energy in terms of calories, and we can talk about energy in terms of the cellular energy that's generated by mitochondria, called ATP. But there's a different level of energy that we should all think about: energy fields. It's a part of medicine that we don't fully understand, this relationship between the energy inside the cell and the energy outside the cell. . . . It's these energy fields—your life force, your chi, your intangible aura—that we believe will be the next great frontier of medicine. (Michael F. Roizen 2007, 79)

This is the level at which the kundalini force operates, and where it demonstrates its most salubrious effects.

The greatest proof that our Self is more that our physical nature can be found in the outcome of pleasure, for overindulgence in pleasure, rather than bringing us closer to happiness, takes us further away. In the pursuit of pleasure, rather than of happiness directly, we get caught in a vicious cycle. The way of pleasure, rather than bringing us closer to our goal of joy, only increases the darkness within, which leads us to desperately seek more pleasure to compensate for our despair, which adds in turn to more darkness and emptiness within. It is as if we were journeying West to get to an Eastern town, but as we travel further, the lights grow dimmer; rather than taking the hint and changing direction, we keep on going, figuring, in some strange way, that more distance travelled in the wrong direction will take us closer to our goal. Our pursuit of pleasure then begins to conform to that common definition of insanity, which is to do the same things over and over again, while expecting a different result.

All that aside, sexuality is one of those areas in which the Principle of Partial Victories most amply applies. To pit ourselves directly in opposition to this force is like standing bravely—yet futilely—in front of a tsunami. To give in partially or in lesser ways, while attempting to transmute sexual energy into its higher equivalents, is decidedly more practical. Freud misled in suggesting that our natures be defined at a purely material and animalistic level. Yet he was correct in identifying the perils and pitfalls of attempting to relegate this inherent part of our natures to oblivion. The result is only a divided mind, not a transcendent consciousness.

To summarize, what is most detrimental about the sex act is the loss of pranic energy, followed by the darkening of those energies overall. So the first line of defense, as we guard the walled city of our minds, is to avoid dissipation; for without a without sufficient amount of prana, we cannot reach enlightenment, any more than a car with an empty tank will be able to travel across town.

It has also been said that, if one is able to refrain from sexual release at the moment of orgasm, the transmuted energy has nowhere to go but up, through the fine wiring or nadis. Mystics have, in this way, used the sex drive itself, as a means of widening the ascending channels. Eventually, the downward impulse becomes controllable as the natural course for the same basic energies is redirected. What thus begins as a troubling obstacle is then utilized, in all its raw intensity, to propel the individual through to enlightenment.

The best control against a darkening of energies is to transmute lust into love or to channel the same energies into creative endeavors, perhaps even combining the two by having an idealistic partner of the opposite sex to work with. Here the partners effectively merge to generate a veritable net of radiated energy, sublimated from the physical to the spiritual, one that binds them and supports them in their higher creative efforts. While this is often an efficient strategy, it is still no excuse to don the hair shirt and to declare sex in its better-known form as "dirty" or "evil." Yet it is by such ideal means that one realizes the true purpose of marriage or any other relationship that can be described in a larger sense as both sexual and spiritual.

The fact remains that in our spiritually benighted society, where sexuality itself is equated only with its most degraded forms, to even become aware of such a connection can be troubling. Those who have a resonant partner, where that relationship is acknowledged and accepted by both parties, are truly blessed, for their ascent is made smoother, while those who must do without it are at an immediate disadvantage, for they are left without a readily-accessible means, within the material range of happenings, for that higher expression to manifest. The lower form, in its raw force, then naturally tends to predominate. This obstacle should not be seen as insurmountable either, or even as decidedly detrimental; it just means that you are enrolled in an accelerated course of development with heavier weights to lift, leading, perhaps in the end, even faster to the most truly satisfying union, the union with one's Source. One also, in moving forward independently, sidesteps the popular delusion that conveniently, yet misleadingly, confuses raw, downwardly directed sexuality with tantra.

Finally, the problem we have with sex is but a miniaturized version of the larger issue we have with attachment in general. In the upper reaches of our consciousness, admiration, love, and beauty are not only given a higher expression, but a more realistic and lawful one, as well. In being aligned with Truth, such higher energies generate realistically positive results, results properly aligned with the workings of Karmic Law, the Law of Cause and Effect.

Were we to witness the unearthly beauty of the Sistine Chapel, surveying its artistry for the very first time, few would say, "I can never appreciate this, as I can never own it or take it home with me." Yet all too often when we identify a potential mate, we are not content to appreciate his or her beauty, but seek in some way to lay claim to it, to lasso it or drag it to our caves by the forelock. This is beauty's appreciation comingled with the force of instinct, and, as such, is even less realistic than the desire to take the Sistine Chapel home, for at least with the Chapel the beauty we are witnessing is something relatively stable.

The Sistine Chapel as we may remember it from a journey, taken in our youth, will be experienced in much the same way should we revisit it years later. Yet years later—and in truth even moments later—the people we set our sights on as objects of our desire will already have changed. Different thoughts move in and out of their minds, different bucketfuls of air are being inhaled, the body and limbs disposed in alternate ways. Yet our instincts would have us believe that all this is all a stable target, and potential personal possession. As the Dhammapada summarizes this misguided viewpoint, "These sons belong to me, and this wealth belongs to me," with such thoughts a fool is tormented, concluding, realistically that, "He himself does not belong to himself; how much less sons and wealth." (Babbitt 2012, location 179, verse 62) Indeed, not only is any objective gain or beauty we wish to claim subject to continuous change, but that part of ourselves that delusively seeks to claim it.

NOTES

1. In the Dhammapada's words, "He whom no craving with its snares and poisons can lead astray, by what track can you lead him, the Awakened, the all-perceiving, the trackless?" (Babbitt 2012, location 377, verse 181)

2. As certain Taoist sources describe, the way this process works is different for men than it is for women. As described in *The Tao of Health, Sex, and Longevity*, "The essential difference between the sexual nature of man and woman lies in the different nature of male and female orgasm. When a man ejaculates, he ejects his semen-essence from his body. When a woman reaches orgasm, she too 'ejaculates' all sorts of sexual secretions internally, but these are retained within her body. For both men and women, sexual essence is an important storage battery for vital energy and a major source of resistance and immunity. In conventional sexual relations, a man ejaculates every time he has intercourse, regardless of whether his partner reaches orgasm or not and regardless of his own age or condition. This habit gradually robs him of his primary source of vitality and immunity, leaving him weak and vulnerable to disease and shortening his lifespan." (Reid 1989, 158)

3. Celibate yogin. See (Prem 1948, 12).

Chapter 22

Self-confidence and Independence

Closely tied to the idea of independence, and what forms its effective base, is an ample degree of self-confidence. There are times when our outward environment is supportive of our efforts, and times when it is not. It is during such times of deprivation and adversity that the inner life reveals its intrinsic value, not only as a means to spiritual growth or enlightenment, but of sustaining our forward momentum, as we pursue our more mundane goals. At times when others say we are worthless, or that we will never accomplish our ends, we must know who we are and what we can do; that knowing, unsupported from without, can only come from within. At those times and others, it is important to realize that no amount of "other-confidence" can make up for a lack of self-confidence, for "we can never have enough of what we don't really want," where what we truly want and need is to sense our own worth. Praise without self-regard is like a burial mound excavated with a lack of self-confidence, and filled with the separate opinions of others.

If we see ourselves as inferior, if we lack faith in what we can do, then receiving an award or promotion may serve as a short terms fix. But the effect will soon fade, leaving us as empty and needy as before. If we wish to be loved, we must have love for ourselves first, and unconditionally.

M. Scott Peck, in The Road Less Travelled, spoke of those individuals who, deprived of love in their youth, seek it in all the wrong places and all the wrong ways, later on. (M. Scott Peck 1978, 104) When we are insufficient in ourselves, the connections we form with others become invariably grasping and needy. The love they then give us can never be enough, and we will rarely be able to avoid severing our strongest and most beneficial ties. From a confident space of independence, emancipated from all that we want, but that would otherwise serve to bind us, we discover truly how "the world is won by those who let it go." (Tzu 1983, 119)

Chapter 23

Worry

Peter McWilliams wrote a book with the vastly instructive title, *You Can't Afford the Luxury of a Negative Thought*. Never a truer statement was spoken or better title chosen. It is also true that if you're going to become preoccupied with nonsense, life will match your mood by giving you something real to agonize about. Start to fret over the radiation emanating from your microwave, the fact that you have a new pimple or gray hair, or that your significant other keeps leaving the toilet seat up, and the next thing you know, someone will hit you with a lawsuit, or you will have an issue with your child at school, because by the Law of Attraction—not to mention the mechanics of nonsense and stupidity—you have asked for an additional problem.

It is equally true that we are all responsible for our own lives, whatever our material circumstances, the size of our bodies, or the color of our skins. If we roll over and play dead by deciding to complain or to place the blame or burden on someone else, or on society as a whole, we will already have lost. And if we don't show care and respect for ourselves, the larger world won't either.

In this transitory play, nothing we own will remain ours forever. What we don't lose along the way, we will certainly lose at the end—all except for character and choice, the enduring impressions on our souls of what we have opted to do, good, bad, or otherwise. Worry, like hatred (as it is described in the Dhammapada), is a losing throw from the start.[1] It consumes the life whose obscured value drove us ill-advisedly into the arms of worry to begin with.

NOTE

1. As noted in verse 202 of the Dhammapada, "there is no losing throw like hatred." (Babbitt 2012, location 411)

Chapter 24

The Principle of "Positivity"

In the Dhammapada, it is reasonably asserted that "If by leaving a small pleasure one sees a great pleasure, let a wise man leave the small pleasure and look to the great." (Babbitt 2012, location 556, verse 290) Implied in this statement is the inestimably pragmatic idea that you can't overcome a negative by a greater negative but only by a greater positive.

Millions of failed dieters have proven that you can't permanently lose weight by torturing your body. But you can by relishing the joyous aspects of eating, by chewing your food slowly (thereby properly appreciating your meals), and by enjoying the rush of endorphins associated with vigorous exercise. That is, by far, a more sensible approach than perpetually courting a visit to the emergency room, as would your typical weekend athlete.

Many people eat just to compensate for a feeling of low energy. Exercise raises your energy level, thereby alleviating that problem. In the East, as previously discussed, erotic addictions are overcome by Tantric practices which raise the sexual feeling to a higher, more enduring, and more refined level of bliss, one that the short-term pleasure of the physical orgasm alone can never equal. Lustful feelings, to the extent that seems natural, are gradually replaced by loving ones. The end result is a greater overall sense of well-being, a deeper happiness. Mere prohibitions against sex as dirty or impure can't even begin to approach the same goal with a comparable level of effectiveness.

The problem with lesser versus greater pleasures—and indeed the central problem of life, when accepted as a spiritual challenge—is in simply getting from here to there. It is in transitioning from that starting point where an immediate pleasure takes precedence, to that ultimate destination where a long-term joy, more arduously acquired, is alternatively embraced. As the Dhammapada states, "As long as the evil deed done does not bear fruit, the fool thinks it is like honey; but when it ripens, then the fool suffers grief." (Babbitt 2012, location 189, verse 69) The Gita likewise refers to those actions, classified as Rajaistic that are "at first a drink of sweetness, but are discovered in the end to be a cup of poison," versus those which "seem a cup of sorrow (but) . . . found in the end (to be) immortal wine." (Mascaro 1974, 119) We can see how such activities as gluttony, illicit sex, recreational drug use, and more, can provide a short-term pop; yet they ultimately and inevitably victimize those who indulge in them. Such activities leave our energies depleted, and our systems, weakened and disordered. Wholesome engagements such as a healthful exercise routine or sensible diet, while difficult to initiate, are as reliably beneficial once reasonably undertaken. This is the central dilemma of life, a fork in the road of choice, and here the force of habit is key; it can either make or break us as we move optimistically in the direction of enlightenment. It can either glide us along our journey, kicking in like autopilot, or lock us into a downward spiral that becomes difficult to pull out of. In overcoming obstacles, it is very important to be conscious of the role of habit, to avoid the pernicious ones, and to deliberately cultivate positive, wholesome actions that ultimately become routine.

It is also important that we utilize the aid of virtue's real or prospective joys in overcoming our harmful addictions, for when we engage in wrong behavior, or cave in to foolish desires, we not merely open the door to unhappiness, only to close it again; we set that door ajar. We create a tendency, thereby exposing ourselves to future danger and unhappiness. We weaken our spiritual immune systems. That is why the Buddha said "Let no man think lightly of evil, saying in his heart, It will not come nigh unto me. Even by the falling of water-drops a water-pot is filled; the fool becomes full of evil, even if he gathers it little by little." (Babbitt 2012, location 278, verse 121) In prescribing the winnowing of desires, the Buddha did not refer to those that relate to our purpose, or to the routine or natural pleasure that we may experience en route to properly fulfilling it, but to the unnatural and obstructive accumulation of all that is superfluous, unnecessary, binding, and destructive.

Chapter 25

The Nature and Plan of Evil

Most people conceive of Evil as the sum total of all those guilty pleasures, representing all the great things they really want, all the sex and wild parties, while they conceive of Good as a kind of kill-joy that would withhold those desired things from them. As Billy Joel sang, "I would rather laugh with the sinners than cry with the saints; the sinners are much more fun."[1] Yet this is a gross misconception, Evil's own definition of what a life of goodness is all about.

To reiterate what the Bible states, "seek first the kingdom of God and His righteousness, and all these things (all else that you need) will be added unto you." (Bible Hub, n.d., Berean Study Bible, Matt. 6:33) The lesser joys will come, in their proper role, measure, and time, when we are centered on the greatest joy of all. When we have the pizza, we will no longer want or need to eat the box. The role of Evil, however, is to keep us ignorant of the greater joy, while tormenting us endlessly with what is of far lesser value. This it dangles on an invisible string before us, making us pay for it with our lives and our souls. The central plan of Evil is thus always to turn the god into an animal or a slave. It torments with outright suffering, those who can conceive of no greater joy than what Evil has to offer, while tempting with fame, glory, wealth, and limited bliss, those who have partially seen through the Deceiver's gross disguise.

Imagine that you have an incredibly deft and formidable foe, one who in full possession of his powers causes you great fear. Imagine you give him some wine, for which he has a particular weakness, and instead of being the menacing adversary he is meant to be, is found stumbling around blindly like a newborn foal. What degradation! What a loss for that person, such a state would be! This—this specifically—is the role of Evil, to reduce us to such a condition where we are less than what Christ and the other Great Masters would have us be, to prevent us from realizing our innate spiritual strength and independence, to keep our vast spiritual resources unknown and forever dormant. And this so that we will be forever enslaved to whatever paltry range of resources such ill-intended "powers that be," in their condescension, cruelty, and contempt for us, are willing to apportion.

In this sense, the infernal "powers that be" function in much the same way as their better-known human equivalents. It their will to keep us weak, dependent, dumb and enslaved. It is their morbid intent to kill our dreams and to make us feel that life itself is nothing but an endless cycle of drudgery. They would have us believe that we are helpless to determine our fates. It is their way, therefore, as well, to keep us distracted by an endless array of mindless entertainments and "busy work" that keeps us moving faster and faster on the monotonous treadmill of mundane preoccupations. Hence, we are rarely afforded a moment to think; for if we did think, we might question, and should we question we might comprehend what our lives are all about, to see how we have been deceived and to realize how we may have been compelled to act repeatedly against our own interests.

This was an underlying theme in Allen Silatoe's *Saturday Night and Sunday Morning*, whose modern antihero manufactured 999 widgets daily at his firm's bicycle factory, finding no better way to prove afterwards he was alive and still, presumably, free than to engage in a compressed period of drunken, lascivious, and reckless abandonment during his limited time off.

People often get angry with God over things they have lost, or never had; but in truth, God takes away only a paltry handful of relative trifles so that we can fully and finally experience the absolute joy that these outer things can only dimly reflect. In fact, in enjoying them properly, centered now on what you should most value, the core of your spiritual being, you enjoy them with less anxiety, with far less at stake, and with far greater balance. Once you taste the greater pleasure by which the lesser can be relinquished, the unalloyed joy resulting from the ever-increasing depth of your spiritual practice—you are already at a strong advantage; thus the Buddhists say that by experiencing ever-higher levels of enlightenment, you are saved from rebirth in the lower realms. The greatest danger is for people who know little spiritual joy, who instead of discovering that God was never cruel, that he was only taking a few tawdry trinkets away, so that they can know and enjoy the best of better things, fall back upon their anger. Like Ramses, the Pharaoh in "Exodus," they seal their doom by hardening their hearts. They thereby descend to a deeper and more profound level of spiritual degradation.

While indulgence in sense pleasures can be distracting, "there is," as the Dhammapada notes, "no losing throw like hatred . . ." In fact, the worst thing about sensory indulgence is that, in encouraging satiation and isolation from the spiritual, it makes way for these worse, more hateful possibilities to arise. By becoming angry and resentful over the loss of what, from the outset, could never have made you genuinely or permanently happy to begin with, the dark door is opened to the next degenerative step downward, the one that truly leads to hell, in some form or another, both here and hereafter.

Another great misconception of the spiritual life is that there is, in fact, a mutually-exclusive here and hereafter, that what operates one way on earth functions differently in the higher realms. The truth is that what is wholesome in this world is wholesome in the next, only harder to apply here; "as above, so below." Having a body and mind subject to stress and pain, can twist our otherwise benign thoughts in a decidedly malignant direction. We can become angry, impatient, and irritable. We may thus find ourselves at odds with others in our immediate environment, others similarly burdened and afflicted. For every human being who has ever existed, physical embodiment is the cornerstone impediment to virtue, life's greatest inherent challenge and obstacle, as it was for Christ, Himself.

As the Dhammapada states, "The virtuous man delights in this world, and he delights in the next; he delights in both. He delights and rejoices when he sees the purity of his own work. / The evil-doer suffers in this world and he suffers in the next; he suffers in both. He suffers when he thinks of the evil he has done: he suffers even more when he has gone in the evil path . . ." (Babbitt 2012, locations 97–99, verses 16–17) Those who have been seduced by the lures of our perverse advertising culture tend to view this differently. They think that they will be happy in heaven, but only at the cost of all that makes life on earth worthwhile. As Napoleon Hill and others have convincingly affirmed, what leads to success and joy now are the same sort of virtuous traits that lead to our salvation or enlightenment ultimately. Material benefits are but the icing on the cake, in a greater, more spiritualized life of service and success.

NOTE

1. This is a line from Bill's Joel's hit single from 1977, "Only the Good Die Young." (Joel 1977)

Chapter 26

The Principle of the One

We often allow ourselves to become discouraged by statistics, ballooning them out into ironclad obstacles. We then proclaim our lives to be irremediable states of permanent misery and disaster. All men are "pigs"; all women are "gold diggers"; all bosses "suck." In the misplaced declaration of these false absolutes, and others like them, can be found, weakly-inscribed, the terms of our surrender. In America, though there may be fifty channels of crap on the TV, there only needs to be one presenting valuable programming, as we will only be watching one at a time. Most spouses may, at any given time, seem lousy, but you only need to marry one who generally isn't, for you will only be with one at once, and hopefully that one for life; most radio stations may be boiling over with gossip and pabulum, but we only need to tune into one that is presenting valuable programming. The Principle of the One applies to virtually any and all circumstances, and will ultimately bear itself out in an improvement in our lives and prevailing situations. The Principle of the One requires only that we apply two ancillary rules, the rule of space and that of time. We must allow enough time for good things to happen, and we must cast a wide-enough net. Here the Principle of the One defies the odds, by playing a larger field.

Observe a squirrel in New York and one in California, and you will notice that they behave in much the same way. They carry nuts around in their mouths and flit about with a nervous, jerky motion. There is little noticeable variation—noticeable to us anyway, though perhaps noticeable to the squirrel—within the constraints of this particular genotype. Yet human beings are almost infinitely variegated.

One time, I took a train from Rutgers to Manhattan, and struck up a conversation with a girl whose hobby was ringing church bells. Church bells! How unique is that!! The difference between different people, between a Charles Manson and a Mother Theresa is so great as to be wider than that between separate species. An aging or overweight woman might be pining away at home, assuming that no one wants her; yet the variety of erotic sites dedicated to MILFs and BBWs suggest otherwise. They may not be—and almost certainly are not—the statistical norm. But they don't have to be, for you only need to find that one amid the many.

The Principle of the One says that it's okay to be dis-appointed, so long as you keep all of your other appointments, or maybe just one important one! Like Babe Ruth, it is fine to strike out, perhaps as much—or even more—than anyone else, so long as you score more home runs along the way.

Genealogically related to the Principle of the One is the ability to view alternative scenarios and to identify their separate advantages. There are, for example, advantages to be married and to being single, to being twenty and to being forty, to living in one place, and to living in in another. There seem to be few notable advantages toward the very end of life, yet it is a time of letting go, one that prepares the individual for the stage beyond death; so even that phase is useful too. Work is generally better than unemployment; yet through retraining while out of work, you may find your ideal occupation. The loss of one romantic relationship may lead to the formation of a better one, one meant to last a lifetime. Recognizing that there is a reason for what happens, keeps us balanced between extremes. It removes the vice-like grip of attachment we would otherwise have on what we would otherwise fear to lose.

The search for the one further reveals the existence of the many in the abundance of options we typically have. There are many jobs that are interesting and that pay well, many partners and friends we could be happy with, many activities worthy of our time. Here our attachments reveal themselves as limiting to our growth and destructive to our happiness. By confounding a single option with the entire range of available opportunities, we limit the scope of what we might otherwise, and very reasonably, hope to achieve.

Chapter 27

The Principle of Notable
Victories in Partial Gains

I once had a graduate friend who was able to complete the New York Times crossword puzzle in ten minutes or less. Possessing a brilliant mind, he nonetheless spent much of his time his time lolling around the student lounge rather than shooting for academic excellence. His reasoning: "whatever he could do, someone else could do better; so why bother?" Yet such a viewpoint is misguided, for the challenge in life is to always do the best we can with what we have, to meet the obstacles and challenges confronting us, and to delight in so doing, whether we are playing with a winning hand or with only a few cards. A good chess player, likewise, is delighted to solve a wide variety of puzzles, some where his opponent ostensibly has the advantage and some where he does, some in which there are many pieces on the board, and some in which there are only a few. It is ironic that while Milton Bradley's "Game of Life" is the second most popular board game in history, many people find it more engaging than the real thing. Perhaps if they saw life itself more accurately as a category of game, they would similarly come to appreciate it more.

If life is a game, a passing show, and a learning journey, it makes sense that we will find ourselves in many different scenarios, perhaps even, according to some, through numerous lifetimes. In some narratives, we may have brilliance instead of beauty, in others we may have ability without wealth. For those who believe in reincarnation, as I do, as many gnostic Christians did, it is recognized too that what we have is karmically determined, and that we ourselves set the stage for what is to come by how well we respect, are grateful for, and properly utilize those benefits we now have. What is clear, regardless, is that we always make things better, both here and now, and hereafter, by facing the challenges on the battlefields of our lives directly, turning obstacles into opportunities, and acknowledging progress in partial victories along the course of a wondrous journey that may hypothetically take a very long time. The main competition, and the road to victory at its close, is always against our own limitations, and not against someone or something else, upon whom we would rather place the blame. As Max Ehrmann states, "If you compare yourself with others, you may become vain and bitter; for always there will be greater and lesser persons than yourself."[1]

In the symbolic and profoundly meaningful story of Gulliver's Travels, when Gulliver is among the Lilliputians, he is a Giant, but among the Giants, he is (effectively) a Lilliputian. We all come across looking like Giants or Lilliputians depending on the crowd we ride with. We may be the top student at our rural grammar school, then find it tougher going at the urban high school we graduate to. We may be able to trounce our neighbor's kid at chess, but find ourselves struggling against the average opponents at our local chess club. Still, as the Tao Te Ching asserts, "the way is gained by daily loss," (Tzu 1983, 119) where the humbler—and thus more teachable—we are, the more we will be empowered to grow. In this ongoing process of development, the real competition is against our own limitations.

In the Star Trek universe, there is an all-important rule known as "the prime directive." It fictionally derives from the actual experience of colonialism, and is based on the observation that whenever a less-advanced culture abruptly collides with a far more advanced one, the results are invariably catastrophic. The impacted, more primitive culture is suddenly thrown into chaos. It is pitifully torn from its traditional moorings. It loses its core beliefs, its self-assurance, its goals, and its gods.

If aliens journeyed to earth who were smarter and more capable than we are, if they became responsible for all the latest innovations, and appeared to be physically and mentally more evolved to boot, would we not be inclined, as a result, to simply sit on our hands? Would we not be apt to say, along with that grad student I once knew, "why bother?" Would we not cease to be creative, cease to strive, cease to become more than we are? Would we stop trying to be great, in perceiving others to be greater already? If superior and benevolent beings such as archangels are largely unknown to us, it may be for this very reason. While a foundation in humility is beneficial and desirable, to think too little of ourselves is not. We should never lose sight of our larger, more hopeful ends. There is still meaning and significance to being the proudest ant on the ant hill, although that hill may not be a mountain, for the will to evolve prepares each life for a greater future, and we will never know how far we can go until we try. Whatever our limitations or obstacles, we must stop eating the "bread of shame"; we must zip up our vests and march on. Here the principle of satisfaction in partial gains and in lesser—yet significant—victories, applies, and as much to our spiritual progress as to our social and intellectual attainments.

In this context, the Bhagavad Gita refers to the three gunas, or forces of nature, Tamas, Rajas, and Sattva. Tamas is the principle of darkness and inertia. Rajas, that of restless activity; Sattva, the domain of light, clarity, and calmness. The first is said to lead a soul downward, the third upward, and the second to keep it in a spiritual holding pattern. When the Dhammapada observed that "Few there are among men who arrive at the other shore (become Arhats); the other people here merely run up and down the shore," it had this principle of Rajas effectively in mind. (Babbitt 2012, location 216, verse 85)

In America, we know all about Rajas. We are, on average, a "Rajaistic" nation. We are constantly working up a sweat, consumed with an endless array of "urgent" tasks, few of which would pass muster as having any enduring value. The ultimate dissatisfaction associated with Rajaistic activity was ideally captured in the Pink Floyd line, "Run, rabbit run. /Dig that hole, forget the sun. / And when at last the work is done/ Don't sit down it's time to start another one."[2] Our complicated lives are often very much like that. We have little time to reflect on the value of or to delight in the attainment of what we have already accomplished, before we are off and running again, on to the next goal, or striving for an outcome we are compelled, by others, to secure. Here the ignorant frantically proceed as if they had a purpose, to disguise, usually more to themselves than to others, the unpalatable fact that they really have none, for as the Tao Te Ching states, "high virtue is at rest; it has no need to act; low virtue is a busyness, pretending to accomplishment." (Tzu 1983, 106)

At the end of the "Rajas rainbow," should be more than just another rainbow. Perhaps having come this far commercially, we would do better, as a culture, living without thirty varieties of air freshener in favor of more time to just live and to breathe the fresh air. At least, it would be nice to think that after creating those thirty varieties we could collectively envision something better, something more exalted and edifying to our souls, than creating thirty more. Like a snake that would consume its own tail to support its own life, we twist and tumble distractedly though countless glittering moments of time, stretching wistfully for the "Holy Grail" of a retirement "someday" that, once it arrives, hold far less promise than a larger productive life well-lived.

Musing thus on the 3 states, you might be inclined to say, "okay, great, let me strive to always be Sattvic. That would certainly be better." But—no—it doesn't work that way. As the Gita further explains, at one time or another, one or another of these mind states will predominate. Like everything else in nature, they alternate in shifts.

The Gita offers an interesting response to this dilemma. It says, not only to overcome Rajas by Sattva, which, from what we already know, seems sensible enough, but to overcome Tamas by Rajas, to overcome inertia or depression, not by aiming immediately for the highest state of mind, but for the one directly above the one you are experiencing now. As much as the ends of restless seeking may not represent the ultimate goal, as much as they may not glamorously encapsulate that perfect set of conditions that would lead us into the light, they can nonetheless help us to overcome the darkness.

At times when the Bible would admonish us to love our neighbor, we would be hard pressed simply not to hate him. Here tolerance can suffice as a short-term goal and respectable intermediate attainment. Of course, if we were able to love our abusive neighbor in the midst of his abuse, it would put us directly into the exalted company of the wise. It would mean that we had reached a point where ordinary material gain and loss mean little to us. Jesus, even as he was sacrificing his physical existence, was able to say, "Father, forgive them, for they know not what they do." (Bible Hub, n.d., King James Bible, Luke 23:34) Such a supreme love has been rightly celebrated throughout the ages by men and nations. It is a testament to Christ's transcendent nature and miraculous life that one who was a carpenter by trade should have had such a profound, pivotal, and enduring influence on the world.

On a similar note, in Tibet, there was a monk who was said to have made great spiritual progress within a short period of time. He had been captured, imprisoned, and tortured by the Chinese; During his internment, his greatest fear was that he would lose the capacity to love his tormenters. This is love indeed, and at an extremely exalted level; until we get there ourselves, tolerance can be celebrated as a partial gain and admirable mid-tier victory. Before we learn to love, we must more obviously cease to hate. Fullness of sympathy and compassion come later when we have matured spiritually and are ready for them. To act as if in our ignorance and self-preoccupation we have already fully secured them is just more posturing on the part of our pretentious egos. Such posturing obscures an accurate self-view. It takes us even further from where we need to go and be.

In The Lord of the Rings, Gandalf and company are called upon, at one point, to defend the walled city of Minas Tirith. That city, forever within range of its mortal enemy, was designed in a series of defensible layers, built upwards from the ground. At one point in this fictional adventure, the enemy, possessing a superior force overwhelmed the town's peripheral defenses. The defending forces then fell back to the next layer. They conceded something, to preserve something, and to achieve a greater end.

Sometimes a habit or addiction is too powerful to immediately overcome, in which case, if we have delayed its onset or succumbed in lesser form, we have a partial victory upon which to build and from which we can successfully recover. Yet in our excessively competitive and cruelly exacting society, we don't always see things that way. When we don't succeed 100 percent of the time in 100 percent of our goals, we tend to become excessively self-critical. We jump immediately to the unjust and masochistic conclusion that we have failed ourselves utterly, or are simply no good.

The Principle of Partial Victories is expressed in the Gita through Arjuna's initial dilemma and doubt. As he voices his concerns to Krishna, ". . . if a man strives and fails and reaches not the End of Yoga, for his mind is not in Yoga; and yet this man has faith, what is his end . . . / Far from earth and far from heaven, wandering in the pathless winds, does he vanish like a cloud into air, not having found the path of God?" (Mascaro 1974, 72) What Arjuna is basically asking is, "if I focus all my energies in an effort to attain enlightenment, and I don't get there, won't I then have lost everything, both heaven and earth, with the goals of each left substantially unattained?" Krishna's immediate, and the Gita's larger answer is twofold: 1) that no effort is lost; no cause without its effect, now or ultimately, and 2) that overall success in all departments of your life is best assured by making God or Spirit the centerpiece of your strivings, for not only does your spiritual success depend ultimately upon God, but the vast multitude of worlds as well.

The alteration of the three states, as the Gita describes them, is a further and pointed reminder that the goal of our spiritual quest lies beyond all alternating states of cosmic relativity, beyond those that can be described as heavenly and those that can be dreaded as dark, and that the absolute and relative good are two different things. It is not so much a future state that we should be looking to, for that, when it arrives, will certainly change too, but the transcendent reality that exists in force even now, and that remains in effect when life's game pieces have been restored to their cupboard, when the film laps off its reel and the theatrical illusion ends. It is then that we will understand, and fully appreciate, the meaning and purpose behind the preceding game and drama.

NOTES

1. This line is from Ehrmann's popular inspirational poem Desiderata.

2. This line is from the song, "Breathe," by Pink Floyd, part of their *Dark Side of the Moon* Album. The mournful conclusion in the lines that follow: "For long you live and high you fly/ But only if you ride the tide/ And balanced on the biggest wave/ You race towards an early grave."

Chapter 28

The Nemesis

The Nemesis is our most prominent obstacle. It is the one that, in giving us the most trouble, offers us the greatest opportunity for growth. Like the grain of sand in the oyster, the Nemesis is what allows us to produce the pearls of character and wisdom. Without the irritation posed by the Nemesis, the pearl would remain no more than an undignified grain of sand. Thus, our worst enemy, our greatest obstacle, becomes, in a way, our greatest asset and friend. Opposition to our strivings is the resistance against which we build our strength of character. And it is here that the Nemesis gives us "the biggest bang for our buck."

Our Nemesis could be just about anything. Often it is a habit or addiction that we find endlessly hard to shake. Sometimes it is a mind that falls repeatedly into a negative or destructive groove. It may even be a physical or mental handicap or limitation.

It has been speculated that Napoleon was driven to great "heights" of achievement, in part, to compensate for his diminutive stature. When taller people spoke to him, they would stoop to his physical level, and, in the process, involuntarily bow! He was also, like other great people throughout history, driven by the need to surmount the limitations imposed by his hereditary class. He rankled, as a member of the "Corsican nobility," under the condescension that his classmates, as members of the native French nobility, displayed toward him. This circumstance drove him to prove that he was not only as good as them, but, by his own standards, better. He ultimately crowned his efforts by crowning himself emperor.

Sometimes the Nemesis can appear in the guise of a person who has something we admire, but notably lack, such as physical beauty, or skill in a particular area. This would be something that we don't want to see or be reminded of, but which, because the energy of our aversion is so strong, we seem to confront, in one form or another, everywhere we go.

Maybe we are hanging around our dorm room, tormenting ourselves with our loneliness, while desirable potential partners are ringing our more attractive roommate's phone off the hook. Maybe there is someone we know who demonstrates a natural genius or proficiency in an area to which we have dedicated a substantial portion of our lives. And we are forced to sit back, and to writhe in our discontent, as we impotently watch their greater star rise.

The relationship between Mozart and Salieri was reputed to be this way. Even while he was young, Salieri's musical talent was recognized, applauded, and, by his family and supporters, encouraged; yet it couldn't begin to match what Mozart was more naturally able to do throughout the whole of his short life. Sometimes, someone who continues to try our patience, will encourage us to accomplish the higher end of being more skillful in our responses, for such situations are not merely—or even mostly—a challenge of skill, powers that are, at best, wasting assets, but of character. To respond deftly and appropriately, we must be prepared to meet our signature challenges with openness, courage, patience, and love, and with a willingness to boldly engage, like Arjuna, in those struggles that are appropriately ours. We must be mindful of what our circumstances demand, so as to emerge from the battle of life, victorious.

Chapter 29

Michelangelo's Guide to Life

Michelangelo once claimed that the sculpture he wished to create was already buried in the stone. He needed only to flick away the extraneous chips to arrive at the intended image. What we are left with, in the end, when all the extrinsic matter in the stonework of our souls has been laboriously chipped away, is the essence of who we are. In a spiritual sense, where our lives are our art, and where, as the Tao Te Ching claims, "the Way is Gained by Daily Loss," (Tzu 1983, 119) the sculpting we must do involves divesting ourselves of the limited ideas that constrain us. We must, in the words of Yoda, "unlearn what we have learned." (Kershner 1980) By separate analogy, we need to empty the glass of prejudice and preconception so that it can be refilled with the nectar of truth.

Chapter 30

Mindfulness

Mankind, in the modern world, generally operates in one of two basic states: 1) a condition of relative (and distracted) awareness, accompanied by restlessness and anxiety, and 2) a state of relaxation bordering upon or merging into sleep. Yet there is a third state, the relaxed, yet keen awareness, known as mindfulness. The benefits associated with mindfulness are so profound that they can, not only assist us in traversing the landscape of our hectic daily lives, but lead us, under the proper conditions, all the way to enlightenment.

In the East, the practice of mindfulness (Vipassana) is accompanied by that of virtue (Sila) as muddying the waters with sensual delusion or agitating it with mundane worries works at cross purposes with the calmness and clarity that will allow us to see to the very bottom of the pond.

As with the benefits that accrue from other spiritual practices, there is a mundane and a supramundane form of mindfulness. The mundane form frees us from ordinary carelessness. It keeps us from driving over cliffs, neglecting our bills, or missing our appointments. The supramundane form resides at that level of consciousness where we understand how the moral universe functions. It is here that we become fully aware of the underlying realities of change and impermanence. It is amazing how much benefit can come from simply being present and alert in this way. As we learn from the behavior of others, mindfulness also contributes to a kindred trait, one critical to our development—self-honesty. Self-honesty is one of those virtues which, in the paradoxical tenor of the Tao Te Ching, is easy to comprehend, yet difficult to apply.

Chapter 31

Mindfulness, Acceptance, and Inquiry

There are three traits in life that will speed us past whatever obstacles we need to overcome and whatever lessons we need to learn, and this quality of mindfulness is one of them. Mindfulness, as we may now summarize it, consists of a heightened level of awareness, of ourselves, of our attitudes and responses, of what course we are taking in life, of how we relate to others, and of what lessons life may subtly or desperately be trying to teach us. The second is acceptance, and, acceptance, in particular, of what mindfulness itself reveals. This may at first seem contradictory, for in wanting to change something, we must first find it, at least to some degree, "unacceptable." What we must accept, however, is the factual reality of conditions, not their perpetual stranglehold upon us. Acceptance doesn't mean interpreting the unfavorable as favorable, but accepting the factual existence of whatever comes our way. Should we hope to dispel the darkness, we must cast enough light to properly identify it. Imaginary utopias built solely upon the ideal, become, as a result, the ideal that fails. We must perceive our lives accurately to improve them successfully.

The third, which builds upon the second, as the second does upon the first, is to constantly ask, in reference to whatever circumstance we may happen to confront, or within whatever instructive relationship happens to develop, "what do I have to learn from this?" The question seems even more pointed, when we realize that the people and situations we learn the most from are those we most resist, and that, like a tight pair of galoshes, life will pinch hardest where the demand for growth is greatest.

One of the great joys of the spiritual life is the ability to look back on the journey with satisfaction at having lived in a thoughtful, mindful, and merciful way, at having resisted the temptation to be angry or unkind, and at having consistently done our best. We realize such satisfaction in being maximally helpful. To reiterate what the Dhammapada claims, "The virtuous man delights in this world, and he delights in the next; he delights in both. He delights and rejoices when he sees the purity of his own work. / The evil-doer suffers in this world and he suffers in the next; he suffers in both. He suffers when he thinks of the evil he has done: he suffers even more when he has gone in the evil path . . ." (Babbitt 2012, location 215) As it is painful to recall the harmful events of the past, one, by the same token, carries a legacy of optimistic joy forward into the future, by having thought and acted well.

It is a tragic, yet inherent, part of life, that those systems we would wish to preserve can only be maintained in a certain way, but can be destroyed or disrupted in numerous other ways. A house of cards can be toppled from many sides, but remains intact only if its precarious base rests sufficiently undisturbed. Our bodies strive to renew their patterns and are, in this sense, different; but when that pattern is lost, we die. It is a pattern that can only be maintained within a limited range of conditions. Our organs work together in a specific way, with heart, lungs, liver, brain, and kidneys all dependent on their joint activity. When one set of organs irremediably fails, all die. This simple fact, that of life's tenuous nature should alert us to the very real possibility that things may not always go our way, and that we will need to maintain a positive attitude amidst circumstances that are not always ostensibly so. Yet even more than this, it reveals the crucial role of mindfulness, for in one moment of carelessness, recklessness, or distracted awareness, something priceless can be irretrievably lost. This should not serve to make us paranoid, for paranoia wreaks its own brand of havoc. It obliterates our good in a different way. The agitation that attends it causes us to lose sight of that inner clarity which is the only full and reliable guide. But its basis does accentuate the need to, in the words of the Tao Te Ching, be "as cautious as men crossing streams in winter." (Tzu 1983, 76)

If we reach for an image of the moon in the water, we won't grasp the moon, only water. If we seek happiness within the confines of illusion, we will discover only illusion. "Looking for love in all the wrong places" is not only a line from a 70's hit tune, it is a common, yet mistaken, way of life. (Lee 1980) A more mindful approach, a deeper analysis, should allow us to "separate the seed from the chaff," for it provides the means to determine what is valuable and, ultimately, what is Real.

Chapter 32

The Power of Not-Doing

The Tao Te Ching claims that ". . . the Wise Man knows without going, / Sees without seeing, / Does without doing." (Tzu 1983, 118) It is a statement that acknowledges the persistence of the Universe's underlying Flow. By "not doing" we are not "doing nothing," but are instead harmonizing ourselves with the movement of Life that is already there, meandering its way through the subterranean regions of silence.

In a state of non-doing, there is a natural release of tension. With the release of tension, our internal knots are untied; breathing slows. As the breath softens and mindfulness intensifies, pranic energies automatically begin to rise, and to open and occupy the upper chakras, the higher centers of consciousness. Calmness leads to clarity, and through clarity we are able to plumb the minds greater depths, accessing the broader resources of our subconscious and superconscious minds to achieve our positive aims. The wave feels its connection to the ocean, and through this deeper joining, a clear and illuminated mind is now confidently poised to accomplish great things.

A mind that, by contrast, forces its way through life, makes a good show of accomplishment, but its actions, when not in harmony, do not produce any lasting good. It expends itself rather quickly, always scattered outside the moment, lost in regret, worry, agitation, and frustrated egoistic ambition. These painful states lead it into the realm of unhealthy distractions. Such an agitated mind is afflicted, lacking the ability to see clearly and incisively. Then, as like attracts like, we find ourselves, when excessively contentious and belligerent, occupying a space filled with people who, like us, are contentious and belligerent too. Soon, we end up with collective problems whose origin is obscure, and whose solution remains troublingly elusive. The power of "not doing" works because, in a real sense, the universe is already doing, and we, as parts of the cosmos, are one with that larger unfolding. The great paradox of the Tao is that in a state of non-doing, properly appreciated, understood, and applied, everything gets done.

Among the more obvious examples of results achieved through "not doing," life, in its various forms, including that of our own bodies, develops without our prompting. Thoughts enter our minds in completed form from the dimension of our subconscious. This indicates that there are deeper processes going on which our conscious mind need not control, and would not benefit from micromanaging. For these processes to work, all we have to do is direct our attention mindfully in a certain way, and our brains will at once begin to evaluate that situation's requirements. To avoid all that is contentious, inharmonious, and resistant to our goals, we must realize the power of not doing; we must become one with the Flow. In thereby generating and encountering less resistance we will have more energy with which to achieve, and can continue to work tirelessly. As the Tao Te Ching states, "The world is won by those who let it go!" (Blakney, 48, p. 119)

The Gita refers, in an identical context, to the yogi "who unperturbed by changing conditions sits apart and watches 'the powers of nature go round,' and 'remains firm and shakes not.'" (Mascaro 1974, 105) These two references combined define a state of spiritual detachment. Detachment is not indifference. It doesn't imply losing interest, but gaining control. In a paradoxical universe, control is lost, not gained, by grasping. The method and modes of grasping, which still predominate, and to which all the world's ills can ultimately be traced, refer to what Gary Zhukov terms, "inauthentic (or external) power." (Zukav 1989, 224–33) Through inauthentic power, we attempt to manipulate events as if they were centered on us rather than existing for a larger purpose all their own and in accordance with their own laws. As the Tao Te Ching states, ". . .the world is a sacred vessel/ Not made to be altered by man./ The tinker will spoil it;/ usurpers will lose it." (Tzu 1983, 95) All the demons and dictators throughout recorded history who attempted to make Life conform to their own controlling model have ultimately been flushed from the universal system by the lifeblood of the Tao, yet only after inflicting colossal devastation upon lives, souls, and the larger world environment. In the end, their way doesn't work. By letting go, as the means to genuine power and accomplishment, we seat ourselves securely on the throne of daily existence. We begin to "live life as life lives itself." In not allowing our responses to be distorted by egoistic bias, we will know the best way to be, and thus, how best to serve the ends of both world and self. Right action proceeds from a calm center with breathtaking precision, appearing, after a point, as if it were performing itself. Work then becomes conjoined craftsmanship and worship. We finally reach a level where we rest behind our own dedicated actions as captivated, yet compassionately detached, observers.

This is the state known in Hinduism as "witness consciousness." While falling short of the ultimate beatitude associated with full enlightenment, it furnishes a strong foretaste of freedom, is a precursor to that greater state, and is an important milestone on the path. Mindfulness is required beyond that point to reach total enlightenment, as there remain parts of one's own mentality which, like errant children, are still scampering about, doing their own thing, still trying to gain the world by grasping and manipulation, and which, to use the Tibetan phrase for the basic chore of mindfulness, have yet to "be brought face-to-face with reality." Yet, despite our residual ignorance, we learn at this point how Life living itself is truly the best way to be, and has been the best way all along, how all along we have only imagined ourselves the doers, where our every decision has merely been the result of a preponderance of natural forces with our minds, much as the movement of the winds is the result of a variation in atmospheric temperature, one that makes the breeze blow in a predicable way one way or another. All the time that we have been pompously asserting ourselves, we have only been distorting Life's Flow through us, garbling the script of the universal drama, and attempting to play God's directing role as only God can.

Chapter 33

Rashness

Joseph Goldstein, in his book, The Experience of Insight, quotes Herman Hesse's Siddhartha in identifying the 3 qualities of a warrior. As Siddhartha states, "I can think; I can wait; I can fast." (Goldstein, The Experience of Insight 1983, 63–64) Goldstein equates the last attribute more broadly to "fasting of the mind," to a mentality that can reflect on the needs of a given situation without proceeding rashly. Rashness is a great enemy of success.

It is, as already noted, one of routine life's tragic realities that a particular structure, a car or building, for example, can only be held together in basically one way, yet destroyed in numerous other ways. In a comparable sense, our core relationships can only be sustained by maintaining a tempo of positive actions and behaviors, but can be destroyed irretrievably by one rash word.

There are times when we lose our perspective. Then nothing that once seemed good in our lives, for a time, seems good anymore. A dissatisfying verbal exchange with one key person can taint our outlook comprehensively for a whole day or more. It can tarnish our view of an environment that we had, until then, found pleasant and congenial. At such times, it is important to recall the need to be patient, to withdraw and to hold back, for our responses then are unlikely to be skillful; at such times, we are not completely ourselves. When your mind is strongly contaminated by the kleshas (negative emotions), you are like a drunken man standing before his vehicle with the ignition key in hand, contemplating whether to turn the engine over and to drive off. When we cannot proceed safely, it is usually best not to proceed at all; when we cannot respond skillfully, it is better to remain silent, "to think, to wait, and to fast."

Chapter 34

Anger

Pop psychologists encourage us to "express our anger," but as Mr. Spock of Star Trek fame contends, the individual's "healthy release of emotion is frequently very unhealthy for those closest to you." (Alexander 1968) A finer examination typically reveals that it is not very healthy or beneficial to the heated individual either. This assertion applies equally well to those self-righteous expressions of "idealistic" anger we would otherwise tend to defend.

There are two unskillful extremes when it comes to anger; one is repression and the other, indulgence. With a clogged drain, it may be necessary to force-fully remove the block. Similarly, where repression of one's deeper emotions has become habitual, a sharp burst of anger under controlled conditions may be necessary to pierce through to an awareness of our underlying feelings. But under more ordinary circumstances, an acknowledgment that anger is present, without undue identification with anger, in all its volatile unpredict-ability is better. Anger, like lust, is reactionary. It obscures our issues through avoidance and illusion rather than resolving them through precise and effec-tive means.

Goldstein describes anger as something that is "neither me nor mine"; it is just another part of life's flow. It is a "factor of mind" which, like a muscle, can be exercised or allowed to atrophy. (Goldstein 1983, 53, 55) As it typi-cally manifests in highly unskillful ways, ways that defeat our purposes, the latter is usually preferable. We typically get angry when someone tells us something we don't want to hear. But that something could well have been stated for our own good. Anger further sparks words and actions whose nega-tive outcome cannot later be undone.

Even certain Buddhist sources advise us to deal with our anger with full acceptance as a part of being human. Yet the Buddha himself suggested a more proactive approach. As the Dhammapada states, "He who holds back anger like a rolling chariot, him I call a real driver; other people are but holding the reins." (Babbitt 2012, location 446, verse 222) Holding back the chariot requires both strength and resolve.

In deliberately checking our anger, we see something else occur; we progress in the development of its antidote—patience. As the Dhammapada states, "Angry speech breeds trouble, thou wilt receive blows for blows," (Babbitt 2012, location 300, verse 134) and "If a man commits a sin, let him not do it habitually; let him not rejoice therein; sorrow is the outcome of evil. / If a man does what is good, let him do it habitually, let him rejoice therein; happiness is the outcome of good." (Babbitt 2012, location 274, verses 117–18) Here the Buddha's signature approach of always pragmatically seeking the greater joy directly applies.

Patience is a very refreshing emotion. It is like a cool breeze blowing through us, and is akin to the energy generated by meditation itself. Once we experience this, then, rather than deliberately avoiding situations that make us angry, we begin to use them as opportunities to develop this positive and uplifting quality of patience. Accumulation of the energies associated with patience will make us a soothing influence on those around us, and they will increasingly value and seek our company. This is a more productive way to deal with the obstacle of anger, and with the contention it sparks than allowing it to flow freely.

Chapter 35

Poverty and Wealth Consciousness

If you have a wealth consciousness, you believe in the underlying abundance of the universe; if you have a poverty consciousness, you are convinced of an abiding scarcity. Since your capacity to receive is based on your willingness to give, each of these beliefs becomes a self-fulfilling prophecy. If you have a poverty consciousness, you will greet the world with a closed fist; if with a wealth consciousness, with a welcoming and contributing hand, and each view will manifest its corresponding results in keeping with the Law of Karma.

If you have a poverty consciousness with regard to food, you will bolt your meals as you will never know when the opportunity to eat will come again. In thus enjoying food less, you will inevitably eat more. You will simply eat more anyway, not knowing where your next meal might come from. So, to sustain your life through food, while harboring a poverty consciousness, you immediately proceed to destroy it, along with any associated joy and contentment within. If you have a wealth consciousness with respect food, you will eat only what you need, knowing there will inevitably be more. You will thoroughly enjoy the experience of eating, and thus be satisfied sooner. This will cause you to consume less as well, thereby promoting your sustained good health.

If you have a poverty consciousness regarding love, you will seek love desperately, thus attracting only undesirable mates, mates who are just as needy and desperate as you are. Your excessive need and unbalanced approach will put the "stench of death" around you. This will repel all suitable candidates and attract only those for whom "misery loves company." Most individuals hope to attract a mate that they can depend on, if necessary, not one who is himself dependent and clingy. Such clinging predictably repels, for as the Tao Te Ching states, "grabbing misses . . ." (Tzu 1983, 138)

If you have a wealth consciousness regarding love, there will be a balance and grace to your actions, one that will be automatically attractive. Potential mates will wonder what you've got that makes it so easy for you to get along without them. With females especially, such mystery and curiosity can be an almost irresistible draw. In all subrealms of its effective application, with a consciousness of wealth, we invoke the Principle of the Vacuum. We give, emptying ourselves, that life may refill us with its underlying abundance.

What the New Thought literature refers to as a wealth consciousness is also pragmatically related to the Buddhist notion of nonattachment. For why do we cling? It is essentially because we feel that without the experience of what we are clinging to, we would be left unfulfilled; we would be empty; we would be broke. We tend to feel that way because 1) we have not sought first the wealth within against which nothing else compares and 2) because, when we have a poverty consciousness, we feel that, if we lose this experience or that possession or our current dissatisfying relationship, it, or something like it—let alone something better—will never come again. A person with a poverty consciousness feels that tomorrow will always be lacking, so he must cling to today with a desperate ferocity. A person with a wealth conscious-ness is confident that what he needs will be there tomorrow, if he does what is right today.

There is a poverty consciousness implied in many of our most unbalanced actions. There is, as already described, a poverty consciousness in gluttony which impels us to gobble up now as much as we can, for it might not be there later, and as fast as we can, for even the existing gluttonous opportunity itself might be snatched away suddenly and unexpectedly. But, there is a more obvious poverty consciousness in a more generalized greed, in the thought that we must grab something up before someone else does, and nail enough of it down, because some of it might elusively slip away, and this thought leaves us insecure. Since like does attract like, this scenario becomes, like "the long spoons depiction of Heaven and Hell," a self-fulfilling prophecy. Our nega-tive thoughts draw us toward negative people, people who tend to think the same way we do. Also, and often, we are like baseball players who think they won't be safe so long as they stay on base, whereas the opposite, in fact, is true. Only in being centered spiritually are we secure from lack, secure from fear, secure from the excess of pain in its extreme of out-and out suffering.

Most of the evils we commit arise from a sense of lack and lack of inde-pendence. We don't trust Life to provide us with what we want or need, so, we tend as a species to lie, cheat, steal, and manipulate. We cast our lot, effectively, in with the Devil, choosing to depend, not on God, but on those who care little for our interests. These are people whom, we feel, we must nonetheless please and praise to survive.

A mind that gives up on the noble way of attainment to be enslaved by the whims, will, and opinions of others, cannot offer itself right guidance, let alone the happiness that issues from it. And the price of such slavery is always the same—fear. We become again like that beaten dog. We never know then when the door will fly open, and a Life that then can no longer protect us will administer a savage blow. And such sustained fear will destroy our health and sanity long before any direct ruin comes. The alternative, devoid of mendacious complexities, is simply to do what is right. Right action is kingly, and in a society whose foundations—if not always its deeds—are good, right action is respected. It earns us the protection of those people who can be relied on to actually be there when times get tough, not those modern-day pirates and thieves among whom there "is no honor." But the protection alluded to is not merely social; it extends much farther than that. As the Tao Te Ching states directly, "If you work by the Way,/ You will be of the Way; / If you work through its virtue/ you will be given the virtue; Abandon either one/ And both abandon you." (Tzu 1983, 87) As *The Voice of the Silence* comparably observes, "Help Nature and work on with her; and Nature will regard thee as one of her creators and make obeisance." (Blavatsky 2011, 12) The protection of God, of our Source, is the most reliable protection of all. Even if, after performing conspicuously right actions, you are still not socially esteemed, then it is obvious that you are simply running with the wrong crowd, one whose companionship you have earned through past unwise and unwholesome actions. By correspondence within the Law of Attraction, you have entered the hell-side variant of the long spoons realm; your task then must be to try to make your way out.

Imagine what it would be like to have a million dollars. Short of violating the law (which would only serve to take that million dollars or our free and effective use of it away) what would we fear to say or do? What cherished project would we hesitate to initiate? Would we not have the moral fortitude to be honest and sincere with others and more importantly with ourselves? Would we not have the courage to be true? Yet even a million dollars, which life and others can still take away can give us ultimate security. Only God, Life, or our Source, can.

Many of us would go to great lengths—even to the extent of violating our priceless integrity—to secure that million dollars, even when the likelihood of obtaining it is slim; yet God is available now; and only God, Life, or our Source, however we choose to define the underlying Reality of the universe, can truly make us secure and free. Nothing else can. Nothing.

Chapter 36

Procrastination

In the opening scene of the Bhagavad Gita, we see procrastination ideally modelled. Arjuna is presented with what is identified as his "plain duty," and he doesn't want to do it. Fortunately, he has Krishna, his supremely-wise mentor, by his side to coax him back into the game. The rest of us generally have no such advantage. We have only our own minds, those same minds that are ignoring the problem and inventing countless imaginative excuses. Still, as we well know, and have each on numerous occasions experienced, ignoring the problem doesn't make it go away; it only makes it worse. Ignoring the mortgage doesn't result in the end of mortgage payments, but in the loss of home ownership. Ignoring the rent doesn't lead to the end of rent payments, but to eviction. In such cases, as in a larger range of issues that we must confront and not ignore, first life will give you a tap on the shoulder, then a shove, then, a swift kick in the behind. Finally, if you are still not listening, it is likely to throw you off a cliff!

There is a lightness and satisfaction that comes with completing a needed task. It arises in addition to the obvious awareness that once you have adequately dispensed with it, you won't have to deal with that particular chore again.

Chapter 37

Despair

There are times when, recognizing the futility of our anger, either with circumstances or with someone who is persistently hounding us, we succumb to an alternative form of negativity: despair. It is a state that is very destructive to our success and well-being. We latch onto a legitimate emotion—sadness—and then drown ourselves in it. We emotionally surrender, thereby weakening our wills and capacity to overcome.

There are three things we need, in sufficient degree, to succeed: faith, ability, and the willingness to act. Along this spectrum of attributes, ability is usually the least of our deficiencies.

I once heard of a supposedly average chess player who, after being hypnotized into believing he was a master, began performing immediately at that level. What is most remarkable to me about this story, is that, if he didn't have that capacity to begin with, buried somewhere within, he couldn't have demonstrated it, any more than a sky without clouds can hope to produce rain. Very likely, you have all the ability you need. More often what is lacking is faith, the will to proceed, and the courage to act. Despair can weaken your resolve. Should it become habitual, it will dash all your hopes for success.

Chapter 38

The Most Dangerous Words
in the English Language

There are times when we make less than optimal choices. We are entitled to do so, and under most circumstances, there will be no one around to object, least of all God. But we will then be compelled to own the result; we must live with the consequences of our choices; we must reap what we have sown.

Let's say that a friend invites us to participate with him in a long-term, vigorous exercise routine. We tell him that, due to health concerns or other reasons, we can't; we'd certainly like to, but we really and truly can't. Our objections may be sound, sensible, and prudent. They may even be based on a doctor's professional advice. All well and good, and okay you have your reasons. But when a year from now your friend is on the beach attracting the attention of the opposite sex with his washboard stomach and rock-hard pecs, it would be pointless and foolish of you to envy him.

It would be similarly idiotic to envy your neighbors for the sparkling renovations to their home when both husband and wife trudged out to work each day, both laboring extra hours, while you and yours opted for more "me time" on the couch. Your priorities will determine your results.

The man who spent his time accumulating a fortune should not be despised by the one who didn't, while he who spent his time reading the great works of literature should not be envied for being significantly more cultured. Each is the result of the seed that he, himself, planted.

It could be that the man who says he can't work, can't, or perhaps a parent who might ordinarily work must stay at home to care for the children. But there may be ways that neither of them originally considered to effectively reach their goals. Maybe an extremely busy man can learn vocabulary or a new language in his car, rather than listening to celebrity gossip on the morning radio.

The words "I can't" are very dangerous. They may well be the most dangerous words in the English language. They are the greatest of obstacles,

and self-created ones at that, for they condition the mind negatively as assuredly as the contrary assertion "I can" does positively. You might think, for
example, that someone without legs could never run a marathon; yet there has
been more than one who has run swiftly with artificial limbs. It is an amazing and inspirational sight to behold, one that should embolden the rest of us,
more impressed by the strength of our obstacles than by our own capacity to
overcome them.

Through the words "I can" the "impossible" becomes possible, while
through the words "I can't," we place even our own more ordinary goals
tragically out of reach. Nor should we envy those whose lives appear to be
without obstacles, for such obstacles can be just the opportunities we need
to progress.

Chapter 39

Everyone is Selfish

Neither the spiritually, nor the materially-motivated man acts against his own self-interest; each merely defines that interest, the nature of his own good, differently. If we were told that the entire world would be saved, but only at the cost of our being damned, without our enjoying even the satisfaction of knowing that our sacrifice contributed to that honorable result, who among us would honestly be willing to opt for such a condition? It would never, of course, arise as it would be founded on the unlawful premise that our sacrifice for others wouldn't serve us, with the greatest sacrifice known—that of Christ's crucifixion—contributing, finally, only to His greater beatitude. Even then, the term of that suffering was relatively short, a lifetime extinguished (physically) at thirty-seven, or so, as compared to a vast eternity of glory.

The reason why so many nations have so often been brought to the brink of war is that they continue to operate, in whole or in part, at that narrowly selfish level at which each defines its interest in opposition to the rest. They shun that higher, happier, heavenly level at which all separate interests are one. They operate from the wrong side of the long-spoons scenario.

Many spiritual authorities advise us to think of others rather than of ourselves. This can be an effective prescription for dislodging that ingrained selfishness that for most of us has become routine. But here the semantics can mislead, for we don't dis-serve ourselves by serving others, but benefit ourselves, thereby, in the best possible way. To be accurate in meaning, as well as in intent, our actions are most correct, most in harmony, where, through meditative awareness, we act from what Zen practitioners call our "essence of mind." This is the level the Gita describes as freeing us from rebirth by liberating us from the dualistic sense of self and other, and thus of self-versus-other too. In place of separation, including a separation of interests, there is instead a traceless unity from which right action naturally proceeds. There is no resulting sense of "noble me acting unselfishly," which is, in a sense, a contradiction in terms, for, so long as there is a self in the equation of action, there is "self-ishness." We simply realize at the point of at-one-ment that the service we render others automatically benefits us. We are just following our individual dharmas, and there is no longer any difference between what we do for us, and what we do for them.

Where there is no longer any sense of self, other, and acting, but, in its place, a traceless harmony—a non-doing in the Taoist sense in which nothing is left undone—a mode of action in which we do not, as the Gita describes it, perceive ourselves as the ultimate doers, it is then—and only then—that we can begin to talk meaningfully about a genuine degree of unselfishness. Uneducated views of what it means to be selfish or unselfish are all that arise when we operate at the crass level of duality. At that level, we are either torturing ourselves, mistaking our self-abuse for a laudatory virtue, or taking advantage of someone else. At the level of at-one-ment, we don't make a big deal about any of that. Right action just occurs unaffectedly. Just as it is in our nature, when functioning at the animal level, at the level of the lower chakras, to be markedly selfish and egotistical, it is just as natural from the higher levels to serve, and to do so without fanfare. All that we do at that level is genuinely unselfish—and unselfishly genuine.

A novel way of expressing this is that the selfishness of materiality is a false selfishness anyway; it doesn't really serve us. It doesn't fulfill the deeper needs of who we genuinely are, only the fleeting and insatiable appetites of the impostor self. To be spiritual is to be selfish, properly and accurately, by being Selfish!

Chapter 40

Gratitude

One thing that the Law of Attraction crowd seems to express better than many traditional religionists is gratitude for benefits already received. To awaken on a crisp Spring morning and to smell the brisk air redolent with new life, to bask in the glow of a beautiful sunset, to immerse yourself in the wonder and intricacy of language, all these are gifts from God, no less than salvation or enlightenment. Though they may not represent the end-all or be-all of our existence, the "godly" approach is to be grateful for them anyway. We don't say to God, "they are not the heaven I am looking for; take them away!" If you are hungry, and a stranger who owes you nothing, out of the goodness of her heart, takes you in and feeds you, although what she has to offer may not be much, although it may not even be enough to nourish you, the correct response is to say "Thank you; I am grateful for your kindness."

Some years later, you may be blessed with something you once wanted very badly. Perhaps it is a new car, or a new love who is beautiful and kind. Although you may have matured beyond the need for such gifts, the correct response, there as well, would be to pause and to say "thank you." As you do, you will find your own sense of joy expand as you realize how much you have received. You should engage in this salutary practice routinely, acknowledging benefits large and small as they successively appear, for the more you acknowledge and affirm them, the more they will abundantly arrive.

Alexandra Solnado, in *The Book of Light*, states that when you realize that you really own nothing, and that all that you have, you have received as a gift, you begin to feel overwhelmed with gratitude, and, as you express that gratitude, you ascend. (Solnado 2011, 185–86, 192) You become increasingly inclined to give of yourself, of your services and even of your wealth, out of the gratitude you feel for all you have received. It is then that, by the Law of Attraction, you draw God, Himself by functioning much the same way He does—which is to give freely through the joy of serving and giving, expecting nothing in return.

This joy in giving methodology highlights the flaw in our customary approach to our own betterment and salvation. So many see salvation as a benefit they individually (i.e., selfishly) receive. They worry about whether or not it will be there, much as they might worry about owning or not owning a Ferrari, or receiving or not receiving a promotion.

The Tibetans say that "the path of altruism is a path leading to the realm of the conquerors; the selfish know not of it." (Evans-Wentz 1967, 63) *The Voice of the Silence* likewise speaks of those who "lost among the host" continually serve, while, Jesus states that "not everyone who says to me, 'Lord, Lord,' will enter the kingdom of God, but only the one who does the will of my Father who is in heaven." (Bible Hub, n.d., New International Version, Matt. 7:21) Here the substance of truth, in a life well-lived, rather than any intellectual assent to a creed, is what's regarded as essential.[1] Verbal acknowledgments alone are no more meaningful than Pilate's "what is truth?" where there is no real fervor or desire behind them, or any compassionate concern for others.

NOTE

1. The full quote, from *The Voice of the Silence* is, "Point out the 'Way'—however dimly, and lost among the host—as does the evening star to those who tread their path in darkness." (Blavatsky 2011, 31)

Chapter 41

The Right Goal

When we examine the typical structure of morality, we find that its key supports overwhelmingly pertain to our relationship to other people. The remainder deal with our relationship to God, with our connection to our Source. Whether it be the Ten Commandments or the Buddha's ethical precepts, injunctions against lying, stealing, adultery, harsh speech, etc., all point to the reality of oneness, to the fact that when we harm others, we are really, at the deepest level, just harming ourselves. This is because at the deepest level we really are them. We are all one at the level of our Source, and only free individually when residing there, in that center of silence that encompasses all.

Yet when we envision the end of salvation, it always seems to be gift-wrapped as something we attain for ourselves, or that is bestowed upon us alone, like a title, a degree, or a vacation, in a determination of a fate that ultimately excludes others, though we continue to see the way there as cobbled with the tenets of a communal morality. There is even a sense, popular nowadays, that most people are destined to burn in hell, and that only a few will make it through to a better state. Perhaps so in the short term. But as Evans-Wentz notes in particular reference to the Buddhist faith, "the belief that one part of the whole can enjoy happiness for eternity while another part suffers misery of the most terrible character conceivable, is quite unthinkable . . ." (Evans-Wentz 1967, 11) And perhaps that is why so few of us get there sooner to begin with, for even in matters of faith it is hard for us to think unselfishly. In a universe where our goals are attained by indirection, the following paradoxical statement from the Tao Te Ching would seem to be most apt: "Denying self, he too is saved, for doesn't he salvation find by being an unselfish man." (Tzu 1983, 66)

Heaven has been metaphorically described, in terms borrowed from an more autocratic age, as a future kingdom, rather than as a timeless state of being, existing, even now, beneath the rubble of our wayward minds. This popular misconception raises several immediate problems. The first is that everything in and of time, every dualistic state, everything we set our sights on as separate individuals, is permeated through and through with change; however blissful it may be, it cannot help but prove itself to be limited, temporary, and unsatisfactory; the second, is that it may cause us to live in and for a future that hasn't yet arrived. This distracted mindset threatens the awareness we have of—and value we assign to—the present. It is thereby likely to dilute the urgency and intensity of our efforts. Seeing the present predominantly in relation to the future cannot help, except in rare cases in which the individual is highly disciplined, rob his current efforts of much of their significance and of his attention. Religion, rather than being what it is meant to be, then becomes, as Marx described it, an opiate for relieving our pains in the here and now, blotting them out in favor of a more fanciful here and now that hasn't yet arrived.

In Paradise Lost, Milton quotes his Devil as saying, "the mind is its own place, and in it self can make a Heav'n of Hell, a Hell of Heav'n." (Milton 2011, location 114) The tragic irony was that the Devil carried his hell along with him. It was a portable misery. It had nothing to do with time or place, which are relative states of physicality, and everything to do with consciousness. So why do we look to the future for Heaven, when Christ, Himself, told us we would find it within? Was He any further away from the Kingdom of God at the time he was crucified? Perhaps physically he was, but in Spirit he was never closer.

The narrow gate to Heaven is unselfishness; it is discovered when we are, as *The Voice of the Silence* observes, "lost among the host." It is glimpsed when we are, whether in relation to past, present, or future, which are all parts of a shifting time frame anyway, less concerned about our exclusive good, and more inclined to assume a broader focus. When we are immersed in a good cause, we are engaged in the sort of conflict which the Bhagavad Gita claims, "opens the gates of heaven." (Mascaro 1974, 51) This is the way of the Great Ones, of Christ, of Krishna, of Buddha, who had nothing to gain for themselves by hanging around this limited earth and blamelessly suffering for us, but who did so anyway, because, in that way, each affirmed the Spirit that they all joyfully embodied. When we think about the goals we have set for ourselves, versus those that benefit others, what is the moral distinction between desiring a heavenly paradise filled with private enjoyments and a life of terrestrial luxury? The quality of self-preoccupation is very much the same; the only difference is that one aims at happiness now and the other at happiness later. The focus is still selfish.

The Bhagavad Gita recognizes this astutely in observing, of those misguided, that, "their soul is warped with selfish desires, and their heaven is a selfish desire." (Mascaro 1974, 52) Dark-hearted souls can be quite conscientious in honoring the standard rituals of faith, for they sense the need to hedge their bets in case there really is an afterlife; they are nonetheless focused predominantly on what they are going to do in it, rather than on the fate or condition of others.

The immature soul longs for heaven the same way that people trapped in their jobs long for an early retirement, or for the next approaching vacation. They search for the answer within the confines of duality, within a state where incomplete experiences waft endlessly over their isolated selves. They do this without ever recognizing the structural deficiencies inherent in that particular approach to life and its conception of their ultimate beatitude. In the final analysis, we may even grow tired of being us—of being separate personalities; hence the natural perfection of life, with death at its close. No one yet has been able to properly test the theory, but if we had the chance to physically live forever, while treading "the path of desire," would we not ultimately long for the death that we had been unnaturally denied?

We often refer to someone who proceeds through life inattentively as "having his head in the clouds," those same clouds where heaven has been reckoned to reside in traditional religious imagery, rather than in the here and now as the eternally existing Kingdom of Truth within. Where heaven is localized elsewhere than within the depths of our immediate experience, how can we do otherwise than to devalue that experience? Where what passes for religion blots out the present, how could it serve other than as "the opiate of the people?" And how can we be expected to do more than falter in our current, defining struggles, when belief alone is expected to see us through? Wrong attitudes and actions issue immediately from that "elsewhere-than-here" mentality, making it suspect, in this way as well.

Eternity has always existed, and we have always been a part of it. Once relieved of the burden of self, we will reside there fully again. By ceasing to tarry in the darkness, we will dwell again in the Light. And we will feel that connection within, wherever we reside.

Chapter 42

The Way is Not Complicated

We live in a society that is overly conceptual and materialistic. Our approach to faith reflects this cultural imbalance. The substance of the inner life has been sacrificed on the altar of ritual, where prophets, pastors, and priests are expected to know it all and you, as the spiritual focus of your own unique struggles and challenges, practically nothing. In a similar way, a mere verbal consent to the idea of salvation has substituted for the value to be realized in a strenuous life of character and truth.

The idea that those who adhere to a particular form of worship are saved while all the rest are damned raises some immediate and serious rational dilemmas. It would place such noble individuals as Mahatma Gandhi or the Dalai Lama on a hell-bound path, despite their being ideal embodiments of traditional Christian virtues—albeit cloaked in the alternative garb of foreign cultures. At the same time, mafia chieftains, who despite their bad behavior, believe (and who is to say that they don't believe sincerely) in the category of the saved. This assumes that all are merely human, and thus all, from the outset, unworthy; whether it is a ten-foot leap to the moon or a quarter of a million miles, it is still too far to jump unaided. Yet as some are clearly worthier than others, such distinctions are critically important.

Between those Muslims who regard Christians as heathen, Jews who see Gentiles as "goyim" and Christians who see all nonbelievers as damned, God's own view would seem to be one of tolerance, and those tests we undergo on the road to enlightenment, tests designed to erode our biases and overcome our flaws so that we may become more genuinely godlike attest to that greater unity. Here Hinduism, in being more catholic, at times, than Catholicism—more willing to admit to a diversity of approaches all aimed at one central Truth does not as easily confuse the form with the substance, the meat with the husk, but acknowledges that anything which inspires genuine devotion naturally leads one Godward. The form that devotion takes is peculiar to the individual and matters far less than the spark of illumination it fans.

Chapter 43

Right Speech

There is a sense of brotherhood and generosity implied in the act of speech. We all agree to process sounds in a certain way, to attribute shared meaning to specific utterances. In the process, we agree to let others hurt us with their words. This is, in large part, what makes the abuse of speech so reprehensible. The remainder has to do with the power of words themselves to project the energy of thought encapsulated within them. This makes wrong speech essentially a form of necromancy. The domain of verbal morality is one in which Buddhism particularly excels, dedicating an entire ethical subcategory to it.

The Bible and the Tao Te Ching both recognize the value of speech that is direct, sincere, and unembellished. Jesus said, "Simply let your 'Yes' be 'Yes,' and your 'No' be 'No.' More than this comes from the evil one." (Bible Hub, n.d., Berean Bible, Matt. 5:37) He further referred to those "pagans" he observed who "think they will be heard 'because of their many words.'" (Bible Hub, n.d., New International Version, Matt. 6:7) The Tao Te Ching comparably asserts that ". . . honest words may not sound fine, / Fine words may not be honest ones." (Tzu 1983, 158) None of this is intended to deny the intricacy and beauty of language, but actually has a common touchstone in a number of linguistic rules. Right speech is clear. It is direct. It is sincere. Like the man of the Tao himself, it accomplishes its purpose, and stops at that. It doesn't cheapen its coin by spending itself too lavishly.[1] This parallels Suzuki's idea that pride is extra. (Suzuki 2005, 59) With speech, pride is expressed in language that is pompous and labyrinthine without being instructive or effective. It is encapsulated in spiels that reek of false advertising, that bend an argument deceptively rather stating one directly.

One of the flaws of speech, noted in Buddhism is the error of overtalkativeness. As a specific vice, it has no direct parallel or similar prominence in the Christian tradition, though it is implied in that tradition's overall approach to virtue. It is a flaw that relates directly to one of the most insidious obstacles on the spiritual path, the need to convince others of the correctness of our views. Many religious people are unfortunately very big on this idea; it is as if everyone around them were falling off a cliff into hell, and they needed to grab as many of them as possible—by hook or by crook, by fear or by indoctrination—until all resistance to a particular viewpoint is overcome.

More helpful, by far, is the alternative view expressed in the Abraham writings of Esther and Jerry Hicks, that we are "on the Leading Edge of thought, experience, and expansion . . . The Non-Physical aspect of this Leading Edge you is experiencing the expansion, also, reveling in the new ideas, and joyously joining you as you continue to move into your powerful future." (Hicks 2006, 3) The larger point, as it pertains to our spiritual lives and practices, is that we may only hope to know, and that incompletely, what is best for us; we cannot legitimately determine what is best or most appropriate for anyone else.

The typical reason why people impose their views upon others, is that they lack faith in those views themselves, and in their personal degree of commitment. At the initial stage of the spiritual journey, a known pleasure is renounced, while the joy to be realized is not yet obvious. It is merely the light that threads through the clouds, noted in *The Voice of the Silence*. This is indeed the most difficult part of the journey—the uncertain beginning. Our ignorance and the Truth's obscurity are greatest then, our bad habits most distracting and binding, our confidence, lowest. If we persevere, we will find what we are looking for in a bliss greater and more constant than anything the senses can provide. Then we will become, as the Dhammapada describes, one who "climbing the terraced heights of wisdom, looks down upon the fools, free from sorrow he looks upon the sorrowing crowd, as one that stands on a mountain looks down upon them that stand on the plain." (Babbitt 2012, location 121, verse 28); we will then have the assurance of the divine that Sri Yukteswar referred to, "convincing to our very atoms." But until then, we will have sacrificed something seemingly for nothing, and may thus feel compelled to beat others' value systems into submission to convince no one so much as ourselves that our choice has been correct. This self-righteous proclivity should be conscientiously avoided, while, for an immediate remedy, we retreat into silence, where we will become one with Truth at the nondual level. This approach will get us faster to where we need to go, and assuage our current doubts.

NOTE

1. The specific reference from the Tao Te Ching is, "the good man's purpose once attained,/he stops at that . . ." (Tzu 1983, 96)

Chapter 44

Memory

Among Buddhists, it has been asserted that "forgetfulness is the way of death."
(Goldstein 1983, 120) They advise us to live in the moment, to honestly and
boldly confront the reality of circumstances as they arise, lest we dive off a
cliff or sign away our inheritance; but within that moment we bring to bear
all we have experienced before. To lack memory is to function without the
benefit of experience. But it is far more than that. Memory is like a time cap-
sule through which we playfully visit previous versions of ourselves. We see
how the scenery of the past, along with so much that had once caused us such
colossal pain, has transitioned lightly onward, and how the present, however
unbearable it may now seem, will likewise come, eventually, to relinquish its
hold. Part of the enthrallment of what Hindus call Maya, the magical play of
our constantly shifting experience, is that we can never regard it as anything
but fully and excruciatingly real at the time that we are experiencing it. So,
while anything karmic may be said to eventually pass, we should consider
all of our actions—and their foreseeable consequences—very, very seriously.

Still, from our immediate vantage point, the vantage point of the present,
a salutary journey into memory's departed vistas can keep us from taking
ourselves and our obstacles too seriously. We realize, by this means, that we
have passed through other corridors, operated from other contexts, emerged
from other wombs of experiences to arrive at where we are today, and that
today will give birth to tomorrow in much the same way. As divine thespians,
we have played other roles, starred on other stages, dreamed other dreams,
achieved other victories, bemoaned other losses. And now we are beyond the
reach of all that, except, perhaps, in memory. This understanding can, if we
let it, give us the courage to move on to new and more hopeful beginnings.

Chapter 45

Know When the Time to Go— and to Let Go—Has Come

When fame and success / Come to you, then retire. / This is the ordained Way.

—Tzu (1983, 68)

One of the ways of acknowledging life's flow is to recognize when it is time to move on, whether it be with relationships, jobs, or other rites of passage. "Kiss the joy as it flies," let it go lightly—if you can—but, most importantly, just let it go.

Most people, however, resisting the flow, tarry for far too long. They let the sweet fruit of circumstance languish on the vine until it eventually turns sour. They allow an originally good situation to deteriorate utterly before they finally agree to relinquish it.

When the heat is intense, and you smell your own flesh burning, it is time to step out of the fire, to preserve yourself, to live and to fight another day. Chances are that life has to clear your plate to make room for better offerings,[1] that it has something newer and timelier to present to you. But for that transition to occur seamlessly, you must make room for it. Hopefully, one of the metaphors in this mix, will convey the desired message!

As the Tao Te Ching comparably observes, "The good man's purpose, once attained,/ he stops at that." (Tzu 1983, 96) Here we can take an instructive page from the salesman's playbook. What do you say to the customer at the other end of the line once you close the sale? You say "thank you and goodbye," not "How's the weather out there in Houston?" or "I just bought a new car," but "thank you, and goodbye." Linger on the phone any longer, and you risk having that "yes" turn into a "no," or perhaps a "Um, tell you what; I know I just said 'yes,' but let me think about it a while longer."

We allow life to just as easily turn our yeses into nos by not leaving the field after the battle is won, by hanging around too long. This is particularly evident in the realm of professional sports, where former pennant winners, just a few years down the line, can be seen lumbering pathetically across the field, casting an incremental shadow across the record of their previous attainments.

Part of the enduring mystique surrounding John F. Kennedy, though by no means intentionally fostered, is that he died with his youthful promise, brilliance, and charm intact, tantalizingly immortalized in the form of an unrealized promise. Thank you and good bye, in this case tragically and unwillingly, yet the effect has been just the same.

NOTE

1. I made a similar point in *Guideposts to the Heart: Observations from the Spiritual Path* (G. Hallett 2011, 30) when I stated that "Sometimes life must clear our table, so to speak, to make room for better entrees. This becomes a problem only when the person then thinks that he has nothing better to do than starve."

Chapter 46

Self-Confidence Must Come from the Self

Silently shall I endure abuse as the elephant in battle endures the arrow sent from the bow: for the world is ill-natured.

—Babbitt (2012, location 611, verse 320)

That the world is, or can be, ill-natured is clear enough to most of us. It is even clearer to those who are innately sensitive. The same depth of feeling that allows creative people to respond to injustice or beauty, causes them to be vulnerable to hurt. For such sensitive souls, the cruelty of the world can cut too deep. Some lose their vital warmth, become callous, and never recover. As a case in point, note the following from Vladimir Lenin on the beauty of music. As Lenin observed, "I can't listen to music too often. It affects your nerves, makes you want to say stupid, nice things, and stroke the heads of people who could create such beauty while living in this vile hell." Such is the tragic viewpoint of a brilliant yet thoroughly dehumanized man. Of a refined and delicate nature to begin with, such people can too readily find themselves throwing their "pearls before swine" and being systematically plowed under by a dense and unappreciative society. Their only remaining solace lies in those recorded words and elevated thoughts that like a dim and distant echo, speak to them reassuringly from the luminaries of the past.

Herman Hesse wrote about just such a sensitive soul caught "beneath the wheel" in the regimented and increasingly mechanistic society of turn of the century Germany. As Hesse notes, in that brilliant work of the same name, so poignant and applicable to our time:

the struggle between rule and spirit repeats itself year after year from school to school. The authorities go to infinite pains to nip the few profound or more valuable intellects in the bud. And time and again the ones who are detested by their teachers and frequently punished, the runaways and those expelled, are the ones who afterwards add to society's treasure. But some—and who knows how many?—waste away with quiet obstinacy and finally go under. (H. Hesse 1968, 100)

A comparable situation exists in today's American society, where intelligence is valued only as it adds to a narrowly-defined range of neatly-delineated realms and preapproved endeavors. Those who answer "how" with their lives and intellects by building mindless trinkets or genocidal weapons are rewarded with posh suburban homes and exclusive country club memberships; those who ask "why" these are the things we think about and invent, are ostracized, minimized, and scorned. Where this inevitably occurs, the idealist must sustain himself in a different way through the strife. The correct response, for the spiritual aspirant, is, first, to be prepared, to know that the truth and not any particular viewpoint or social custom is what ultimately matters. Our fate will be determined by karma or by God, not by how closely our thoughts and actions resemble everyone else's. As for the opinions of others, Kipling said it best when he recommended that you "trust yourself when all men doubt you, but make allowance for their doubting too."[1] Self-confidence, by definition, can only come from the self; it cannot be borrowed or transplanted from another.

NOTE

1. This is a line from Rudyard Kipling's poem "If."

Chapter 47

The Easter Egg Hunt that Never Grows Old

Life, beyond eighteen, can still include an Easter egg hunt, an Easter egg hunt for adults. As opposed to the child's Easter Egg hunt, where we search for red, yellow, or blue-dyed treasures hiding in obscure corners, what we search for as adults are those things that work for us. We look for those practices, professions, foods, exercises, relationships, jobs etc. that suit us best. In the course of discovering them, it is a lack of confidence in the validity of our own beliefs, an uncertainty we hide from ourselves, that causes us, as previously noted, to denigrate other people and their practices. It insists that they think as we do, to assuage our hidden doubts, our regrets, and our nagging sense of uncertainty.

What other people believe need not challenge our own way of life; it is only when we are unsure of what we should think that we are inordinately pestered by others' contrary views. If we are wise, we won't revamp ourselves overnight either, but will apply what may be termed "the principle of the steering wheel." Skillful drivers don't veer erratically from left to right but compensate incrementally for bends in the road. Thus, the process of driving becomes seamless and smooth, the tar, one steady ribbon that leads us reliably to our chosen destination. It is much the same with life.[1]

NOTE

1. For more on "the principle of the steering wheel," see also *Guideposts to the Heart.* (G. Hallett 2011, p. 31)

Chapter 48

To Go Unmurmuring

The highest goodness, water-like/ . . . goes/ Unmurmuring to places men despise;/ But so, is close in nature to the Way.

—Tzu (1983, 67)

When we define our happiness energetically, we draw our attention away from those objects and goals that cause us to contend with others; as previously suggested, if there is a Mercedes in your garage, you won't envy your neighbor his Ford. If we have sought and found a higher happiness, the kingdom of heaven within for which the man in the Bible sold all his goods, then we won't despise others for the lesser goods they possess. No, this doesn't mean "here you take the presidency, I'll go mop the floors," for we will still have our dharma, that immeasurable blessing which weds talent to purpose and keeps us from "hiding our lamps under bushels." What it does mean is that the guy who does mop the floors, for whom mopping is his dharma, and who does so in harmony with the rest of Life, is far more likely to find happiness in that endeavor than the pompous ass who occupies a position of authority, yet whose ever act is contentious and whose every response is out of harmony, as rendered through the falseness of his ego.

Chapter 49

Be Here Now

One of the great keys to happiness is living in the here and now. But there is much more to this beneficial practice than simply being present. You can work with memories and still be in the here and now. To live in the here and now is to be sharply in tune with your experiences, whether they be sense impressions, memories or ideas. In fact, as Ram Das and others have noted, we are always here, always now anyway; there is really nowhere else to go. Being here now doesn't mean funneling our perceptions down a narrow corridor of experience, but of penetrating, in real time, to the root of the timeless.

At the intersection of here and now, we are either living mindfully, or not. By being present with our experiences, we discover consciousness as the unchanging backdrop to everything that occurs. In discovering consciousness, we find it to be something that transcends all dualistic distinctions—past and present, self and other, and the really big one: life and death. We discover it as the force which sustains all existence, the ultimate hidden solution to all our problems.

A short and well-known prayer, one that has offered comfort and encouragement to many, is "God give me the strength to change the things I can, patience to accept the things I can't, and the wisdom to know the difference." The last is usually the tricky part, though it doesn't have to be. Accomplishing it is largely a matter of awareness, of living mindfully in the present. When we are fully aware, we will then fully know what to do. Denial is the bigger problem. But living in the present doesn't imply lacking foresight, of living for the moment only. Such an idea is a genuine obstacle. Conversely, when the Tibetans say that all future lives are greater than this life, they are not implying that we complete our actions anywhere but within the time frame of our present involvement. Still, part of what we call "the future" is contained in that present. Here time resembles a great outstretched rubber band in which elements of what we call "the future" extend their way gradually into the range of our current awareness.

A large part of defensive driving is looking to the road ahead to see what hazards may be approaching. This is different from leaving the moment behind in favor of a separate reality, of climbing into another car or of driving backwards. It means coping with the onset of slight or potential hazards before they become major or actual ones. In short, a perspective on the future's immanent arrival is part of the present's current reality.

While the mold is setting, we can change it; we can see it taking shape, and can be confident of the form it is likely to assume. It is not yet finished, but exists now only as a coagulating substance; after it is set, it is, only then solid, and we can only change it, at that point, by breaking it. The lesson of the Tao is to remain as fluid as possible. While this abundantly applies to our perceptions and experiences, our bones are, of course, more fragile and less fluid, and part of a mindful approach to living is to continue to avoid breaking them.

To reemphasize, what has been termed "living in the now," is simply being aware, in a balanced, sharp, and thorough way. From a prohibitive standpoint, it is not about retreating into the past or leaping into the future, because that is not immediately possible anyway. The idea of mental time travel remains an intriguing possibility, but from the current standpoint of our physical capabilities there is really nowhere else to go; the eternal now is all there is. So, from the perspective of someone participating in the same events as us, we don't suddenly climb onboard the Star Trek transporter and beam back into the past, or into a future shared with Montana Wildhack on Tralfamador,[1] but are simply zoning out. We have positioned imaginary obstacles in the form of memories or fantasies between us and our immediate experience. We are engaging in a crafty process of avoidance. By refusing to live in the present, we render our actions in that present less effective, thereby jeopardizing as well "the future" we are recklessly dwelling in.

Should we find ourselves in a difficult situation, whether with a bad boss or an oppressive government, it is only natural to want to get away, to be somewhere else entirely; here part of our task and test may be to muster up the courage to pull up stakes and move on. But, if there is something we genuinely need to learn from these or other experiences, then we are bound to confront them in analogous form everywhere and anywhere we go, for what we can never truly escape is ourselves. As the Dhammapada affirms, "Not in the sky, not in the midst of the sea, not if we enter into the clefts of the mountains, is there known a spot in the whole world, where if a man abide, he might be freed from an evil deed." (Babbitt 2012, location 610, verse 127) Many times, like Arjuna on the battlefield of Kurukshetra, when we face our designated obstacles, we are momentarily hesitant. We are then, by avoiding action, just evading our essential tasks.

If you look at life in any given moment, not through your regrets or your fears, what are you most likely to see? A wonderful panoply of movement.

Blue skies and other colorful scenery. Little to nothing deficient in itself, except as unduly compared to other moments passed or yet to come. Yet our regrets about the past and fears for the future are like bungee cords tethered to our hearts, stretching painfully into other times. And why do they do this so easily? Because, with regard to the past and the future, we expect to find something therein of permanent value. And why do we expect that? Because we reify the passage of time, through anticipation and through memory, through hope and through fear. We see what is gone as eternal. Yet when have such flickering moments ever been anything but transitory? The blunt answer is "never." This is the natal and prenatal ignorance that Buddhism talks about. We are born into a world of change anticipating from it a permanent happiness. But because that world itself is impermanent, and our birth into it but a solidified expression of change, that world, at least in our current mode of experiencing it, can never provide what we took birth into it to have. But be not concerned, for in the depths of the here and now, is the limitless sea of all times, and it is there that we will view ecstatically, once we are fully enlightened, "our original face, before we were born"—with all merged times complete as one, and nothing at all deficient.

NOTE

1. The reference here is to Kurt Vonnegut's *Slaughterhouse Five*.

Chapter 50

Work

One of the greatest obstacles to living in the here and now is having the wrong occupation, for the wrong work encourages us to be elsewhere in our thoughts than we are in our actions. Engaged in the wrong work, we feel the need to anesthetize ourselves inwardly to make it through the day. The Bhagavad Gita makes such a big deal of this as to state outright, "to die in one's duty is life: to live in another's is death." (Mascaro 1974, 59)

When it comes to selecting their proper occupation, many people choose to opt out, taking on unsuitable work that they think will earn them more money, so they can enjoy themselves more on the weekends. But this is a flawed strategy; you only need so much money to be happy. Beyond that, the happiness that money can buy rapidly enters the realm of diminishing returns. Increasingly lavish possessions begin to constitute a new norm at which our happiness again levels off, stabilizing itself at no greater a plateau effectively than before, while their increased expense necessitates that we now work even harder, and depend on more money and obligating ties to satisfy our growing collection of wants. These wants become new fetters that newly bind the soul. Since material things can never themselves buy happiness, they often merely distract from the inner wealth which alone can ultimately provide it, and from the inner work we may still need to do to uncover it.

Taking the compromise road to work also skewers us on the horns of an agonizing dilemma. We look forward to the next vacation or the next day off, only to be whacked on the behind by the return paddle of Monday's approaching waterwheel. The more we live for the weekends, the more painful our return to work becomes. Yet what many people view as an obstacle or barrier in their lives, the work they are obligated to do, can indeed be the greatest of blessings. This frequently annoying obstacle, regarded correctly, can be the supreme opportunity in disguise.

When we work, we earn enough money to eventually go on vacation. Most of us come to regret our subsequent return. We then must work more to go on vacation once again. The solution to this repetitive dilemma is to enjoy the work as much or more than the vacation. This would seem, to most people like a facetious answer, but it isn't. In fact, it contains one of the greatest keys to success and happiness ever devised. That most people aren't aware of it is why most people are not truly successful or happy, irrespective of their accolades or titles.

This is the approach of the Bhagavad Gita, which advises us to focus on the work rather than on its fruits, and tells us that when we find purpose in our work, there we will find God. Once we find God, then lesser things won't bind us. Then we will, in fact, end up valuing the work more than the vacation. A larger version of the vacation example concerns all those people who work hard for the day when they can eventually retire; then, without some form of alternative work, or a systematic plan, they go stir crazy within a year. As the famous (and original) essayist Montaigne, humorously—and accurately—wrote:

> Lately, when I retired to my home, determined so far as possible to bother about nothing except spending the little life I have left in rest and seclusion, it seemed to me I could do my mind no greater favor than to let it entertain itself in full idleness and stay and settle in itself, which I hoped it might do more easily now, having become weightier and riper with time. But I find . . . that on the contrary, like a runaway horse, it gives itself a hundred times more trouble than it took for others, and gives birth to so many chimeras and fantastic monsters, one after another, without order or purpose, that in order to contemplate their ineptitude and strangeness at my pleasure, I have begun to put them in writing, hoping in time to make my mind ashamed of itself. (Montaigne 1965, 21)

What meditation and work have in common is that they each provide a focus and enhance alertness. That is why at the end of both a long meditative session and a vigorous work day, while the body may be achy and tired, the mind is typically calm and clear. It becomes even more so when, after a good night's rest, the body has recuperated as well. This allows the mind's resulting radiance to burst forth unobstructed. Indolence, by contrast, dulls the mind through random overuse of the senses. Where the mind is allowed to proceed lazily through the day, and where every desire is pursued pell-mell, in a head-long and undisciplined fashion, one's thoughts, like Montaine's in retirement, become chaotic. A chaotic mind is the fertile seedbed of neurosis and misery. That is why Krishna characterized yoga as "wisdom in work." (Mascaro p. 52) Undertaken in the right spirit, work, like meditation, becomes an avenue to both worldly happiness and spiritual enlightenment.

Regarding the fruits of one's labor, the Puritans believed that wealth was an indicator of salvation, a sign of God's favor. This assertion would seem to be contradicted by the significant number of people who have wealth but no apparent morals. Still, like similar ideas that have endured the test of time, it contains a kernel of truth.

Those who seek joy in service through purposeful work, no longer focus, to the same degree, on lavish spending. This allows them to save more for the future. The Bible says "seek first the kingdom of God and his righteousness, and all these things (all else that you need) will be added unto you." (Bible Hub, n.d., Berean Study Bible, Matt. 6:33) thereby asserting, more directly, that when you put the horse before the cart, the spiritual before the material, material prosperity will be drawn along too. This approach also dispenses with the troubling issue of "paradoxical intent."

Paradoxical intent is a brick wall that practitioners of the Law of Attraction collide with when they begin to fear losing what that law has apparently given them. While excitement, enthusiasm, and positive expectation draw what we want to us, fear and doubt push it all away. The only real solution to the problem of paradoxical intent is to keep your center true. It is okay to want things that are limited by nature, only not so much. Once we do, it soon becomes clear that we have veered from the True North of our spiritual strivings. We then proceed, through the Law of Paradoxical Intent, to drive all of these positive incidentals away. By keeping God and Truth enthroned, rather than the golden calves of our material ambitions (which we need not abandon either), we keep the Law of Paradoxical Intent at bay.[1]

The right work, undertaken in the right spirit, combines two of the main purposes of life, to develop our talents and to serve others. The right work only becomes a burden when, like the wrong work, it keeps us stuck in duality. Wrong work does this by locking us into the futile endeavor of seeking one side of the experiential coin at the expense of the other, to avoid the pain of work only through the thrills of our time away from it. Right work becomes aversive when we get hung up on its outcomes.

Once the ball is struck, and is sailing through the air, there is really nothing more that the batter can say or do about it; he must hit the ground running. As Christmas Humphreys states, with regard to dutiful action, "Look at it, do it, drop it"; (Humphreys 1962, 162) it will produce its own karma in its own good time. It is pointless to fuss over things that are outside of our control, yet takes a great deal of discipline not to; but that discipline is well worth cultivating, and is key to the Gita's recommended approach. It is what allows us to ascend through our work beyond all realms of duality into the domain of genuine peace and satisfaction, the abundant inner domain where God and Truth dwell.

If we know we have done our best, then that is really all we can do, for as the Bible similarly asserts, "And who of you by being worried can add a single hour to his life?" (Bible Hub, n.d., New American Standard Bible, Matt 6:27). Even work that is less than ideal can become an efficient avenue to happiness, should we train ourselves, in the midst of it, to be present and mindful. We can take great joy in small things. We can generate new ideas that enhance the productivity of our firms or make our assigned tasks easier. This would be equally true whether we work for McDonald's or for NASA. Still, the right work, the work that engages our strongest talents and through which we can ideally serve, should be a primary objective in our lives, and a cornerstone in our spiritual foundation.

Much like the ideal relationship, the ideal job is not necessarily the one without obstacles, for such obstacles, as in other realms, typically become a catalyst for self-development, and the more we improve, the happier we will be. Unlike many avenues to enlightenment which prescribe retiring to a distant mountaintop, the Gita's approach sets us directly in the midst of what we Americans specialize in most—activity. It takes such activity, often frivolous, obsessive, misdirected and unrefined, and hones it into a precision tool for reaching our highest ends.

Most people who would otherwise be happy with their jobs find them burdensome due to strained relations with coworkers. They find themselves repeatedly interacting with others who have either compromised on their individual dharmas, or are undertaking work in the wrong spirit, choosing to be pestered by uncontrollable outcomes. Maintaining the right course, yourself is the best armor to don in such an environment.

It has been said that bad things come in threes. The simple, mundane reason for this is that we are stunned by the first blow into being precariously thrown off balance. Pestered by what the boss said, we may find ourselves forgetting a key or an appointment, our email or laptop. Maintaining the right perspective on outcomes will allow us to recover faster from our momentary setbacks. Such a desired perspective is realized by following the Gita's recommended approach of performing our work as an act of devotion, without egoistic attachment.

The only thing more tempting than temptation is the thing in life we are most meant to do. Once we pursue it, it is like we are riding a beam. In a reversal of a popular aphorism, the Gita states that where there is fire, there is smoke.[2] In all work that we might opt to undertake, there is an inevitable element of drudgery, and a fair share of annoying obstacles, whether in the form of deadlines to meet, or challenging coworkers to contend with. In such instances, it is the love of what we do, the pure element in an otherwise impure process, that will ultimately see us through.

In the *Star Trek* episode, "Elaan of Troyious," Captain Kirk falls under the spell of an alien seductress by coming into contact with the pheromones in her tears. At the end of the episode his friend and physician, Dr. McCoy, comes up with a medicinal cure for the biological aphrodisiac, only to find that Kirk has broken the miasmic spell on his own, through the greater love he has for the Enterprise, the ship that he commands. (J. M. Lucas 1968) Being devoted to our work is powerful. It is only by undertaking what Stephen Cope calls The Great Work of Your life that you can overcome your Nemesis and reach the end of enlightenment. (Cope 2014)

NOTES

1. As Sandra Ann Taylor defines this term, one she uses repeatedly in her books, ". . . the more desperate we are to achieve our goals, the more our needy energy will push them away, creating the opposite—the paradox—of our intentions." (Taylor 2011, 94)

2. Offering the complete reference, ". . . a man should not abandon his work, even if he cannot achieve it in full perfection; because in all work there may be imperfection, even as in all fire there is smoke." (Mascaro 1974, 119)

Chapter 51

The Principle of the Staircase

The Tao Te Ching states that a journey of a thousand miles begins with the first step forward, or with the ground beneath our feet. Although our objective may be to ascend, to proceed to an upper floor, it would be as unlikely that we will get there in one gargantuan leap, as it would be for us not to get there one small step at a time.

The Principle of the Staircase[1] implies that the next thing to do, whether it be taking out the garbage, mowing the lawn, or winning the Nobel Prize is what we need to do attentively, undistractedly, and without impatiently dwelling in a moment that hasn't yet arrived. It has a lot to do with staying in touch with reality, with proceeding in a way that will enlighten us, for only in the living moment is reality itself focused.

The principle of the staircase entails living in the here and now, for it encourages us to "live life the way life lives itself," one instant, one mindful leg lift, at a time. It also dovetails with the Buddha's recommendation to "make haste gradually," which means, in practice, to stay both patient and squarely focused on our chosen objective. It implies engaging with obstacles on life's battlefield unflinchingly, for through it we cease trying to avoid what exists by attempting to evade the specific step before us. If we do withdraw, as we must at times, from bad company or from noxious or destructive influences, it will be because we have made a carefully-crafted decision to do so, rendered in the moment, or in a series of moments, without avoiding the need to make that decision either. The principle of the staircase is further implied in the well-known "Lord's Prayer," which exhorts God to "give us *this day* our daily bread" (emphasis mine);—not, specifically, to shelter our tomorrows with the advantages of long-term annuities.

In *Star Wars*, a movie heavily influenced by religious thought, both East and West, Obi Wan Kenobi tells Luke Skywalker that he cannot avoid his destiny; that he must face his father, Darth Vader, again. (Marquand 1983) In a karmically-determined universe, we will undergo trials that center on our fears and attachments. If we refuse to engage, as Arjuna originally did at the opening of the Bhagavad Gita, our evasiveness will prove futile, and we will, finally, succeed only in making circumstances worse for ourselves. As Krishna explains in the Gita, "If, in your vanity, you say: 'I will not fight,' your resolve is vain. Your own nature will drive you to the act. For you yourself have created the karma that binds you." (Isherwood 1972, 129) The obstacles and elements of destiny that we futilely seek to avoid will only present themselves more insistently and annoyingly later on. They arise inexorably from the flaws in our own natures, demanding from us an appropriate response. What Buddhism refers to as "heavy weighty karma" concerns actions that have been—not only committed in ignorance—but for which we ignorantly refuse to atone. Its unmitigated force is what then must inevitably strike us. To mindfully and constructively proceed with the specific step in front of us, is the fullest assurance we have, an assurance in the here and now, that the future—what is not currently here and now—will favorably arrive.

NOTE

1. "The Principle of the Staircase" was first introduced one of my earlier books, *Guideposts to the Heart*. (G. Hallett 2011)

Chapter 52

Develop Your Talents Outwardly

Imagine a musician or an actor who never performed. Imagine a chess or checkers player who only learned strategy, but never played a game. At least half—if not more—of the joy in developing a skill is in serving and engaging through it, in productively sharing it with others. Such a broadened emphasis also serves to take the neurotic edge off our standard preoccupation with where we are going, and just how fast we are getting there. Our gifts, what is, by definition, given to us abundantly, exist so that we may in turn give to others. In the process, we find that all is gained and nothing lost; "denying self, he too is saved, for doesn't he salvation find by being an unselfish man." (Tzu 1983, 66) This approach, firmly adhered to, also ends any inordinate concern we may have about the afterlife. We are just too busy doing what we need to do that automatically leads there. We are focused on the now and not on the end. This leads more seamlessly to an end that's blessed, versus one that has been marred by inattention.

Chapter 53

Completeness

What we often say, in our highest and happiest moments, is "I am complete." In a fractured universe, the prospect of genuine completeness appears elusive. It can only be realized by restoring our lost unity with others and with God. The two are in fact one, to "love thy neighbor as thyself," and "to love God with your whole heart, soul, and mind," for when we are one with God, we are one with each other, and only in being one with each other are we truly one with God. In that unity alone is found freedom.

As the Katha Upanishad states, ". . . What is here . . . the same is there; and what is there, the same is here. He who sees any difference here . . . goes from death to death." (F. Max Muller n.d., 16) When we arrive at that point where we find our fullest happiness and ultimate enlightenment, we will find everyone else in there too. We are all "on the same bus." The problem arises when we seek to enjoy the bliss of divine unity as a separate attainment, which, as an inherent contradiction, is effectively the same as saying I want to be complete in my separation. Once we cling to the state of oneness, its associated bliss vanishes, because we have erected the dividing wall of our exclusive identities once again.

Before many earn their first million, they are desperate to see an equality of access. Afterwards, they run off with their wealth to enjoy it alone, building mansions in recesses surrounded by tall pines in places that others are not aware of, let alone, invited to. And boarding there with them is the gremlin of their fear, a fear that can never be assuaged by any amount of money, a fear which is a sure sign that they are relating to their good fortune and to their less-fortunate neighbors unwisely. While, as spiritual people, we might condemn their actions, we behave similarly when we attempt to enjoy the fruits of the spiritual life alone. As *The Voice of the Silence* asks, ". . . Compassion speaks and saith" "Can there be bliss when all that lives must suffer? Shalt thou be saved and hear the whole world cry?" (Blavatsky 2011, 56)

It is in the nature of dualistic experience that it be forever incomplete. You may hate bad days, and determine never to have a bad day again, but you are unlikely to keep that promise for long, let alone, forever. Your physical nature too is part of life's duality. And still we long for completeness; so how do we resolve the paradox of yearning for an enduring harmony and peace in a world that is interminably conflicted, oscillating endlessly between a limited "good" and "bad"?

Identifying this as a problem is the first step toward resolving it. Then, finally, when we discover the nondual, amid the dual, we will have the best of both worlds, both colorful variety, and enduring meaning.

Chapter 54

Concepts and Reality

From one standpoint at least, all concepts are equal. They are just more traffic that flows continuously along the highway of the mind. The Buddha revealed his psychological depth when he said that "the Tathagata (Buddha) has no theories." He thereby proclaimed his Dharma to be a skillful means of engineering enlightenment, and not just another logically consistent theoretical viewpoint. Buddhism is very drastic in its approach to enlightenment in that through the easily misunderstood notion of anicca ("no self" or "no soul"), it kicks the legs out from under our ignorance, giving us no place left to stand than upon the naked and indescribable foundation of Reality itself. In saying nothing directly about God, in not speculating about what we will find when we truly let go, it discourages us from clinging to a construct of God in lieu of God's more substantive Reality.

Hinduism and Christianity offer a more gratifying verbal description of the Ultimate in talking directly about God; the problem here is that whenever we speak of God, we put Him in the box that our limited concepts have constructed; then what we are left to commune with are our own ideas, and not God anymore. We halt, mentally satisfied, outside the gate of spiritual satisfaction. It is a dilemma that is virtually unavoidable.[1] That is why Buddhism sidesteps it entirely, remaining silent on the topic of metaphysics and even of God. In the final analysis, which recipe is best for you depends on how your mind responds. If the sharp psychological vivisection of Buddhist methods only leads you to perceive people with a cold and flinty indifference, it may best be avoided in favor of another approach, one which poetically muses on the eternal, is inspired by the beauty of temples and cathedrals, and which exalts God "to the heavens."

As moderns, we dwell in a sanitized domain of polymers and peptides where what we describe, while conceptually accurate, doesn't always capture the wonder and beauty of our experiences. Hence an approach to God through Nature, through Music, or through Art can be an excellent practice as well. In each instance, the cure must reflect the needs and disposition of the patient.

Joseph Goldstein shared a well-known story about a man who, in the Buddha's time, would stare enthralled at the Great Avatar, who was the reputed embodiment, through his incomparably favorable karma, of not only mental but physical perfection. One day the Buddha admonished the man, saying, "you can stare at this form all day and still not see the Buddha." (Goldstein 1983, 153)

The Bhagavad Gita, in similarly emphasizing the superiority of substance over form states:

> Many are they, who saturating themselves with the letter of the spiritual writings and teachings, and failing to catch the true spirit thereof, take great delight in technical controversies regarding the text. Hair-splitting definitions and abstruse interpretations are the pleasures and amusements of such men. Such are tainted with worldly lusts, and, therefore, incline toward a belief in a heaven filled with objects and enjoyments in accordance with their desires and tastes, instead of the final spiritual goal of all great souls. Flowery words, and imposing ceremonies are invented by these people, and among them, there is much talk of rewards for this observance, and punishment for that lack of it. To those whose minds incline to such teachings, the use of the concentrated, determined reason and the still higher Spiritual Consciousness, is unknown. (Yogi Ramacharaka 1930, 84–85)

In India, Christ is regarded as a Divine Incarnation, as a perfect embodiment of the highest Truth, and is duly venerated as such. The Hindus have no problem with this, and with seeing the same Truth personified in Krishna and Buddha as well. They can do this, but we, in the West, not as easily, because they operate predominantly at the level of substance, and we at that of form.

When we look at the substantive outcome of religious conflict, whatever form it may take, whatever tradition it may ostensibly serve, it is always hatred, division, and conflict. When we look at the substantive outcome of religious tolerance, as one with the essence behind all forms, it is always love, peace, and light. Should we wisely attempt to know the tree by the fruit it bears, as Christ advised, this observation should tell us something.

This same distinction between form and substance underlies the peculiar Biblical statement of "resist not evil," (Bible Hub, n.d., King James 2000 Bible, Matt. 5:39) for implied in the modus operandi of religious conflict, whether it be a Muslim conversion at sword point, or a Christian crusade, is a substantive violation of Christ's words, of Krishna's words, of Buddha's words. In not resisting Evil, we substitute for Evil's methods, Good's harmony and love.

There have been religious wars in the past, and there may be many more in the future, but there has never been a spiritual war. In Spirit, and in its unspoken attainment of unity is peace, and that peace can only be found within.

There is ultimately, as Alan Watts described in *The Spirit of Zen*, but "silence, and a finger pointing the Way."

Each of us has a set of parents. Through them, if they be good and noble parents, as is typical, each of us learns what maternal and paternal love are all about. The love we have for them is special. We would not and could not change it out, like a worn-out set of tires, for the love of any other set of cherished guardians. It is unique to us, yet not unique overall, for through parents much like ours, other people are learning what parental love is all about. We dare not say that they can't really love their parents the way we love ours, that only our relationship to our own set of parents is valid or real. Yet we do something very similar when it comes to religious faith.

God has spoken through the ages. He has communicated through the colorful guise of numerous and varied cultures. Through them, the One Law that is perpetually operative, filters its way through. This is not a violation of spiritual understanding; it is not an abomination or aberration. It is the way the unified Truth of Spirit, in a world of material diversity, is meant to be expressed. Spiritual diversity is as noble and valid as that among races and nations. Everyone, through the unique context of his own culture and society, through its distinctive forms and peculiar practices, finds his own understanding and his own way home.

There is a passage from the Bhagavad Gita and another from the Dhammapada that apply particularly well, and in a complementary way, to the value of Christian worship: As the Gita asserts:

> For the salvation of those who are good, for the destruction of evil in men, for the fulfillment of the kingdom of righteousness, I come to this world in the ages that pass. / He who knows my birth as God and who knows my sacrifice, when he leaves his mortal body, goes no more from death to death, for he in truth comes to me. (Mascaro 1974, 61–62)

And from the Dhammapada:

> Whosoever pays homage to those who deserve homage, whether the Awakened or their disciples, those who have overcome the hosts of evils and crossed the flood of sorrow, who have found deliverance and know no fear—his merit can never be measured by anyone. (Babbitt 2012, location 399, verses 195–96)

Joseph Goldstein, in a profound yet simple statement, clarified that "the Buddha didn't teach Buddhism, he taught the Dharma, the law." (Goldstein, The Experience of Insight 1983, 151) Just imagine all the lives that would have been saved by our collectively comprehending the truth behind this basic and straightforward assertion. It is a truth that Buddhism acknowledges particularly well, that concepts are one thing and reality something else, something ultimately indescribable. All the conceptual "isms," "ologies," "anities" and inanities we have desperately embraced throughout history, in deference to which countless lives have been sacrificed and to which all life on earth has, in the nuclear age, been periodically ransomed, are like bags of rocks we carry around. Some bags contain blue rocks, others green, and others a varied mix. We swing at each other with these bags of rocks, arguing to the point of death over which is better or more valuable, while continuing to bear the burden of carrying them all around. Best to just put that burden down, to realize our ideas for what they are, i.e., limited conceptual tools, merely aids to understanding—some more useful than others—and to live and dwell within the speechless confines of a higher and deeper reality. This is the Reality in which God and Truth dwell. They will, from there, most assuredly guide us.

A typical balance sheet contains both tangible and intangible assets. Tangible assets are, by definition, those we can touch and feel, like cars and kinetic watches. Or they have a precise and measurable value, such as money or investment shares. Intangible assets are those we can't dent, rewind, or burn. They are not concrete, yet valuable nonetheless. Internet domain names and architectural blueprints fall within this category.

Concepts are the intangible assets of the mind. While ethereal and elusive, they may be worth more to us than our more tangible possessions, and we can become just as easily attached to them. Wars have been fought over such intangible ideas as "Liberte," "Kulture," and "the Divine Right of Kings." As with the ideas we espouse individually, such motivating concepts conceal as much as they illuminate, casting into the shadows the more tangible, yet less-appealing realities that insidiously undergird them. A good part of the enlightenment process involves dissipating our conceptual smoke-screens, both individually and collectively, in order to accurately perceive and evaluate what is.

NOTE

1. For a comparable description of this idea, see *Guideposts to the Heart.* (G. Hallett 2011, 7–11)

Chapter 55

Substance and Form in the Mind

The further you go, the less you will know.

—Tzu (1983, 119)

In saying this, Lao Tzu didn't mean to imply that a second grader should know more than a college graduate. His statement relates instead to what has been termed "epistemology," to how we know what we know. Only absolute knowledge, knowledge derived from the Tao can bestow an absolute certainty. It is knowledge we experience directly, knowledge we feel in our bones. All the rest is but relative understanding. We have a tendency to get immersed in our concepts to the point where we think they are real. But in truth, in thinking about things, all we are doing is building models.

If I construct a model of a tank or car, it will resemble the actual item in certain identifiable ways, particularly in its shape and visual appearance. If it is a car model, it will probably have rubber tires much like a real car does. The better the model, the more it will resemble its archetype. A model that precisely duplicates all the essential features of its original becomes a replica. Yet it remains separate and distinguishable from the original design nonetheless, as I am not about to climb into my model car and take a casual spin around town.

That concepts form systems of thought, which we can then apply to our communal activities, adds greatly to their seeming veracity. For example, my boss and I may have a mutual understanding that I am to arrive at work at precisely 8 a.m. So, if I am late, and without access to any means of reporting my whereabouts, I might get nervous contemplating the consequences that my tardiness might bring. But neither that workplace design, nor its consequences, are part of any immutable system of physical laws, like those of flight or gravity. Maybe when I arrive late for work, my boss will not be there, or will be so preoccupied with a pressing issue of his own, that he doesn't notice my absence. Perhaps I will have an opportunity to convincingly explain my delay, resulting in consequences less severe than those I had previously imagined.

Society, as a whole, has similar, yet more reliable and weighty constructs in the form of laws to which all are expected to adhere. Significant penalties are attached to their violation. So, should I find myself driving on the left side of the road in New York, I am likely to experience a heady rush of fear; but it is the same fear that someone in London would experience driving on the right side of the road. It is all based on the model of acceptable behavior that has been collectively affirmed.

In Nazi Germany, a citizen would have faced consequences more severe than those associated with running a stoplight, by harboring refugee Jews, or in the American prewar South by sheltering runaway slaves, even though such activities, from the perspective of a Truth deeper than man-made law, are fundamentally right.

Diverse conceptual schemes often come into conflict, once they have been identified as such. Is it better, in fact, to drive on the right side or the left, or by extension, is Communism or Capitalism, Enlightenment Rationality or Romantic Idealism correct, and to what degree? Yet, all of these systems are ephemeral. They are like snowflakes that present themselves to the world in their unique and intricate patterns, as they arise, glisten, then lightly melt away. In 17th Century Russia, controversy raged over whether the sign of the cross should be made with two fingers or three, even though contention over such a vapid issue involved a more substantive violation of Christ's message than any such procedural hairsplitting could have been.[1]

The insight developed in meditation raises us beyond the level of model-building to the plane of Truth itself. It blends our souls with the living substance behind our conceptually-catalogued schemes. After Truth is realized, we still retain the capacity to build models; we "still carry water and chop wood," but we are more likely, when we arise from our mats, to accurately identify the dualistic nature of that experience, to view our separate, limited, and relative activities for precisely what they are.

As the Zen Patriarch, Hui Neng declared, "all distinctions are falsely imagined." (Humphreys 1962, 90) All relative and partial truths create and affirm each other and are identified and sustained only by their mutual opposition without which they would be to one another, and to us as observers, entirely unknown. In meditation, concepts are accurately seen as just more "stuff" that drifts along the Flow. We realize this clearly whenever when we try to grasp them. Whenever they are contradicted by life or by others, we get mentally burned, as we would be physically burned by grasping at that moving truck tire, and this regardless of the nature of those ideas, or their seeming veracity to us. We learn that the way to relate to them is by not clinging to them at all, as if they were permanently, or independently real, because at the most basic and substantive level, they are not.

It is marvelous to rise to the level of balance, bliss, and understanding that is beyond the conceptual battleground, beyond the more limited dualities of life, beyond the opposite, revolving, and contending sides of the Yin Yang symbol, a symbol representing elements that are in constant and dynamic interchange, one giving way continuously to the other without permanence or finality. As *The Voice of the Silence* states, "To reach the knowledge of that SELF, thou has to give up Self to Non-Self, Being to Non-Being, and then thou canst repose between the wings of the GREAT BIRD. Aye, sweet is rest between the wings of that which is not born, but is the AUM throughout eternal ages." (Blavatsky 2011, 7) This is the level of the Tao, of a subtle knowing that manifests as a supreme deftness in action, because it remains balanced between any and all extremes. To realize it is to bring eternity into the realm of time, to where, when the Zen Master ties his shoes, it is the entire cosmos doing it. Few people ever reach this level, in any given lifetime. "Few there are among men who arrive at the other shore (become Arhats); the other people here merely run up and down the shore." (Babbitt 2012, location 216, verse 85) They are continually trying to assert one half of a unified duality at the expense of the other.

It has been suggested, by some, that Eastern meditation is inappropriate for Westerners; in fact, it is most appropriate for us, for it serves as an ideal corrective to a persistent cultural imbalance, one that leads us to overly idolize and idealize our concepts.

The highest form of knowing exists in the unity of subject and object, a confluence through which consciousness itself manifests. If I am one with what I observe, it is no longer out there for me to observe it. It does not even empirically exist, for it is no longer in any way distant from who I am. Thus, from the standpoint of a subject/object modality, it cannot be demonstrated, any more than without a mirror you can see your own eyes, though they, themselves, are the basis of sight. Yet it remains, and perhaps for this very reason, the most immediate, the most real and the most unassailable (i.e., nonrelative) form of knowing. It is this that we can most fully rely on for our realization of both Truth and happiness; it is not a knowing set apart from us; it is us. We know most deeply and truly that which we inseparably are.

Rousseau spoke of those who have "reason without wisdom and pleasure without happiness." (Rousseau 1964, 245) The first is the shadow; the second, the substance. To have knowledge without wisdom is delusive. It is to understand a lot about things, without understanding any of them directly, to have "head knowledge without heart wisdom." That is why external knowledge, rather than leading to wisdom often conduces to arrogance and presumption. Pleasure without happiness likewise appears to get us somewhere while actually getting us nowhere. It corresponds to the notion that "painted cakes do not satisfy hunger,"[2] that nothing without ultimate substance can ultimately satisfy.

Pleasure has a short lifespan and a surface appeal without taking us anywhere we really want to go. It is, ultimately, more of a palliative and a distraction than a meaningful objective. A contrasting life of simplicity, a life unencumbered, characterized by what Paramahansa Yogananda called "plain living and high thinking"[3] leads to the readier attainment of happiness through a realization of the greater joy within. From there you embark on an authentic mode of existence where your greatest treasures rest secure. To reiterate what the Tao Te Ching asserts, "One can never guard/ His home when it's full/ Of jade and fine gold." (Blakney 9, p. 68). The Bible too exhorts us not to build up our treasures "where moths and dust corrupt."

The Tao Te Ching parallels the Bible in speaking of the wise man who, when he discovered the kingdom of heaven, sold everything he owned for it. This unqualified enthusiasm for an invisible yet compelling domain of fulfillment may appear perplexing to those who are still beating each other up over relative, material trifles; but it is the road to real happiness, the road the Gita claims to be bitter at first, but sweet in the end, of discipline, work, and then onward to the deepest joy, a joy that that will render all the years of arduous effort and of harsh and rigorous discipline a triumph. And the great beauty of this process is that no one will contend with us for its advantages, the way they do for money, power, or any other of life's dim material alternatives.

The remarkable thing about "knowing" versus "knowing about" is that spirituality—and by extension religion—if aligned with its own core substance, deals with a higher, deeper, and more fundamental level of truth than science does, for the conviction of the soul is greater and more profound than that of the senses. In Saint Paul's words, it is "the substance of things hoped for, the evidence of things not seen," that faith encompasses. (Bible Hub, n.d., King James Version, Hebrews 11:1)[4]

The problem with modern religion, and the main reason, arguably, for its notable decline in the face of a science that alone cannot fill faith's role is that it too is more about "knowing about" than "about knowing"; it has confounded faith as the substance—mark the word SUBSTANCE—of things hoped for—with mere belief. In this latter, more limited, capacity, it cannot help but appear inferior in quality to a science which, without knowing in the deeper, intuitive sense that true spirituality implies, at least knows about its own subject matter very, very thoroughly. With belief versus faith, we simply take someone's word for what we believe, or we don't, which doesn't imply knowing in either sense of the term. The truths of spirituality are nonetheless there to be discerned, to be demonstrated and to be proven to ourselves. Here the proof is to be found within, and not through any form of outward experimentation or expression. We will not discover God or Truth in a test tube; but we are able to discover them.

To summarize, in the West, through science, we have developed theories that help us to increasingly account for more of what we experience. But none of it can equal the level of conviction to be found in Truth itself; it is, at the end of the day, only thoughts about thoughts. No matter how much the cake in the magazine resembles the cake from the oven, it can never duplicate its texture or flavor. There is and can be no conclusiveness to knowing about, the way there is to knowing directly.

As the Tao Te Ching states, "the way is gained by daily loss; loss upon loss until there comes rest." (Tzu 1983, 119) What we shed along the way are our preconceptions which, as we relinquish them, make way for fresh knowledge; we release our excessive attachment to what has already occurred, thereby making room for new and deeper experiences. Like the pounds we shed while dieting, what we lose is not only superfluous, but obstructive.

Ram Das, in a skillful expression, once referred to the rational mind as the "golden calf" of the culture. (Das, Grist for the Mill 1987, 4) In our innately acquisitive society, we see knowledge, like happiness, as something to be grasped rather than something to be realized when all obstacles have been overcome, all obscurations removed, and all preconceived ideas relinquished.

We learn, through meditation, that our senses have a merely symbolic relationship to reality. They present us with data about life that is logically consistent, that keeps us from bumping into walls or wandering in front of buses; but none of what we experience through them is the thing itself. This is indicated by the fact that, although each sense processes the same experiential environment, it reports on that environment differently. Just as a blind man who has never seen (only one who once had sight) can imagine a visual object, there may in fact be other sensory means of relating to life beyond what any man has hitherto experienced, or can currently even imagine. Yet all of them, too, would be merely symbolic, providing no more than a logically consistent relationship to Reality. What makes the enlightenment experience so ecstatic, even if glimpsed only briefly, is that through it we are finally one with the substance of our experiences, we are finally tasting the cake and not just looking at it through the pastry shop window in a way that accentuates our separation from it. In that moment of merging, we actually know.

Through the practice of meditation, I have experienced various phases that are precursors of a full enlightenment. I have benefited from a vastly heightened level of sensitivity and bliss. My senses have been washed clean, so that I can now perceive life sharply and clearly. My mind has stabilized at the level of "witness consciousness" so that, even amid extreme hardship, it is able to rest inwardly firm and calm. These hard-earned results, the results so far attained, are enough to fill me with amazement and confidence, and to justify my continued exertions. Yet there was only once in my life when I got a glimpse of what it will finally be like at the end of the long journey, a glimpse of that full enlightenment which is the unmistakable and true goal, the resting place of deliverance.

During that one moment of time out of time, I was neither reaching with anticipation for an uncertain future, nor clinging to a recollected past. I was not consumed with any artificial sense of who I was. At that moment, it was as if a fine bubble burst, a bubble that had always separated me from a direct perception of life. Suddenly I was immersed in a boundless field of light, immeasurably bright, brighter than "the light of a thousand suns," yet clear without any differentiating qualities.[5] I felt in that clear glimpse of Reality that as a separate individual I was dead, yet never more truly alive, for what makes for separate existence other than that dividing line separating experience from experiencer? I also felt in that moment of merging, before slipping back into "the fitful sleep of ignorance,"[6] the delusive state of everyday life, that all I had experienced in the sensory world from birth onward was but a dream by comparison, and that for one brief yet unforgettable moment in a time beyond time, I woke up. I then realized too that a lot of the conceptual nuances that cause people such torment, such as the idea of "no-self" or "no-soul" in Buddhism, are nothing to be feared. They are but the ingredients of a recipe that cannot, in itself, capture the actual experience. Such concepts become obstacles only when we rely on them too much and wrongly, needlessly tying our thoughts into knots. We need to analyze them less, and live them more, and just "keep on keeping on."

NOTES

1. See James Billington's *The Icon and the Axe*, for a detailed description of this particular controversy. (Billington 1967, 133–36)

2. This inscription immediately precedes the nonpaginated "additional reading" section of Ram Das's *Be Here Now*. (Das, Remember: Be Here Now 1971)

3. One of the stated aims of Self-Realization Fellowship, as set forth by its founder, Paramahansa Yogananda, is "To encourage 'plain living and high thinking': and to spread a spirit of brotherhood among all peoples by teaching the eternal basis of their unity: kinship with God."

4. The identical point was made in my earlier book, *Humanity at the Crossroads*.

5. "Suppose a thousand suns should rise together into the sky: such is the glory of the Shape of Infinite God." (Isherwood 1972, 92)

6. This is an expression Yogananda used in his Autobiography to describe the unenlightened state that his guru Sri Yukteswar, through the latter's frequently indelicate methods, aimed to dispel.

Chapter 56

Seeking Substance from Illusion

Ram Das once spoke of a man who, having lost his watch in an alleyway, was searching frantically for it on the sidewalk. When asked why, he said "because the light was brighter there." (Das, Grist for the Mill 1987, 4) He employed this metaphor to describe how we conceptualize our experiences to gain knowledge, knowledge that can never be secured through conceptualization alone.

This same metaphor can be applied, not just to understanding, but, by extension, to happiness. While certain circumstances and people can function as triggers, or reminders, of happiness, that happiness—or even Love in its essential nature—is not localized in those people or objects but in the divine realm within. It is from there that our receptivity to them and to the value they hold for us arises. Through our spiritual practice we move beyond the mere symbols of existence as we seek love and happiness, each in its own nature and on its own ground. When we seek happiness externally only through objects and people, we are happy only when they behave the way we want them to. When happiness is found within, we have direct access to its underlying source at all times.

The Gita analogizes this as "the use of a well of water where water everywhere overflows"; we surmount the need for scriptural guideposts once the inner knowledge has been secured. (Mascaro 1974, 52) Much the same could be said of happiness. In realizing the highest happiness, we don't cease to appreciate all the other joys in life, but we no longer value them so highly that we become enslaved by them or dependent on them. We can't obtain that fuller reality, "we," as Kalu Rimpoche asserts, "are that reality"; (Goldstein, The Experience of Insight 1983, 32) we are one at the deepest level and at all times with all those things we would hope to have, and with all those people we would long to embrace.

So, which is better—brushing against life or being one with it? This is where we realize the distracting and ultimately dissatisfying role of a merely sensory pursuit of happiness, of it being the light that glimmers off of Mara's jewel, captivating but not ultimately fulfilling. We don't have to own the Sistine Chapel to appreciate it. The sense of appreciation and that of ownership, though often confused, are widely separate things.

Chapter 57

Life is Composed of Both Light and Shade

In the Taoist Yin Yang symbol there is always a bit of Yin in the Yang, and of Yang in the Yin; what can this teach us about life? That even in our darkest moments there is a faint glimmer of light; that even in the nearly perfect, there persists a shadow of the unwanted. This valid appreciation directs us to seek the fullness of peace and satisfaction, not in the swirling spectacle of continuous plays or malleable destinies, but more reliably within.

Where there are dark letters on a page against a white backdrop, there is meaning that can be discerned and expressed; if the page is all white or all black, nothing is thereby manifested or conveyed. It is the same with our material experiences. In the moment that one thing exists in relation or opposition to another, in that moment, time begins. But with that dynamic tension, that opposition of one thing to another, of Yin to Yang, there is born with time itself, a built-in incompleteness.

In the Yin Yang symbol, there is furthermore not just opposition, but dynamism, the movement of each opposite carving into the domain of the other. Eliminate the opposition, and there is nothing that can be expressed or experienced in any ordinary linear way, nothing to see or to learn on the plane of duality. Time itself vanishes. But that experience of no-thing is not nothing; it is the Infinity and the balance of all things, the arrival in time of a timeless perfection. It is life resting in its original nature. Once we finish reading, once the sentence ends with the dot on the page, we make the carriage return home.

It is often said that "seeing is believing," yet the deeper realities are ones we cannot see. Not convinced? Well, have you ever seen a falling leaf or branch? Of course, you have. But have you ever seen gravity fall? I would guess not. Yet while the leaf or branch is likely to be long gone by now, swept away or mulched back into the soil, gravity itself endures. Have you ever seen two pears or two cars? Of course! But have you ever seen the number 2 walking around out there? No. Yet the quantity 2 is something we can refer to constantly, something more naturally enduring, while the two pears may already have been eaten, the two cars rusted away. It is almost as if the leaves and branches, the cars and the pears, are part of an experiential domain in which the workings of a higher, more constant and consistent reality are demonstrated. They are like in nature to symbols. Richard Bach stated this outright in *Illusions* when he said, "The world is your exercise-book, the pages on which you do your sums. It is not reality, although you can express reality there if you wish. You are also free to write nonsense, or lies, or to tear the pages." (Bach 1977, 127) Plato said much the same thing, in referring to his Realm of Ideas, out of which visible creation is formed. And the Tibetan Buddhists acknowledge this truth, as well, in their Yoga of the Great Symbol, where the perceptual world is portrayed as the symbol of a deeper underlying Reality.

The Buddha, in his search for enduring happiness, first ran into the daunting obstacle of not finding anything enduring at all. He concluded, soon enough, that anything formed was not the object of his search, that all created things, all objects of sensory experience, were subject to change and dissolution, and thus unsatisfactory. To borrow a line from *Star Wars*, they weren't "the droids he was looking for." (G. Lucas 1977) That is why he spoke of

> an Unbecome, Unborn, Unmade, Unformed; if there were not this Unbecome, Unborn, Unmade, Unformed, there would be no way out for that which is become, born, made, and formed; but since there is an Unbecome, Unborn, Unmade, Unformed, there is escape for that which is become, born, made, and formed. (Evans-Wentz 2000, 68)

In the final analysis, even Time and Space, as Einstein asserted, are not absolute, but part of a relative relationship known as Space/Time. It is God, or the Tao, the formless and timeless, that is without opposite and correspondingly without end.

Chapter 58

The Obstacle of False Renunciation

There is a form of pseudo-renunciation which is none other than a cowardly and ill-advised retreat from life. It is a suicide, in effect, by spiritual means, a sort of death while one remains, by all appearances, living. The world has hurt us, so we try to expunge it. But the fact remains that we must continue to engage with life and its obstacles; we must continue our worthy struggle to its very end, should we realistically hope to succeed, both in life and in our spiritual quest. As Suzuki's popular Zen saying goes, "there is nothing infinite apart from finite things." (Humphreys 1962, 60) Being here is what takes us there; understanding fully by not just knowing but becoming Truth, takes us home.

When we become enlightened, we return to the unity that can be found, no less than anywhere else, exactly where we are. As the Isa Upanishad states, "Into deep darkness fall those who follow only the immanent. Into deeper darkness [yes deeper!] fall those who follow only the transcendent." (Mascaro 1974, 18) Spirituality is not meant to be a means of escape but a method of engagement to secure our victory and success in life no less in the here and now than in the uncharted, vast beyond. It is not just a means for our distracted egos to go on vacation.

"Why," the false ego argues, "do I have to deal with this bill, this jackass neighbor, this annoying coworker when I could be sitting in a corner meditating peacefully." Yet such challenges are the very essence of the path, meditation, the means of treading it with ever-increasing patience, tolerance, and equanimity; the places that pinch most, reveal where the direction of and need for growth are most pronounced. Things will get better as we move towards the better, but they may not seem to do so at first, as we tightly bend the wheel against the inertia of all the obstacles within that we need to overcome to advance. Here the way we develop spiritually is indistinguishable from the way we pragmatically progress through life; for once we have paid the bills, mollified our neighbors, and cooperated with our coworkers in a skillful and effective way, we will no longer know them obstacles, as challenges to be met or as barriers to be overcome. We will, by then, have made them part of our larger, more peaceful, more balanced, and more effective approach to life.

Judging by every recorded legend and experience, when one realizes the goal of the spiritual quest, he doesn't say he has attained a "Buddhist enlightenment," a "Hindu Enlightenment," or a "Sufi Enlightenment;" he is simply enlightened. He may even opt to say nothing, as what he has attained cannot be adequately described.

The Buddhist idea of "no-self" is the "glass half empty" version of the Hindu idea of the individualized self in one evolving into the Self in all. When we are no longer so narrowly and futilely obsessed with shoring up that relatively drab and minuscule portion of the universe with which we have become inordinately identified, we will realize our seamless and conscious unity with the One. It is a completeness that has always been there, but that we have hidden from ourselves behind a delusional curtain of self-generated ignorance, perhaps for innumerable lifetimes. That oneness is not a new attainment. God has always been there. The universal consciousness has always been extant, poised to spew new galaxies of experience from its kaleidoscopic loom of change. This remains true, whether we are cognizant of its workings or not. When a person is focused intently on a particular task or project, the sounds of the external world are still there; they have merely fallen off of his personal radar. When we dream at night, the waking world is still there. And so, when we awaken, we remember it. It is the same with the Divine Realm.

Chapter 59

A Seeming Contradiction

In the Dhammapada it is stated that "If a man . . . meditates on what is not pleasant, he certainly will remove, nay, he will cut the fetter of Mara," (Babbitt 2012, location 665, verse 350) while the Law of Attraction suggests that we focus on good feeling thoughts as a means of attracting correspondingly favorable circumstances. So how do we reconcile this seeming contradiction? I believe that the answer lies in the indirect (i.e., Taoist) approach to happiness implied in "Cliff Klingenhagen," a poem by Edwin Arlington Robinson. As Robinson sagaciously wrote:

> Cliff Klingenhagen had me in to dine
> With him one day; and after soup and meat,
> And all the other things there were to eat,
> Cliff took two glasses and filled one with wine
> And one with wormwood. Then, without a sign
> For me to choose at all, he took the draught
> Of bitterness himself, and lightly quaffed
> It off, and said the other one was mine.
> And when I asked him what the deuce he meant
> By doing that, he only looked at me
> And smiled, and said it was a way of his.
> And though I know the fellow, I have spent
> Long time a-wondering when I shall be
> As happy as Cliff Klingenhagen is. (Robinson 1887, 18)

We all want to be happy, and as soon as humanly possibly; yet we retain the causes of unhappiness, and the memory of past unhappiness, within our minds. Ignoring the negatives entirely is like trying to save money by not paying any bills. That strategy, as one might easily foresee, would quickly backfire, leaving us with more problems than we originally had—and no fewer bills.

We also carry around, to one degree or another, what psychologists call cathected material, vestigial memories of experiences so painful we hide them from ourselves. This manifests in each of our lives as what I call "the problem that's not the problem." We obsess over some trifle that for the moment serves to dominate our attention before becoming equally, and as pointlessly, obsessed with something else. We may even, in the extreme, find ourselves engaged in neurotic rituals, essentially meaningless routines that our minds tell us we have to enact, but which merely serve to divert our attention from what is really bothering us. These are all signs of a much deeper problem, a problem we still must face.

At one time, I worked at a brokerage firm in New York City. One day the manager came rampaging through the aisles, slamming cabinet doors, and complaining about how messy the place was. I asked a colleague of mine, one whose instincts were better attuned, why, all of a sudden, the boss was so worried about the condition of the office. He responded by suggesting, that this wasn't the problem, that something else was. We soon learned that our Manhattan office was about to be closed. Those currently employed there were given the option to either relocate to the company's headquarters in Boca Raton, or to leave the firm entirely. The problem that's not the problem.

All of this cathected material, all of these troubling feelings we elaborately hide from ourselves, are like mental adware that consumes our internal resources unproductively. We may find that some of our trials concern the need to repay karmic debts, to balance the scales of justice once again. But others relate to a more basic need to overcome some personal limitation that is continually holding us back from all that we could otherwise become. Imagine how fast we would advance in our own psychological and spiritual growth if we were to become, amid this ineluctable process, deliberately proactive. Imagine how many obstacles we would thus avoid experiencing, by dispensing with them before they arise. In so doing, we would realize that what we were so preoccupied with and agitated about from within our stash of cathected material, are just feelings about feelings; while they can create a lot of commotion in our own minds, most of them would seem meaningless or comical to someone else.

One known and positive way to clear emotionally charged events is through the Sedona Method. It is a technique by which you ask yourself two basic questions with regard to any cathected memory you would otherwise tend to repress: "Could you allow yourself to welcome this feeling as best you can?" and "Could you allow yourself to let it go?" (Dwoskin 2009, 84) It isn't even necessary to answer "yes" to the second question. The main idea is that we have finally undertaken the daunting task of grappling with our personal demons directly and honestly. We are finally allowing ourselves to feel.[1]

Because we tend to push them repeatedly from our minds, it would be worthwhile to keep a journal of such emotionally charged events, maybe using a personal shorthand, one that would remind us of them, yet be indecipherable to someone else. "Remember the incident at the prom," or "remember what happened on the field trip." Be gradual in this process, as the willingness to confront repressed material may lead to the release of additional traumatic memories too abruptly. We should allot a specific time to deal with repressed experiences, spending the rest of our day, consistent with the Law of Attraction, focusing on those pleasant things we optimistically hope to manifest, for confronting obstacles and unpleasantries is never an end in itself, but part, whether within the context of Buddhism or in keeping with the Law of Attraction, of the larger quest for happiness.

NOTE

1. The full lineup of questions, per the method, is, "Could you allow yourself to welcome this feeling as best you can? / Could you allow yourself to let it go? / Would you let it go? / When?"

Chapter 60

Reasons to be Happy

Most of what we need, if we are healthy and whole, we already have: sight, hearing, mobility. Even those of us who lack one or more of these precious attributes will still typically find a way to be happy, given how great a blessing the remaining benefits are. Yet we still tend to focus inordinately on the negative, on the absence of what we don't have. Why?

Buddhist Master, Chogyam Trungpa, in *Shambhala: The Sacred Path of the Warrior*, refers, in this context, to life's "basic goodness." (Trungpa 1985, 11) Basic goodness is, in fact, so basic, so ordinary, so much a part of our everyday lives and deepest being, that we usually take it for granted. Yet it is the loss of that basic goodness that we fear in the prospect of death. We are thus secretly terrified that a day might pass without our being here, without our sensing the air in our lungs or the wind on our faces, without our appreciating the blue of the afternoon sky or the orange warmth of an evening sunset. We don't think much about these things while they are happening—with the possible exception of the sunset; but we sorely miss them when they are absent or gone.

Our modern focus on the negative is to some extent natural, yet nonetheless misguided, and all-too-likely to balloon out of control if we let it. In an earlier State of Nature, the threats we faced were often to life and limb; thus, we were naturally inclined to dwell on them. In the modern world, we face far more numerous challenges; but rarely is what we grapple with, during the course of a typical day, as critically dire. Instinctively reacting to these numerous small crises can make us habitually stressed and negative, as we repeatedly contend with them within the agitated domain of the "fight or flight" response. Still, in the end, and as Mark Twain sagaciously noted, in reference to his own experience, "I've had a lot of worries in my life, most of which never happened."

The problem we habitually face with negativity resembles that which many of us have with food. Our instincts were formed in a primitive environment in which food was relatively scarce. So, whenever the opportunity for a good

meal arose, we stuffed ourselves to the gills. We also profited from the mitigating benefit of travelling a great deal on foot in search of food and other
resources needed for our basic survival. So, we automatically got plenty of
exercise too. Nowadays, we repeatedly gorge ourselves on snacks that are
typically no further away than the nearby fridge, before climbing into our cars
to travel to work on a machine's motive power, rather than upon our own.

In terms of what we actually need, even our longing for love is not
quenched elsewhere than within our own hearts, with the sight, voice, or
perfume of another serving merely as the catalyst for igniting that amorous
fire which is localized within. Yet in further pondering this distinction, we see
how the truth may run deeper than this more superficial observation implies.
It can help to identify what it is about Evil itself that is so essentially dark
and tormenting.

Referring to the "Yogi of harmony," the Bhagavad Gita states, "He sees
himself in the heart of all beings and all beings in his heart." (Mascaro 1974,
71) As Chuang Tzu comparably noted, "the heart of the wise man . . . is
the mirror of heaven and earth, the glass of everything." (Goldstein 1983,
65) All of Life, indeed the entire cosmos, can be found by closing the eyes,
quieting the mind, and peering deeply within. Our illusory connection to
Reality is through the senses; the substantive one, subtly hidden behind the
senses' restless activity, is initiated via the heart and spiritualized mind. That
is where our truest and deepest connection to others can be found. From this
perspective, and ironically, the yogi sitting alone on a mountaintop may be
experiencing a far greater and more satisfying relationship to Life than someone isolated in a crowd at a superficial gathering. From within, the greatest
adventure commences, the loftiest peaks are scaled, and the highest happiness
of Nirvana is ultimately attained. As the Moody Blues sang, "the lovers, and
the fighters/ And the risks they take/ Are on the other side of life tonight."
(Moody-Blues 1986).

In the movie, Poltergeist, the Beast held a group of departed souls in a tan-
talizing limbo away from the True Light by distracting them with the lesser
light of what they could no longer hope to have. (Hooper 1982) Similarly,
through lust and greed, we are driven to pursue the shadow of things that have
made a fleeting impact on our senses. It is a shadow we can never grasp, a
shadow we can never own, a shadow that is forever passing, even as we are
experiencing it. All along these shadows distract us from the all-satisfying
vision of that unity which can only be found within. Once seated there we are
gods. Once centered there we are kings. Begging after shadows, we remained
enslaved, enslaved in the way that the demons of hell and the demons of
this world would prefer us to be. From this perspective, as well, we see that
most of us still live amidst the deceptively comforting shadows cast upon the

walls of Plato's cave, chasing forever after insubstantial mirages, false and pale reflections only of a truer and deeper happiness to be found in a more substantive mode of Life.

Chapter 61

Revisiting the Past to Rekindle a Sense of Love

As people get older, they often experience what one observer once called a "hardening of the hearteries." As a spiritual person whose life experiences have taken on new meaning, it would be valuable to go back and examine the causes of past lovelessness, to find the reasons why you later hardened your heart. As our rationalizing typically begins, "my heart is cold because I lost/didn't get _____" (fill in the blank for the missing person, place, or thing).

It is important to realize that the universe is a loving teacher, one that is instructing us through all of our experiences, whether we are willing to learn from them or not, whether we courageously embrace our challenges or just stomp our feet and complain. The people we are connected to, they too are learning, even if they appear not to consciously appreciate their roles. In the midst of this divine play-acting, we often behave like spoiled children who cry for what is not best for us—if not for what is downright harmful. We then proceed to compound our misery through the negativity of our thoughts, not realizing their ability to subsequently manifest into reality.

Chapter 62

Virtual Realty

Perhaps the main reason why human beings have emerged as the dominant species on earth has been our ability to cooperate as members of a team, to function as one, while retaining our distinct identities. Separately considered, large brains and prehensile thumbs might not have been enough to propel us ahead of other creatures physically stronger than us. Individually we remained weak; but together we employed language and used it to advance a common ideal or good, collectively perceiving it as Truth. This ability, so central to our survival, has, if anything been hyperdeveloped in modern times, to where we are now able to accept a commonly-held belief as right, regardless of its accuracy, and to interpret a popular course as moral—however reprehensible or disastrous it might otherwise seem—and be.

A recent documentary was released centering on some newly-discovered letters found in Heinrich Himmler's safe. (Lapa 2014) If the viewer didn't know better, he might be convinced he was privy to the thoughts of a historical personage with untarnished moral sensibilities, one who worried about his son's lying, for example. Here a decent set of values cohabited with the most reprehensible type of actions imaginable, actions which participation in a notoriously corrupt regime allowed Himmler to unflinchingly interpret as good. This hypnotic "groupthink," to which Himmler—among others—was routinely subject, is why, as in Joseph Campbell's "hero's journey," the individual seeking wisdom retreats from society to cultivate his inner truth alone.[1] It also appears, in terms of the evolution of thought, and of the species itself, that the purveyor of new ideas is, in most environments, except the most open of them, automatically alienated. The alienated individual's departure allows him to interact with and to develop his nascent vision in optimal experimental isolation. Then, if he survives, chances are his vision will as well, and will represent, at the end of its own trial by fire, a useful contribution to humanity and to Life.

As noted in *Beyond Success*, our sense of ourselves is heavily influenced by others' views, and especially by what the leaders of our particular group, think we are and are capable of accomplishing; living down to others' expectations, we rarely discover what we can genuinely be and do. As stated by "the seer Almine," "When the human soul feels alienated from Source, it seeks a situation that offers a sense of 'belonging,' as in a tribe. The tribe, however, stunts growth because it requires conformity. Solitude is the price of greatness." (Almine n.d.)

The often blinding ability we have to generate new realities, to act collectively upon a common ideal and to perceive it as the unassailable truth, and the often deleterious and hypnotic effect of following prevailing trends, reveals the need to access that faculty within us that dwells deeper than our collective delusions and surface-level strife, beyond the divisive notions of black and white, male and female, East and West—beyond any other dualistic distinction or popular ideal upon which we may hang the hats of our separate identities, including those between ostensibly distinct faiths. We need to penetrate beyond to the level of our Source, to access the storehouse of Truth within.

The increasingly destructive manifestation of our misguided collective ideals, as demonstrated by Nazism and Stalinism, among similar modern movements, highlights the evolutionary need to reach beyond and within ourselves, beyond our dualistic preoccupations to that selfsame Source collectively. Without a renewed, nondogmatic connection to Spirit or to God, and to the elevated values and virtues they harmoniously represent, this planet will simply and certainly, eventually and perhaps sooner, fail to survive. We need that fundamental evolutionary change in the way we think to which Einstein prophetically referred, to move securely forward.

NOTE

1. For more on the hero's journey, read *The Hero with a Thousand Faces.* (Campbell 2008)

Chapter 63

The Need for a Guru

It has been suggested that self-realization is 40 percent individual effort; 60 percent God's and guru's; the truth about needing a guru is right in one way at least—you yourself would not have chosen or even been aware of the often difficult and trying circumstances needed to correct your flaws, otherwise they wouldn't have dominated your life for so long; God, the universe, and your spirit guides had to orchestrate that improvement; without the catalyst of that external prod, you would have continued to founder in error without any more awareness of what to do to correct yourself than a drunken man would have in driving himself home; thus you should continue to seek the help of your spiritual guides, as well as your more-mundane mentors. You should be grateful for them, and honor them.

A Master's nature is always both 100 percent genuine and 100 percent in tune with the greater needs of life. Yet the behavior of Masters often appears contradictory and bewildering to those who inflexibly adhere to a static moral code. A Master, for example, may be heard using withering language to mercilessly berate a disciple. Yet this may be just what a passerby, who yells at his spouse at home, needs to hear. "Wow, is that really how I sound?" he may think. Such an experience would hopefully lead to his making the required adjustments, the demand for which he otherwise would not have recognized, had the Master just smiled politely to everyone on the scene. Another witness, not enlightened enough to appreciate any of this, might simply conclude that the Master is being rude or cruel, and is thus not really a Master at all.

As Richard Bach wrote in *Illusions*, "A cloud does not know why it moves in just such a direction and at such a speed . . . It feels an impulsion. . . , this is the place to go now. But the sky knows the reasons and the patterns behind all clouds, and you will know too, when you lift yourself high enough to see beyond horizons." (Bach 1977, 119) Only Masters see from the level of the sky. Only they know why they do what they do. Still, all of this moral prestidigitation makes it even more difficult to distinguish the false Master from the true.

211

The Dhammapada identifies the wise man as "he who knows the right way and the wrong." (Muller 2009, 184) At first glance, this comment may seem strange. After all, don't we have the ethical precepts of the Buddha or the Ten Commandments to guide us, and don't we know right from wrong on that basis? Well, yes and no. There is, for example, a precept against lying; but, let's just say that you are living in Nazi Germany, and your best friend—who happens to be Jewish—is hiding in the closet. An armed troop of SS officers bursts through the door and asks if you have seen him. Are you going to say, as George Washington reputedly did with his legendary cherry tree, "I cannot tell I lie, he is (pointing to the closet) in there?" Of course not! This doesn't change the fact that the precept against lying still pertains, only that it has to be applied differently where different circumstances themselves apply, living realities to which not all are equally attuned.

There are people who wouldn't enter a "two-person" car lane because there are three people in the car. Yet all but the most fanatical of us are free from the tendency to be so fastidiously literal. But there is another level of concern entirely. The unenlightened, "the stumbling eyeless of the world,"[1] follow the letter of the law, and have such precepts as those mentioned above to guide them. Adepts are spiritually attuned, though their egos are still in play as a potential distortion and distraction. Masters, on the other hand, are a living expression of the Law. Thus, while the unenlightened may or may not know what's correct within a limited range of happenings, Adepts see far more, while Masters see the whole range of interrelationships at once, and in a way that cannot be cognized—or even recognized—by the unenlightened mind.

What I find interesting about such spiritual teachers as Bhagwan Shree Rashneesh is that, although their personal lives and activities have been marked by an ample degree of controversy, they still have much of value to teach us. In other realms of attainment, we wouldn't dismiss the towering works of Beethoven or van Gogh because these geniuses wrestled with their personal demons, or fail to see the beauty in Byron's or Hemingway's works, even though both of these authors lived violent and dissolute lives. Yet with our spiritual leaders, we take a different measure entirely. Why? Part of the reason—and legitimately so—is that with these guides, their lives are their art. But the remainder has more to do with the mistaken way we view them in relation to us and us to them. We demand that their light to be brighter, so that ours can remain conveniently dim.

The single legitimate role of any teacher, spiritual or otherwise, is to ignite the flame of understanding within, so that we will be able to comprehend the truth for ourselves. The guru's function, in this respect, is little different from that of an ideal parent, who hopes that if she plays her role correctly, her children will independently prosper, ultimately beyond the need for any subsequent parental guidance.

We judge others in a way that God would never judge us, though he alone is equipped to judge. In choosing Paul, a former murderer of Christians, Mary Magdalene, a former prostitute, Moses, an awkward and inarticulate man (to lead the Israelites out of bondage), and where Christ himself was criticized for keeping the company of the unworthy, the Bible attests to our capacity to serve and to be inspired, no matter how human we may be, or how many times we may fall or fail. This statement is not intended as an excuse, but to forgo the more common out of expecting our preceptors' enlightenment to be full, so that ours can remain conveniently partial.

The truth is that, since "like attracts like," we attract our mentors, as with anything else, through the nature of who we are. We may thus find their circumstances and even their foibles, past or continuing, to be similar in a way to our own. We will find too, and soon enough as we progress, that we are learning from everything and everyone around us, and that part of our delusion is to expect God or the Archangel Gabriel to be hand-delivering the truths we need to know, rather than our learning less dramatically from the mundane world around us.

In the Empire Strikes Back, Luke initially dismissed Yoda, his mentor, from his sight as the latter appeared to him in a form that he was unprepared to recognize. (Kershner 1980) As we continue to learn, all our judgments including those involving the way we arrive at understanding and enlighten-ment, and of how those qualities are transmitted to us, are challenged. Once, during a walk across town, I encountered a recovering alcoholic living under a bridge who spoke in a discerning way about "the higher power." He served as my guide for that day.

As the Dhammapada states, "Not the perversities of others, not their sins of commission or omission, but his own misdeeds and negligences should a sage take notice of." (Babbitt 2012, 50) As the Bible more graphically admonishes, "first take the beam out of your own eye, and then you will see clearly to remove the speck from your brother's eye." (Bible Hub, n.d., Berean Study Bible, Matt. 7:5) What we get out of the guru-disciple, or from any other mentor relationship, is determined overwhelmingly by what we put in, and in this as in other domains we attract who we are.

In the Tibetan literature, it is said that if we regard our guru as the Buddha, however flawed that person may be, he will fulfill that role for us. As in the New Testament, where the believer's faith rather than what Christ did is what He attributes His miracles to, it is our sincerity and dedication to our spiritual goals that ultimately matters. As for the teacher's faults, to the extent that they are real, they are the teacher's problem primarily, one which he or she, not we, will ultimately have to overcome. We will only fail, in relation to him, where we allow ourselves, through our own flaws, to be misled or deceived.

That being said, choosing the wrong preceptor can be a great obstacle. There are unwitting enthusiasts out there who get sucked into destructive cults with no easy way out. Since, by the Law of Attraction, like attracts like, one of the better ways to avoid this dire fate is to continue working on yourself, to be brutally honest with yourself about your needs and shortcomings, and to make your spiritual choices thoughtfully and independently. Immediately suspect anyone who has an agenda. Those who have only your good in mind will typically demonstrate a "live and let live" attitude; they will never force their teachings on you but, in fact, may be reluctant to accept you as a student until they are sure that you are ready.

On my own path, I benefited greatly from the teachings of Paramahansa Yogananda and Self-Realization Fellowship. Here no one from the fellowship ever rang my phone off the hook scrounging for donations, or appeared at my doorstep insisting that I attend indoctrination sessions or pep rallies. Yet all during the time I profited from the SRF teachings and example, I clearly felt I was guided.

Along the road to truth, the ultimate goal of any valid teacher is to make the student's understanding equal to his own. When that tipping point arrives, the pupil is free to leave. In fact, it would be counterproductive for him to stay, as doing so would only delay his further development, much as it would for a child grown into an adult to continue living with his parents. Until then, the student needs to talk less and listen more. He'll advance faster and better that way.

Akin to the idea that, to make any real progress, you absolutely need a specific type of mentor, perhaps a Rishi with a long-flowing beard or a fierce bald-headed Roshi, is the notion that you must drop all your personal possessions like a red-hot iron, and head off for the Himalayan hinterland, equipped only with the clothes on your back and a well-detailed atlas. Your chances of becoming enlightened are otherwise pegged at nil. Those who so argue suggest that the best one can hope for, out of ordinary life, is to accumulate enough good karma to be reborn under better stars. It is then—and only then—that your spiritual life will begin in earnest, perhaps at a monastery nestled somewhere within the snowy reaches of Tibet.

Yet as Ram Das wisely noted, you can be perched on a mountaintop, purifying yourself until light pours out of your head, but when you return to the city, your attachments will resurface. This valid observation suggests that the real challenge and opportunity for growth, spiritual or otherwise, is where your obstacles are, and in the evolutionary process of enlightenment, everything is potentially useful; nothing is necessarily more so than anything else. It all depends on what you need, where you are, and who you are meant to be. It is only our biases and attachments that make it seem otherwise. Family life is a fertile arena for personal and spiritual growth. So too is your place of employment. If you want to see the face of the guru, take a look at your immediate surroundings. If you want the opportunities you need, make use of the ones you have. It's as simple as that. The journey to enlightenment need not be glamorous—though it could be. There is no standard wallpaper.

NOTE

1. This expression was used by Paramahansa Yogananda in his book *Autobiography of a Yogi*. The complete thought behind it is, "A Saint's courage is rooted in his compassion for maya-bewildered men, the stumbling eyeless of the world." (Yogananda 2003, 144)

Chapter 64

The Tao of Metaphysics

Although enlightenment is pursued like a goal it isn't attained like one. To suggest that it is, is like being an ordinarily intelligent man searching for his wits while drunk. His intelligence remains; it is simply obscured, for the moment, by his drunkenness. The drunk may have horrible visions while he is inebriated, but they dissipate when he is once again sober. It is also, to use a separate analogy, to be like a person on a rainy day hoping for the sun. The sun is still there, merrily combusting in the heavens. It is just obscured for a time by the clouds. A sunny day and a rainy day both have the sun, but one realizes it, while the other doesn't.

The pursuit of heaven as a separate and a distant goal is problematic and has led to much misunderstanding. Christ said the kingdom of heaven is at hand, so many expected that in short order there would be earthquakes and floods, perhaps accompanied by a timely regime change to topple the wicked. At key points in the timeline, prophets of doom have waited in millennial expectancy. In 17th Century Russia, people even crowded into churches, that were then lit on fire, those foolishly immolated dramatically anticipating the end—and bringing it prematurely upon themselves! (Billington 1967, 25) For the drunken man, his intelligence is at hand once his drunkenness has cleared. Christ said the kingdom of God was at hand—but also within—so perhaps He meant His statement to be interpreted this way, as well.

As physical beings we have physical instincts, such as those pertaining to sex and survival. Yet at a deeper level, we all desire something more—a truly enduring joy, that "kingdom of God" that Christ referred to. Our physical instincts, however generalized they may be, however they may better serve the ends of Nature than our own, all pertain to something real, to some valid innate imperative. One may speculate optimistically that, in a universe where "God doesn't play dice," our longing for permanent happiness has its deeper roots as well, that it is something more than just another of life's nefarious cheats. Rather, it is an impulse that guides us onward though a primordial memory of completeness.

Our essential dilemma is that neither permanent happiness, nor anything else enduring is to be found in the realm of name and form, all of which are caught up in the flow of time, change, and impermanence. That is why the Buddha said that "life is dukkha," not because we want to be happy and can never be, but because we are continuously seeking happiness from what can never permanently provide it—an ultimately frustrating and futile endeavor. Sure, we may be relatively happy for a while; we may dwell in a tentative security by relying on that which is relatively stable. But as the Tibetan Buddhists state of all dualistic experience, either what we are experiencing will end—or we (physically) will. Whichever comes first, both will inevitably occur.

For the atheist and the materialist this is the tragic end of the drama. But add the spiritual dimension to the mix, and this negative outcome is entirely transformed; the "Good News" is reported. All the suffering we experience is revealed to be but a means of pushing us beyond suffering to a higher level of happiness, utterly transcending what we have hitherto known and can currently even imagine. As Yogananda stated in *Autobiography of a Yogi*, "If joy were ceaseless here in this world, would man ever desire another? Without suffering, he scarcely cares to recall that he has forsaken his eternal home. Pain is a prod to remembrance." (Yogananda 2003, 320) Or as Ram Das similarly asserts, for those consciously on the journey to awakening, "suffering is grace." (Das 1987, 29)

Someday, when we have had enough of life's chess game, we will put the board and pieces away and return home to God. Until then, we must fight the good fight to get there, as Arjuna was called upon to do in the Bhagavad Gita.

The dualistic nature of our time-space reality has been captured in the familiar Yin Yang symbol, which presents the world in terms of complementary opposites. Critically, and as previously noted, these dualities are depicted as, not just opposite, but dynamic, continuously in motion. The stable happiness we seek cannot be found amidst their unstable tension, lasting meaning within relative truth, the perfect expression as anything that can be verbally described. By being physically dual ourselves, we ensure that all our experiences at the material level will be correspondingly transitory and incomplete. So, in a sense, we take birth in form to seek happiness, but guarantee as a result of said birth, that happiness and all that we experience in our outward attempts to realize that happiness, will remain separate from us as well. It is a cosmic joke, a paradox that can only be resolved in the here and now, by restoring our connection to our Source, also in the here and now. Then it doesn't really matter where our physical form dwells; the connection with the cause of happiness will by then have been permanently secured.

When we experience pain, it is clear to us that it isn't what we want. With pleasure, we jut our heads optimistically above the parapets of hope,

expecting that the barrage of misery has finally ceased, only to have our nog-
gins pitifully shot off; and the hoping makes the outcome even worse, for
pleasure can fool us in a way that pain cannot. Both pleasure and pain have
to do with our dual physical nature; thus, they are as transitory and limited as
that timebound and limited nature is.

Hidden beneath the waves of duality is the ocean of spiritual unity, whose
foundation, as experienced, does not consist of dualistic pleasure and pain,
but of unequivocal joy—"sat, chit, ananda."[1] This is why pleasure can take
us further from happiness than pain, because it keeps us from noticing our
deepest selves. So, what takes us closer? Growth. That growth may even be
painful in a physical sense, but it will be always attended by a sense of challenge, a sense of purpose, and by an increasing sense of happiness. We realize
this mode of happiness by accomplishing what we came here for, which has
more to do with spiritual development—ours and everyone else's—than with
any momentary or trivial ease or discomfort.

While the bad news is that no more than a temporary happiness will ever
be found in pleasure, the unalloyed joy we seek is not something we have to
wait until we are dead to experience, for heaven and hell, life and death, are
just more of Maya's conflicting dualities. The kingdom of God is within. In
a nondual awareness, in the here and now, not someday or tomorrow, is to be
discovered happiness and life's hidden perfection.

NOTES

The heading of this chapter is a takeoff on the title of a book by Fritjof Capra, *The
Tao of Physics*. (Capra 2010)

1. "Existence, consciousness, bliss," what Hinduism defines as our ultimate (and
ultimately fulfillable) needs.

Chapter 65

The Role of Thought

There are two ways in which we influence the world around us: by what we do and by who we are. As the Dhammapada proclaims "all we are is the result of what we have thought," and as the Law of Attraction specifies, change occurs first at the energetic level, before appearing as an effect of thought in the outer world. This gives the thought element, the element of who we are, if anything, precedence over the action itself, should we be pressed to prioritize the two. In karmic terms as well, it is the motivation that counts, making the energetic nature of the thought, rather than its resulting effect in the external world primary.

It would be interesting to speculate how morally culpable a Hitler or bin Laden would be, if, in their own minds, they were convinced that what they were doing was right. A hot stove will burn us, whether we believe it to be hot or not; yet in moral terms, thought and motivation also matter greatly. Ultimately, as we pivot between the balance of thought and action, relatively evaluating the two, one thing remains clear: all our travails, as they are identified in Buddhist thought, can be traced back to a primal and deep-seated ignorance, an ignorance of what's right, an ignorance of what to do, an ignorance of reality's nature, an ignorance of joy's true Source, an ignorance of who and what we are.

Chapter 66

Fear of the End

"Both action and inaction may find room in thee; thy body agitated, thy Soul as limpid as a mountain lake." (Blavatsky 2011, 27) "They who imagine truth in untruth, and see untruth in truth, never arrive at truth, but follow vain desires/ They who know truth in truth and untruth in untruth, arrive at truth and follow true desires." (Babbitt 2012, location 92, verses 11–12) These complementary passages, one from *The Voice of the Silence,* and the other from the Dhammapada, together furnish a response to an obstacle on the spiritual path concerning a fear of what enlightenment means in the absence of ego—the fear of becoming nothing. We may dread that the "end of suffering" in the "extinction of self," as it is conceptualized in Buddhism will be, in the end, but a way of "curing the disease by killing the patient," that we will become either insensate blocks of wood or ant colony drones, not knowing, from the standpoint of our current identities, which is worse.

We don't admire people who behave this way, and for good reason. We have no respect for the person who under wartime conditions, when his commander tells him to "go burn down that village populated with innocent civilians," simply says "will do" without at least raising a perplexed eyebrow or a precautionary "sir?" as a discreet objection. Such an objection is a moral imperative, signaled to the commander by the soldier as a reminder of that leader's humanity and of the soldier's own. By contrast, we admire people whose strong wills allow them to willfully accomplish, whose courage emboldens them to individually object to what is wrong, though in suffering from the derangement of our egos, we can go too far with that too.

Milton argued, in Paradise Lost, that through our own corruption we are drawn to see glamour in evil. He portrays the Devil as driven and cunning, while the angels seem to do nothing but sit around all day strumming harps, blowing trumpets, and intoxicatingly praising God. In reference to *Star Wars*, a cinematic drama that demonstrates this idea within the context of modern-day myth, Jonathan Young observes that "the dark characters always

seem to get the cool costumes, which is to say there is a dramatic reward . . .
an excitement to choosing evil, to choosing the corruption." (Burns 2007)

That being said, what we leave behind as we taxi in to enlightenment are
not all the true desires that are intrinsic to our nature, but all the false and cor-
rupted ones that have been simply pasted on. As Yogananda asserted, "individuality is given to man simultaneously with a soul, and revocable never."
(Yogananda 2003, 283–84) He further observed that even Great Masters have
their personal idiosyncrasies. In enlightenment, we realize the better part of
ourselves by evolving into our Selves. We don't simply disappear.

Chapter 67

Resentment

Most spiritual people have a Kantian sense of justice. They believe that Good should and will prevail, and Evil punished with a certainty and inevitability that is personally reassuring. They expect Sodom and Gomorrah to be razed to the ground; they expect swift and severe retribution, and a gratifyingly happy ending.

While the Law of Karma, over the long run, supports such predictable outcomes, ultimately meting out justice with a breathtaking precision, the wheels of the law turn slowly. Perhaps the good people at one time were not so good, the bad ones not so bad, with both relative good and evil as passing phases that don't immediately yield their effects. Still, because they self-righteously consider themselves to be noble and good, such people regard it as an affront when they are the victim of thoughtless accusations, arbitrary judgments, or simply bad times. They become resentful on a moral basis in a way that no amoral person would. "If I am so good," they reason, "and the universe is so just, then why am I being punished this way?" "Why," they ask, "do bad things happen to good people?"

The Dhammapada, for one, is strewn with statements that dissuade us from expecting any immediate vindication for our virtues; rather, it warns us that a vicious world may well resent us for harboring them. "Silently I shall endure abuse as the elephant in battle endures the arrow sent from the bow; for the world is ill-natured." (Babbitt 2012, location 610, verse 320) "They blame him who sits silent, they blame him who speaks much, they also blame him who says little; there is no one on earth who is not blamed." "There never was, there never will be, nor is there now, a man who is always blamed, or a man who is always praised." (Babbitt 2012, location 610, verses 227–28) Combined, these passages gird us for the worst, as we move forward with continued faith towards a better day and outcome.

The Crucifixion is the premier example of unjustified suffering serenely endured for the sake of a greater beatitude. We are called upon to demonstrate a small portion of Christ's colossal endurance in our everyday lives and dealings as we strive to develop spiritually, and as we struggle to make our way home.

Chapter 68

Forgiveness

You can buy your way to forgiveness, but the ticket price is your willingness to forgive others, to see all as equal before God in their ongoing capacity to err, and in their tendency to repeatedly fall short. The willingness to forgive both oneself and others is rooted in humility, in the honest recognition that perfection is to be found in our Source, in the Ultimate Being alone, and that Greatness is never ours as individual egos to claim.

Lurking behind the unwillingness to forgive ourselves is the supposition that we are especially heroic, that God exists more in us than in other people. For how indeed can someone who is "so perfect," "so special," be forgiven for doing anything wrong? At the root of the unwillingness to forgive ourselves, is the false assumption that we are, in effect, at the ego level, God. Forgiveness allows us to make it past our human mistakes, enabling us to acknowledge, both that we have made them, and that we can and should learn from them. We may thereby grow beyond them to ampler expressions of divinity.

We don't know either, though we can infer from our experiences, how often God works through us to test others, at times when the trials they endure occur through the instrumentality of our own deficient actions and behavior. In this context, the Tibetans deal with the obstacle of angry of people by inverting the situation, viewing these errant individuals as the means by which we develop patience. At the same time, it regards them as the real victims in having to ultimately suffer the karmic penalty for their unwholesome actions, actions from which we have been blessed to learn. These same Tibetan Buddhists also encourage us to reflect on those times when we were angry and to recognize how miserable the angry mind is for anyone experiencing it.

If our lives have a purpose, it is to grow beyond our hobbling limitations, and to complete our journey home to our Source, or God. In this process, the act of forgiveness is key. When others have offended us, we need to forgive them to move past our hurt. When we have offended others, we need to learn from our mistakes, to own up to them, and then, to just as readily forgive ourselves. We will otherwise remain stuck where guilt and self-loathing have uncharitably placed us.

Even the Law of Karma, which has been described as the law of justice, is all about restoring harmony and balance; it is essentially about growth, not retribution. It is the ego alone that seeks vengeance, that demands its proverbial "pound of flesh." It is only the part of us that is ill-equipped to judge that wants to.[1] Through it, we expect an unrealistic perfection from ourselves so that we may remain on our "moral high horse," to be continuously enabled, from that isolated and commanding mount of ethical superiority, to haughtily pass judgement on everyone and everything else. I've known people who learned something about psychology for this apparent reason. Equipped with their newfound knowledge, they put all their friends on the couch, and prescribe various remedies for them from the analyst's armchair of their own presumed omniscience. In devising solutions to their friends' problems, they deftly avoid the more pressing need to grapple with their own.

If there is a balance to be restored on the scales of a universal justice, then that is Nature's business not ours, and it is evident, from the recorded experience of others who have journeyed before us, that if we regret our offense sincerely (not merely to avoid the karmic return) then the scales will be balanced with a lessened—perhaps dramatically lessened—degree of severity. Yogananda, in describing the activities of the exalted Master, Babaji, told, in this connection, the following story:

> Babaji's disciples were sitting one night around a huge fire which was blazing for a sacred Vedic ceremony. The master suddenly seized a burning log and lightly struck the bare shoulder of a chela who was close to the fire.
>
> "Sir, how cruel!" Lahiri Mahasaya, who was present, made this remonstrance.
>
> (Babaji replied) "Would you rather have seen him burned to ashes before your eyes, according to the decree of his past karma?" (Yogananda 2003, 349)

Whether we are sincere in our penitence is something we can tell by peering honestly within. Chances are, if we are dedicated to a spiritual path, we will feel the hurt we have caused others "as if we were burned by fire."[2] Then we will sincerely regret going the wrong way, and will vow not to do it again.

NOTES

1. This idea is similarly expressed in *Guideposts to the Heart.* (G. Hallett 2011, 16)

2. The implied source of this expression is the Dhammapada, which states, "A fool does not know when he commits his evil deeds; but the stupid man is consumed by his own deeds, as if burnt by fire." (Babbitt 2012, location 255, verse 136)

Chapter 69

The Wanderer

Spiritual growth and an itinerant lifestyle have been traditionally intertwined. This is so for a couple of very good reasons. The first is that, as we travel, we learn to be unattached, with an awareness in place that excessive attachment can stunt our spiritual growth. By refusing to let go of the good that is, we fail to make room for the better that is yet to come. If a writer becomes too attached to his first draft, he will never proceed to his second. He will never properly complete his work. Sanaya Roman speaks, in this context, of the need to relinquish forms that no longer serve us. We lightly let go of one to make sufficient room for another. (Roman 1989, 202–3) But there is a further component to this growth and travel connection that is worth noting as well.

If we were to play an association game and I were to mention Richard Nixon, the first thing that most people would think of is Watergate. This is so, even though Nixon accomplished the rare goal of becoming president to begin with, moving forward from there, in his renowned partnership with Henry Kissinger, to rack up some masterful accomplishments in the arena of foreign policy.

The simple truth is that people we know will naturally identify us by our least common denominator. If we have many notable successes and one conspicuous failure, it is by that failure that we will be defined ad nauseam; thus, Christ spoke of a prophet as having no honor in his own town. Hang around the old neighborhood too long, and those who have known us—also for too long—will turn us into caricatures. While not forgiving ourselves will prevent us from becoming better people, others not forgiving us will have the same effect, if we let it, and in our not forgiving them, we similarly deny them the chance to grow.

We can also see how, when we lack forgiveness, we are not "giving forward" (i.e., fore-giving) and are, are, by definition, being rigid; we are refusing to move on, failing to advance with Life's Flow. We thereby delay our own spiritual development. If "all that we are is the result of what we have thought," by not forgiving, we close the door that opens on a brighter future, for what we cling to is not what could have made us happy even then, when that "someone else" offended us, and which cannot satisfy us now, but which leads us to obsess unproductively on negative ideas. As the Dhammapada summarizes the fool's attitude, "'He abused me, he beat me, he defeated me, he robbed me,'—in those who harbor such thoughts hatred will never cease. / 'He abused me, he beat me, he defeated me, he robbed me,'—in those who do not harbor such thoughts hatred will cease. / For never does hatred cease by hatred here below: hatred ceases by love; this is an eternal law." (Babbitt 2012, location 44, verses 3–5)

Chapter 70

Perspective on Persistent Obstacles

If, despite your best efforts, you can't seem to elude a habit or pursuit that, from a spiritual standpoint, you perceive as undesirable, whether it be the quest for romantic love or the drive for social prominence, it may be that you still have something to learn from it. You still have some unfinished business there with life. This assessment, while sometimes valid, should only be made cautiously, for we are all extremely good at rationalizing away our flaws. At the same time, we need to remain honest about who, what, and where we are.

We will notice, as we spiritually advance, that there are many superfluous wants that can be immediately sloughed off. They are remnants of an earlier and different phase of striving. They remain from a time when we were travelling "the path of desire," (Smith 1991, 17–18) with exclusive dedication, when we thought that power and wealth alone were the keys to happiness. These extraneous wants are easy to identify, and fairly easy to abandon. But there are others more innate, more intransigent, more essential to who we are. We may find it hard to separate their pursuit from the central core of our being. They are a part of the soul's "bucket list." They are a piece of who we are.

There are some things we never need to learn, as we already, at some level, know them. Others we must experience fully, to finally and fully understand that, though we have keenly wanted them, and perhaps for a very long time, they are not, in the end, what we genuinely need to be happy. But with this particular category of desire, we can't just say it is so, we must know it, and only experience can provide such knowing.

There is a certain beatitude, temporary though it may be, in not having completed the journey. Augustine was reputed to have said, at one time,— "Grant me chastity and continence, but not yet." (Augustine 2012, 119) In *the Tempest*, Miranda, seeing virile men for the first time after being stranded for years on a deserted island, exuberantly exclaims, "Oh Brave New World

233

that has such people in't," to which a more seasoned Prospero responds, "Tis new to thee." (Shakespeare 1994, 159, Act 5, Scene 1) There is a freshness, an enthusiasm, in such incomplete knowing, and in the dawn of novel experiences that for others have become routine.

How many people start a job, infused with enthusiasm over that position's fresh challenges, challenges involving tasks that others doing the same work are already bored or disgusted with. The latter's advanced position is, in a strange way, pitiable; they remain where they no longer belong, stuck in one place while ready to move on, ready to leave the sandbox for the mountain versus those for whom the sandbox is the mountain.

Anger, lust, and fear may not be the most wholesome and exalted of emotions, but we must recognize them when they arise, and be honest with ourselves about them, if we hope to advance beyond them or to express them more productively. Anger can be transmuted into purposeful drive, lust into creativity, and fear into prudence, but not with an unnatural brutality.

Most every New Englander has, at one point or another, faced the daunting task of clearing a driveway coated with ice and snow. On a day when the temperature rises above freezing, with the sun exiting the clouds, the improved weather will facilitate your task. If every block of ice is adjoined to nothing but more ice, none of it will melt quickly; but if the driveway is partially cleared, with the sun beating down on the smaller resulting pieces, the thawing process will be hastened. Likewise, if we attack our flaws, and succeed in overcoming some of them, then what remains will be more easily chipped away. But if none of them are dislodged, then all will be mutually strengthened and few will be easily overcome.

There are times when we try our best to succeed at something, at a particular job or endeavor, and it just doesn't work out. We may slave away at it for years, yet without apparent success. Numerous obstacles repeatedly confront us, and typically the same ones. Particularly in the beginning, we shouldn't give up too easily, as this may just be a test of our resolve; it may be God or the Universe attempting to determine if what we claim to want is what we really want after all; but if further down the line we still haven't made any notable progress, with obstacles continuing to mount, it may be time to rethink your path. The correct way for us, while it will not always be easy, should always feel right. We should sense that what we are learning, doing, and becoming is valuable. Here the Principle of Flow applies to our work as well. If we are acting against our dharma, against what we are genuinely meant to be and do, with obstacles and setbacks ever increasing, then this may be a sign that we are paddling against the current of who we are, and that we need to step outside our routine, and recalibrate our course.

Chapter 71

Perspective in General

Carlos Castenada, in Tales of Power, talks about "using death as an advisor," as a way of maintaining a proper perspective on life.[1] (Goldstein 1983, 124) As the Tibetans, among others, have declared, our brief human existence is very rare and precious. Yet we squander so much of it away, worrying about what may be lost among the collection of uncertain advantages we must eventually lose anyway. As the Bible similarly observes, "who of you by worrying can add a single hour to his life." (Bible Hub, n.d., New International Version, Luke 12:25)

For those of you reading this book who are 25 or over, one quarter of your physical life—or more—is over. So why waste another moment of it worrying? Much better to get to the point, to discover the reason or reasons why you are here, to clear away the debris of uncertainty, and to live your life deliberately and well.

NOTE

1. The direct quote here is not from *Tales of Power*, but from *The Experience of Insight,* in which Goldstein describes what Castenada learned from his Yaqui mentor, Don Juan.

Chapter 72

Karma and Reincarnation

Our individual lives are like probes sent down by the mothership of our souls to accomplish particular ends. Some probes may be dispatched to sample soil, others to gauge the weather, still others to see what crops can be planted and harvested. We are here to reap the harvest of spiritual growth by overcoming those obstacles that are peculiar to us. Since it would take more than one lifetime to fully overcome them, more than one life to render us suitable companions for our Maker, a scenario of multiple lives seems warranted. It is more logical and compassionate as well.

In the *Star Trek* episode, "Day of the Dove," a Klingon officer boasts to his commander, Kang, that "Four thousand throats may be cut in one night by a running man." (Chomsky 1968) Well imagine such a person who, from the time that he could hold one, used a knife to slit people's throats, one by one in a seemingly interminable row. You would think that he, upon his death, would be consigned to hell forever. Yet think about this fairly. As horrendous and karmically burdensome as such an act or series of acts may be, the evil it represents is finite, is it not? Can a finite cause produce an infinite effect? In a world where, as Einstein proclaimed, "God doesn't play dice," is forever fair?

There have been dictators, such as Stalin and Hitler who, while they may not have held the knife or gun themselves, were ultimately responsible for the death of millions. They may seem to be prime candidates for an eternal booking into hell's infernal resort. Still eternity is much more than just a very long time. It places too great of a strain on God's mitigating compassion to dream of condemning anyone forever. Nor can we rightly speak of justice in such an end, when the measuring scales don't balance. Little justice for sure in judging by the sins of the father, for each person is unique, and different members of the same family often choose different paths, both with respect to careers and to morals.

We are thrown into this finite world of death and uncertainty with few if any answers; yet our established traditions, too often, would have us believe that God would have less mercy than us by warping the sense of universal justice into a series of unjust decrees. And as fully as our bad actions are, our good actions are finite too.

Buddhism, as previously noted, posits the existence of long-lived gods who dwell for thousands of years in states of exalted bliss. Yet when their good deeds are exhausted, they too must return to this limited world of striving to overcome the obstacles, rooted in ignorance, that separate them still from the Light.

When our gas tank is full, we can go a long way. But once it is near empty, we must return to the station to refuel. It is the same with our good and evil actions. The wheel of duality will continue to turn until we experience and release both good and bad destinies; to the extent that they pertain to the individual in separation from the rest, both are finite. One is immediately tragic; the other, as in the case of the long-lived gods, ultimately so. Both are overcome, and the Wheel of Karma broken, by a full return to our Source. When the probe has done its work, the mothership will take us home.

The way we grow though obstacles to the ultimate end of enlightenment was beautifully expressed by Oliver Wendell Holmes in his poem, "The Chambered Nautilus." In it, he wrote:

> Build thee more stately mansions, O my soul,
> As the swift seasons roll!
> Leave thy low-vaulted past!
> Let each new temple, nobler than the last,
> Shut thee from heaven with a dome more vast,
> Till thou at length art free,
> Leaving thine outgrown shell by life's unresting sea!

Chapter 73

Normality

What is normality? It is, by definition, to act in accordance with the norm, with what others commonly think and do. So, what is so precious about that? We advise our children to think independently, to be unique and innovative, and then punish them for being different from everyone else.

What is perceived as normal is based on the underlying assumptions that govern a particular place and time. If those assumptions are wrong, the prevailing sense of morality, as based upon them, will be skewed, as well. In Nazi Germany, it was "normal" to hate Jews; but that didn't make it right, nor did it immunize the haters from the lawful effects of their hatred.

Our society is driven by restless competition, by the endless drive to acquire more and more material things. Those who find this monotonous treadmill dissatisfying may, as listless participants, be perceived as "depressed," or "withdrawn," and thus in need of medication or psychiatric treatment.

Yet just as a person who never lifts a weight will never experience that weight's resistance, the dying ego, that which our society perceives as the true self but which the spiritual aspirant knows to be false, will like a drowning man grasp at any straw; it, as Yogananda observed, "in most barbaric ways, conspires to enslave him." It will throw up any obstacle available to prevent its dominion from being overturned. (Yogananda 2003, 178) This heightened creative resistance adds a set of inner stressors to the social ones that continue to emerge so formidably in the path of the spiritual initiate, appearing to ignorant outsiders as an aberrant effect.

As Humphreys observes, with regard to Zen practice:

the difficulties to be overcome are great in quantity and size, and none the less so for being largely the product of the very force that works to enlightenment. We create our own resistance as we build the power of the pendulum to swing back at us by the power with which we push it away. Mental calm, if we ever had it, will disappear before storms of doubt and despair. There will be psychic eruptions, embarrassing, disgusting, frightening, all of which must be calmly met, faced for what they are, and allowed to disperse. And there will be upsurges from our own and the racial unconscious, mostly unpleasant to the current state of mind. (Humphreys 1962, 147)

The social obstacles associated with the spiritual life apply doubly to those like James Von Praagh, who claim the ability to communicate across the spiritual divide. There are many unusual things that may be experienced on the road to enlightenment—everything from astral projection, to energetic empathy, to telepathy, and more. Such abilities and those who aver them will automatically seem suspect, if not completely "deranged" (for they are certainly outside the normal range) by a society that regards such capabilities as unreal.

To what extent might what the world regards as insanity, not a full-blown howling lunacy, but a touch of angst, of turmoil, of abiding discontent, not be more properly regarded as a sane response to an insane world, than anything improperly out of range? Societies establish their workings predominantly to benefit their elites. They then present the prepackaged result as an ideally-organized structure that is presumed to work effectively for all, like the sharply interlocking components of a fine Swiss watch. Yet what happens when it doesn't, where, as in ours, we are made to "run faster and faster for goals that mean less and less," (Smith 1991, 18) and where the substance of true spirituality, not the rote, distracted, mumbling faith of what commonly substitutes for it, is almost entirely absent? What then? Artists, noted for their eccentricity yet at the same time for the wonder of their attainments have been described, by Ezra Pound as "the antennae of the race." Where the signal of negativity is stronger than before, might not they be the first to warn against it, and to "feel it in their bones?"

Where the societal pattern is untrue, and they know it, the characteristic stance of the elites toward the masses is to keep them continuously distracted, to give them more work to do, then more bills to pay that demand even more work, and of course more mindless distractions, to fill whatever little time remains. In addition to excess work are all the events that must be attended, roofs that need to be patched, meetings that consume time, etc., so that in the end, most of us have scarcely the time to breathe, let alone to think, to ponder why we are here, and what, if anything, we are meant to accomplish. Nor, as a society, have we developed the capacity to think deeply and productively about life's "bigger questions," even when the opportunity to consider them finally arrives. Yet the time is fast approaching, with the dawn of artificial intelligence, when we certainly must consider them, when we must question deeply what it means to be human, and not only from the isolated stratosphere of an imperious social or economic elite, but within society, as a whole. Until then, those at the spearhead of idealism and progressive thought must find a way to deal prudently with a world that never seems to fully understand them—and here is one way:

As the Buddhist Golden Rosary observes, "Much talking is a source of danger: silence is the means of avoiding misfortune: The talkative parrot is shut up in a cage; Other birds, which cannot talk, fly about freely." (Evans-Wentz 1967, 61) The Bible likewise speaks of the dangers of throwing "your peals before swine," who will then only "trample them under their feet, and turn again and rend you." (Bible Hub, n.d., King James Bible, Matt: 7:6) In troubled times, silence is a form of tactical retreat. Those who are socially active often criticize mystics for their withdrawal from life, regarding their departure as selfish. Taoism is, however, and for one, as much a social philosophy as a spiritual one, one that advises people on how to make their way in the world, deftly and courageously, rather than retiring straightaway to a mountaintop. Yet it too recognizes that there are natural periods of ebb and flow, and of resulting darkness in which the wise person's strategy is to sensibly withdraw. Sometimes the mountaintop is simply the best and safest place to be.

To appropriate the Star Trek motto, as we advance along the spiritual path, we will boldly go where few have gone before. It is thus more than likely that we will discover some strange and disconcerting things along the way. They are all part of the larger "hero's journey," where the unique, the creative, and the different are the norm. Psychological health, by contrast, is measured in terms of one's ability to function effectively within that specific environment in which material goals are emphasized and pursued. But what if that one-size-fits-all pursuit is itself, misguided? What if it cannot properly accommodate those operating at a higher level of functioning? What if what we emphasize in our bromidic pursuit of happiness will never get us there? What then?

The great religions of the world believe life to have a goal beyond the material world. They remind us that material goals will at some point prove dissatisfying, as that is what they ultimately are. As Huston Smith argues, they are no more evil than the toys in a child's toy box, but equally true that we will ultimately outgrow them in favor of broader and more satisfying objectives.[1] The goal of spirituality is something other than what it takes to keep our balance onboard the materialistic skateboard; thus, the approach to be applied in attaining our truest goals and in realizing our highest happiness is bound to be different too.

As we grow spiritually, we will be repeatedly thrown off balance until we learn to reclaim that balance at a higher level, until our perspective becomes all-encompassing and wise, and the spark rejoins the flame. The angst we experience en route to that lofty end, is not, as the world would portray it, a sign of maladjustment, but the growing pain of readjustment to a deeper and more expansive norm. The rest will join us in the future, when the ground-breaking way we are spearheading now becomes the norm for them as well.

NOTE

1. As Huston Smith elaborates, "The guiding principle is not to turn from desire until desire turns from you, for Hinduism regards the objects of the Path of Desire as if they were toys. If we ask ourselves whether there is anything wrong with toys, our answer must be: On the contrary, the thought of children without them is sad. Even sadder, however, is the prospect of adults who fail to develop interests more significant than dolls and trains." (Smith 1991, 17)

Chapter 74

Faith and Action

Faith, while good, as a starting point, can lead us nowhere, without effort and determination. It suits the ends of any society, the freest among them included, to encourage you to believe that there must always be someone there to lead you around by the nose, that our role as individuals is not that of roaring lions, but of helpless sheep, bleating plaintively for someone else, someone better, to provide us with our answers, to, in prepackaged form, hand-deliver our betterment or salvation. Hence, we dumbly wait around for instructions and easy, spoon-fed answers, while others insidiously control our lives and destinies. In a different mode of society, such victims would be grist for the mill of dictatorship. Here no one tells you specifically what to do; rather the unwary are seduced into limiting their own options, until laden with debt, and imprisoned within invisible bars of their own devising, they head out on the road of their daily routines like the cooperative drones they have long since become. Civilized man, in Rousseau's words, "pays court to men of power, whom he hates and rich men whom he despises." (Rousseau 1964, 244)

Here the Tibetans emphasize the importance of cautiously "retaining hold of your own nose ring," of maintaining control over your own life and destiny which, in the final analysis, are found—astonishingly—to remain largely within your own hands. They encourage an approach to spirituality that properly serves to keep us centered and empowered.

You can have as much faith as you want in the efficacy of weight training, but if your weights lie abandoned in the corner of your room, they will do you little good. You can believe in a place called New York, having been told that it has mountainous buildings and fabulous shops; but unless and until you travel there, you will never make that remarkable experience your own. As observed in the Dhammapada, "Purity and impurity belong to oneself, no one can purify another." (Babbitt 2012, location 410, verse 165) "The Buddha's enlightenment," as Goldstein observed, "solved his problem, it didn't solve ours . . . except to point the way." (Goldstein 1983, 13)

243

The concept of justification by faith alone, which remains very popular today, sidesteps precisely what it is that may have brought us to this plane to begin with, the neglect of which would keep us from rising higher; that is the need to grapple with the elements of our nature that separate us still from the Light. Why bother, one might argue, to contend head-on with our alcoholism, gluttony, drug or porn addiction, if faith alone is what saves us in the end and if, no matter what we do, God will pull us through? It is like having a rich uncle who, whether we succeed or fail in our efforts to earn a living, will always send us a check in the mail to cover our bills. Without the reliability of consequences, our own efforts are likely to be halfhearted and diluted.

Then there is the simple, logical truth that there are many people who live sound moral lives, and have compassion for others, who do basically everything right, yet are inclined to say quite honestly, with regard to spiritual matters, "I simply don't know." At the opposite extreme are those who reliably attend mass on Sunday, who then spend the rest of the week contradicting everything they've learned there. It would be absurd to think that the first group would end up in God's disfavor and the second in His favor on the basis of faith alone.

It is altogether fitting that we acknowledge, with gratitude, the role and sacrifice of the Great Masters and Teachers, and to call upon their aid and protection when the best of our individual efforts fails to be good enough. But this doesn't mean that such efforts are themselves meaningless, that we are no more than "puny worms crawling in the dirt," helpless to aid or to develop ourselves. We are not dependent on faith alone; here, in a world of cause and effect, our own actions count.

Chapter 75

Life is an Opportunity

This human existence, while rare and precious, as the Tibetan Buddhists maintain, is not an absolute good; it is the instrumentality through which that absolute good can, potentially, be realized. That is what makes it rare and precious to begin with. Approached correctly, it becomes a focal point for wonder and accomplishment; incorrectly, it becomes a burdensome source of fear and misery, with life itself made unendurable in the process.

Imagine a world in which everyone were physically immortal. Here death would not simply be the end of an existence lasting 110 years or less, but the effective loss of an eternity. A severed arm or leg would not be a deprivation to be endured through the span of a short and limited lifetime, but barring the technology to regrow or replace it, essentially forever. The threats that others might make against us would carry far more weight, dramatically increasing the potential for outside control and influence over our lives. Imagine how much fear would be associated with such a precarious immortality!

We become similarly fearful, even now, when we regard our physical existence as a permanent and absolute good. We are best served, as Castaneda's mentor, Don Juan, recommended, by using "death as an advisor," (Goldstein 1983, 124) by living our lives fully and without reserve, in due awareness of the fact that—physically, at least—those lives must eventually end. It is only then that we will have the courage to pursue our dreams, to speak out against injustice, to make our days on earth truly count, and to duly appreciate the abundance we already have. Ironically, those who suffer the most in life are typically those who are most attached to it. In a parallel irony, most people don't believe in reincarnation, but would find the prospect encouraging, whereas Buddhists who do believe in it, see it as problematic.

This existence is a coin that is meant to be spent, not hoarded. As Jesus proclaimed, "whoever will save his life shall lose it . . ." (Bible Hub, n.d., King James 2000 Bible, Matt. 16:25) The Tao Te Ching similarly affirms that "the world is won by those who let it go!" (Tzu 1983, 119) This would seem to imply letting go of yourself and any inflated sense of self-importance, as well. In *The Great Work of Your Life*, Stephen Cope speaks of those individuals who expend themselves through their dharma, and receive happiness in return. As we each pursue our own brand of happiness, we should not attempt to hold what cannot be held, with life itself falling neatly within that category.

Chapter 76

Meditation and Manifestation

Most of the New Thought literature describes the ability to manifest as something we all share, the only difference being that some are aware of it, and apply it consciously, while others wield it unconsciously. Yet as Wayne Dyer suggests, the ability to manifest is tied to our being "on purpose," (Dyer 2004, 147) or as the Hindus would say, to following our true dharma. It may also relate to the reliability of the transmitter in the form of a calm and clear mind, something that meditation directly enhances.

As described by Swami Saraswati, once an aspirant reaches the heart center, everything he thinks of and wishes for comes true. (Saraswati 2009, 165–66) Patanjali's Yoga sutras similarly state that he who speaks the truth habitually develops the corresponding ability to have his words and thoughts manifest into reality.[1] It would seem, on this basis, that the ability to manifest is not essentially the same for all, but relates instead to the underlying economy of the natural, physical, and metaphysical realms. By engaging in activities that are harmonious, the individual heightens his level of vibration, automatically broadening his capacity to draw what is positive into his life. The opposite can be said of negative vibrations, which effectively put the brakes on the ability to spiritually manifest.

Our spiritual practice and the laws of manifestation have a mutually supportive relationship. The type of calm, focused mind that meditation produces, is like a smooth ocean over which we are better able to sail toward those outcomes we are naturally inclined to seek. It will also, inevitably, refine our motivations. Being able to manifest what we want, once we accept that possibility, begs the question of what it is we actually do want. Here the cardinal rule of "be careful of what you wish for, you may get it" aptly applies. At the same time, the ability to manifest would seem to be the missing key in the formula for obtaining that "fixed and unshakable deliverance of mind," that Buddhism sees as the ultimate goal, for we won't have an unshakable deliverance if we are forever quaking before some external authority or internal lack. We must be able to trust in Life directly, to be freed from an

247

unwarranted reliance on anything or anyone at all, to rest secure and godlike in our own natures. The laws of manifestation and karma together allow for that possibility.

A godlike state implies independence. It conveys a sense of both power and responsibility by which we identify ourselves as the ultimate source and author of all our experiences—good, bad, or otherwise. Unless we think that God or an angel is sitting aloft with a scratchpad, keeping tabs on all of our actions, it would be the magnetic Law of Attraction that would deal lawfully with the energies we generate, and account for the process of sowing what we reap in a way that a physicist could well appreciate.

In his *Autobiography of a Yogi*, Yogananda asks his spiritual preceptor Sri Yukteswar, who told him to take no food with him on an impending journey— or to ask for any along the way, "Suppose I never ask for food, and nobody gives me any. I should starve to death." Yukteswar's alarming response, "Die if you must, Mukunda! Never believe that you live by the power of food and not by the power of God! He who has created every form of nourishment, He who has bestowed appetite, will invariably see that his devotee is maintained. Do not imagine that rice sustains you nor that money or men support you. Could they aid if the Lord withdraws your life breath? They are his instruments merely . . . Cut through the chains of agency and perceive the Single Cause." (Yogananda 2003, 104–5) If people on a spiritual path, who are often dedicated to methods at variance with society's ordinary system of rewards and punishments, are to sustain themselves physically without compromising on their principles or integrity, then the ability to manifest lawfully through the power of their spiritual attunement would seem to be a critical element.

In the *Star Trek* episode, "Shore Leave," members of the Enterprise crew, after landing on an alien planet, start seeing their thoughts manifest into reality. Things get out of hand, when the truth that they have stumbled upon an amusement realm, of sorts, is not immediately recognized, and as their own fears and negativity begin to take visible form. This travesty continues until someone, effectively, "awakens them," letting them know what is happening. (Sparr 1966)

"C'mon," you might say; "that's not how my life works." Still, if we sift back through our memories and experiences, we will likely see plenty of evidence of synchronous events, though they may seem all too easy to dismiss as what logicians call "ex post facto reasoning," reasoning by which we attribute a known effect to a plausible cause, whether that effect was the result of that cause or not. The man we run into who loves cars, or chess, or horses, the way we do, that we meet in an environment having little or nothing to do with any of these things. The party we go to that is serving scallops just as we are thinking about how we would like to have some. How much of that is just dumb luck? How many random dice throws does Einstein's orderly universe cast? How many "coincidences" can happen coincidentally before a coherent pattern is identified. As inference doesn't equal truth, such hints of plausibility might not be enough to convince us. Yet we will inevitably and increasingly discover as we spiritually progress that reality reflects both our thoughts and who we are energetically.

If our thoughts are scattered and chaotic, the conditions that reflect them will appear random and disordered too. We will thus come to the seemingly reasonable and matching conclusion that our lives and our relationship to our world are disordered, that events are the product of random chance, the universe itself, spawned from the womb of chaos. We will also likely assume that our thoughts have no influence on our world. Yet that belief itself is a thought which, as such, has the ability to draw the conditions that validate it! This is a remarkable irony about the Law of Attraction, that we look for the truth in outward circumstances whose nature we have, by our own thoughts, predetermined. The conditions we have envisioned then begin to manifest into our lives. In short, what we see through our empirical measuring scopes is there because we put it there to begin with!

If we think all taxi drivers are rude, then, by the Law of Attraction, we will draw to ourselves the rude ones, permitting us to vindictively proclaim, "See, I told you, they're all rude!" Those who believe that taxi drivers are generally kind are more likely to attract—and to recognize—the kind ones. Life contains a large enough pool of outcomes to allow for both possibilities—and more. What we experience hinges on what we think, and on the prospects we permit through our beliefs. This understanding can be enormously liberating and empowering. And what's more, even if the condition opposite the one we are looking for statistically predominates, if the process of manifestation exists, we can still hope to obtain what we seek. This is the Principle of the One revisited. So what, if most members of the opposite sex are bitches or bastards. Even if that were true (which it isn't) you only need to find one who is kind. What if most people are unhappy with their jobs. You can be one who isn't. What if most people aren't fortunate? You can be one who is.

A concentrated, focused and orderly mind will, by the Law of Attraction, manifest circumstances that are themselves orderly and purposeful. We will then see our destinies enacted before us, free of the random obscurations to which ordinary, unreflective minds are subject. When you have a finely developed, concentrated, and focused mentality, you become struck by the sheer number of "miraculous" synchronicities that arise, all of which combined, are hard to explain away; but to reiterate St. Augustine's claim, miracles are not a violation natural law, but demonstrate the functioning of laws we simply don't know.

NOTE

1. In Patanjali's own words, "When grounded in truthfulness, action [and its] fruition depend [on him]," with "him" referring to the truthful practitioner. (Feuerstein
1989, 85, II.36)

Chapter 77

Karma and the New Thought

Some New Thought philosophers take issue with the Law of Karma, for they believe that it limits the ability of thought and choice to precipitate change. But this ignores what the Tibetans call "the three times," the past, present, and future. It suggests that the Law, while in effect now, somehow wasn't operating before, or that Life is devoid of a universal and impartial justice. This is far more of a restriction on the power of choice than a belief in the Law of Karma could ever be.

There are prisoners on death row who claim to have "found Jesus." Some of them may even be sincere in their penitence, much as Saint Paul was in his conversion on the road to Damascus. But that doesn't mean that they are suddenly released; justice must still be served. It is the same with all of us.

A belief in karma also encourages our positive thinking at times when it doesn't yield any immediate results. Let's say you adopt a new regimen of positive thought, then the next thing that happens is that you hit a guardrail, or lose your wallet or your job. What you are likely to declare, in response, is that none of this "nonsense" works. A belief in the Law of Karma would inhibit such a premature conclusion.

That being said, we can hope to mitigate the impact of our past karma through our positive responses in the here and now, much as shooting an arrow through water rather than through air would reduce its velocity and soften its impact; this perspective allows for both a sense of justice and of change (or choice) in the present. When we find that we have been rowing in the wrong direction, we can always turn around; yet we still have to paddle the distance back. We still, alternatively expressed, have to climb out of the holes we have dug ourselves into. It is the same with the impact of our positive thoughts.

Both the Law of Karma and the Principle of Positivity can be perverted, and sometimes are, into something they are not. The principle of positive thought could easily serve, much like formal religion, as an opiate, one that would have us smiling on the way to our own executions. And it would be nearly as wrong to tell a sweat shop worker receiving an unjust wage to take responsibility for his predicament and to just learn to think more positively, as it would to tell the relatives of the 9/11 victims that those victims were merely reaping the lawful effects of their karma. The Laws of Attraction and Karma are real; but they do not exist to promote insensitivity or neglect, particularly in those instances where both empathy and a courageous determination to counter a flagrant injustice or heinous evil are warranted. To operate otherwise is not to apply these laws, but to misapply them. And while they may be co-opted for the wrong ends, their power to effect revolutionary change in people's lives, despite it all, remains.

Gandhi's ability to revolutionize India was founded on the solid bedrock of his own spiritual discipline, and would not have succeeded without it, while the laws of attraction and manifestation have the ability to lead people to a place where they are empowered, not merely to tolerate class distinctions, but to surmount them entirely. It can propel those who apply them well to a higher level of prosperity, evading any need to resort to slavish dependence or moral compromise, but only if such laws are understood, not misunderstood, applied, not misapplied.

Chapter 78

Desire

Where such behavioral guidance systems as Buddhism and the New Thought outwardly differ is in their attitude toward desire; one seems to encourage the pursuit and satisfaction of desire, and the other the extinction of it. Yet the greater difference may be in appearance only. What's left has more to do with an individual's specific level of development.

As the Dhammapada states, "They who imagine truth in untruth, and see untruth in truth, never arrive at truth, but follow vain desires. /They who know truth in truth and untruth in untruth, arrive at truth and follow true desires." (Babbitt 2012, location 92, verses 11–12) This statement contains the key to understanding the proper relationship to desire in general. When the mind ceases its whipsaw oscillations of attachment and aversion, and attains to a state of calmness, the result is not simply for us to occupy space, conforming thereby to the definition of inert matter. What emerges instead is a joyous participation in life's creative symphony; the drive to harmoniously produce and to achieve arises naturally and spontaneously from that enlightened attainment. If you are an artist, you will have a desire to paint, if a writer a desire to write, if a runner, a desire to compete in athletic events. Such pursuits may encompass an ancillary "desire" for all those incidentals that promote that particular endeavor, with the activity itself distinguished by the fact that it is pursued for its capacity to move the individual closer to, and not further away, from his Source. His effort to increase the joyous energy of that connection, has by now become his aim, not the pursuit of anything that would distract from it, that cannot provide it, or that can never favorably compare to it—all which remain, for the unenlightened, the mistaken focus.

Being satisfied within, we no longer sit around inventing things to distract ourselves. This mindless seeking is what Joseph Goldstein, in one of his lectures, referred to as "catalog consciousness." It is akin to what we experience when we randomly flip through a merchandise catalog hoping that our desire will be inflamed by something we see. (Goldstein 2014) In the Enlightened state, catalog consciousness disappears, for there is no longer any demand for it; the satisfaction we seek, is already there. Rather than constituting a benefit, such superfluous desires, for those on the road to enlightenment, are not only useless, but obstructive.

In the enlightened state, we still strive, but no longer do so neurotically. Our sense of self-worth, which, by now, has become inviolate, no longer depends on whether or not we achieve our goals. We labor to attain them because of the value we find in them, versus any we fail to find in ourselves. Krishna, personifying this ideal state, affirmed that, "I have nothing to obtain, because I have all. And yet I work." (Mascaro 1974, 150) In such creative selfless work is joy. As *The Voice of the Silence* claims, "Both action and inaction may find room in thee; thy body agitated, thy Soul as limpid as a mountain lake," (Blavatsky 2011, 27) with that specified approach being both the goal and the path to it.

As the Bible pointedly asks, "For what shall it profit a man, if he shall gain the whole world, and lose his own soul?" (Bible Hub, n.d., King James Bible, Mark 8:36) Here, the larger issue is not what satisfying a particular desire is worth but how fulfilling ANY desire—even the gain of the whole world—could ever compare to what may be lost in its wayward and immoral pursuit. Is it worth opening the three black doors the Gita talks about? Certainly not. After all, whatever else it may be, it is all a passing show. Recognizing it as such, overcoming the ignorance that has taken root at the kernel of our pro-gramming, will allow us to respond without rashness, without anger, without that mindless greed which, far from accomplishing its intent, can only lead ultimately to our further misery and undoing.

Since desire and attachment hit the catwalk together as an interrelated duo, most people miss the fact that we fail to manifest our desires—or otherwise produce negative outcomes in our more ordinary pursuit of happiness—because of our attachments!! We cling to what we have, and thus separate ourselves from the flow of abundance leading to what we want and need. Our attachments generate fear. They precipitate greed. Greed makes a beeline, as Buddhism describes, to the karmic backlash of poverty. Such attachments, themselves, are invariably rooted in a more fundamental and deep-seated ignorance, for we cannot—in truth—cling to the Flow. We can profit from its largesse. But we can no more cling to it than we can head efficiently down the interstate by spinning uncontrollably into the guardrail. While our entire system of commerce is visibly rotted over with a greed for wealth and a fear of declining equity valuations, the flow of abundance leading to legitimate happiness remains lawfully what it is. Its gifts are allied to virtue and truth, making it as true that what we cling to out of greed and fear, while possible to approach that way, will never make us happy.

The central idea that Buddhism and the New Thought share is that Mind resides—or should reside—at a level superior to its material creations; thus, to be enslaved by those creations is to miserably invert Reality. Living in-line with Truth as liberated beings and skillful creators, we reclaim our spiritual lordship and abundantly secure our happiness.

Chapter 79

A Clear Benefit

In examining those things that emerge as spiritual obstacles, it would be encouraging to mention something of benefit, something that can speed us on our way. The Tibetan Buddhists call it as a "joyous realization." It is the understanding that the path is always open.[1] To spiritually progress and to karmically prosper, there is no person you must depend on, no office you must hold, no degree you must obtain, no event or condition you must await, for growth to lawfully happen; it all depends on you and it is all available now. This doesn't mean that the road ahead will necessarily be clear and easy, only that there is nothing to keep you from embarking on it—nothing, that is, but your own fear, disbelief, and reluctance. On your journey into the Light, your destiny is forged in the cauldron of your personal actions and choices. As for the guidance you need, as the saying goes, "when the pupil is ready, the master appears."

Life is a great juke box. What you hear is based on what you play. So where will you put your quarter? What song will you stream through the media player of your life? Will it be a celebratory hymn or a funereal dirge? The choice is yours.

NOTE

1. In *Tibetan Yoga and Secret Doctrines*, this is the last of 10 "joyous realizations" enumerated. The complete reference reads, "It is great joy to realize that the Path to Freedom which all the Buddhas have trodden is ever-existent, ever unchanged, and ever open to those who are ready to enter upon it." (Evans-Wentz 1967, 99)

Chapter 80

Using the Effect to Produce the Cause

We usually view happiness, success, and that grin from ear to ear, as the effect of previous causes, causes leading to results that we must accept at face value if we are to be realistic and pragmatic. But what if the effect can produce the cause we are looking for? If we don a smile, how difficult will it be to be miserable at the same time, how much easier to actually be happy? Either we will lose the smile, or we will lose the misery, and if we insist on the smile the misery may sooner depart! It is, likewise, just as hard to feel motivated when we are slouching and moping around. The entire practice of hatha yoga—in its pristine form—can be summarized as a systematic attempt to proceed from effect to cause, to engender an enlightened state of mind through its effects in those breathing rhythms and postures that naturally accompany it.

In the manifestation literature, it is similarly recommended that we think of ourselves as successful in order to actualize that corresponding condition. To many, this may seem unrealistic, like laughing our way to the gallows. Yet what we are experiencing currently as success or failure is no less evanescent than what we could otherwise envision in our fondest and most hopeful imaginings. Alan Watts spoke, in this context, of being "a genuine fake."[1] What he meant by this, is that what we identify with most frequently as ourselves is but a transient persona anyway, no more real than a part in a play, that personality is one thing, and superficial, individuality far deeper and more substantive.[2] And if mind itself be the deeper cause, consciousness the deeper reality, then grounding ourselves in that reality, refusing, meanwhile, to succumb to despair, would seem to be the road to our ultimate victory and happiness.

NOTES

1. This is the title of Chapter 3 in *The Book on the Taboo Against Knowing Who You Are.* (Watts 1999)

2. As Huston Smith comparably notes, "Our word 'personality' comes from the Latin persona, which originally referred to the mask an actor donned as he stepped onto the stage to play his role . . . This, say the Hindus, is perfect; for roles are precisely what our personalities are . . ." (Smith 1991, 30)

Chapter 81

Better than a Koan

A common phrase, as valuable to attaining enlightenment as an impenetrable Zen koan, is "you can never have enough of what you don't really want." What we don't want is a "happiness" that is shallow and transitory, one that leaves us unfulfilled and yearning. We don't want a gratification that, like the Greek god Proteus, mockingly morphs into the visage of despair the minute we feel we have grasped it, rendering us injured and scarred.

Think of all the limited things you have wanted before and just how badly you had wanted them, only to find that none of them—none at all—was the end-all and be-all of happiness. None could provide the lasting joy you hoped and dreamed it would at the time you originally desired it. So, to thwart your frustration you plunged into the pleasure stream again, hoping against hope and against the reality you sought to avoid that the next fix of materialism would do it for you. All the while, you added to the number of hooks by which the boat of your life would be dragged from the Flow to smash head-long against the shore. You thus contributed incrementally to the world's disharmony, to your own individually, and to the strength of the karmic back-wash. The wayward pursuit of an ephemeral joy that brought you to suffering once, like the inevitable return of the tide, leads you there predictably again and again; the only thing that's changed is the number of times you've tried. We attempt again what doesn't work, as it is the only thing we know.

This vicious cycle is the wheel of suffering that the Buddha spoke about and warned against. Best to experience and appreciate life, in the glint of each shimmering moment, while being wisely aware of the limits to that or any other passing moment's joy. Best to be aware, as well, of the pain that attach-ment to any of them can cause. As "painted cakes do not satisfy hunger;" seek nourishment for your soul only in what can deliver it and, as E.A. Burtt advises, don't "ask of the universe . . . more than it is ready or even able to give." (Burtt 1955, 28)

Chapter 82

Sincerity

I once read a line from a calendar version of the I Ching that has stuck with me over the years: "there is nothing more appealing than the naked genuineness of a person." The individual who is sincere has the courage to be himself; he exudes the charisma that naturally proceeds from an unflagging alignment with Truth, the truth of life and of his own being. Such a person knows who he is and what he must do. While a life of sincerity may seem risky, it ultimately precipitates the most pronounced good fortune in being fully aligned with Life's Flow. The dissembling associated with insincerity, proceeds, by contrast, from an awkward stance of clinging. It is attended by the stress associated with an attempt to be someone other than who you are.

You can usually tell when someone is being insincere, condescending, egotistical, or defensive, for it is written on the face. The glance becomes increasingly objective, the eyes squinty, and the person himself may don a false smile in an attempt to better conceal his motives; but in the end, all of these tells will be clear enough to read. To be happy, and to minimize stress, it is essential to be sincere.

Chapter 83

Simplicity

The Tibetans have compared the commercial environment that now prevails in modern America to the Land of the Hungry Ghosts. In Tibetan mythology, hungry ghosts are an unfortunate category of being in which suffering life chases endlessly after the mirage of happiness, never to truly secure it. Hungry ghosts are said to have huge bodies and pin-sized heads, suggesting that their appetite for pleasure far exceeds their ability to satisfy it. Here the expression "you can never have enough of what you don't really want" comprehensively applies.

Each item that we acquire and cling to becomes something we must shield and defend. As the Tao Te Ching states, "One can never guard/ His home when it's full/ Of jade and fine gold." (Tzu 1983, 68) For the sake of what we desire, we ally ourselves with those who, coincidentally at most, have our best interests at heart; we thus increase proportionately our potential for pain and suffering. As Janis Joplin sung, "freedom is just another word for nothing left to lose." (Joplin 1971) The more we are attached, the more we have to lose; the more we have to lose, the more we have to fear; the more we fear, the more dependent we clearly are. Thus, life itself is anxiously squandered for what is worth far less than life, the many needless goods adorning it. The less we precariously own, the less we are fearfully bound.

Chapter 84

Taking the Bad with the Good

If goodness is taken as goodness,

Wickedness enters as well.

For is and is-not come together;

Hard and easy are complementary;

Long and short are relative;

High and low are comparative;

Pitch and sound make harmony;

Before and after are a sequence.

—Tao Te Ching (Tzu 1983, 60)

At one point in the 1960s, the government of Brazil, eager to create a modern futuristic capital, designed and built the city of Brasilia. This ideal city was to be devoid of the unappealing slums that gloomily encircled Rio and Sao Paulo, the erstwhile cultural hubs of the nation. Soon after Brasilia was built, the slums, like mushrooms, inevitably began to surface. The problem of blight, endemic to all urban centers, soon became a problem for Brasilia as well.

In everyday life, as in urban planning, it is essential to accept the bad with the good, the good with the bad, for both will always be there. The ideal state, the state beyond time, is one that transcends all relative dualities. So long as duality itself exists, these opposites will, as well.

267

This truth should inform our politics too, for even among great nations, acts have been committed that are not so great; but you don't "throw out the baby with the bathwater." Celebrate your ideals, but mindful of duality, be wise and practical about them. Even when a tidal change comes—and there are times when it should and must—to endure, it must be rooted in the traditions of the region to which it applies. Democracy will not flourish overnight in those parts of the world where it never existed before, any more than a new city in Brazil will arise without its slums. Any change that occurs in accordance with the Tao is not only organic, it is simple and nonpretentious—and this as opposed to "band aid solutions" that make the politician look good, but whose real effect is useless or destructive. Harry Truman was a good Taoist, though he would not have identified himself as such. He was simple and unpretentious; yet he was impeccably responsible (with "the buck stops here" being his signature phrase). He was very effective too. Such is the way to lead. But few, in an assertion that the Tao Te Ching challenges us to refute, can follow it.

Chapter 85

Written Goals

As Americans, we live in a society of Contract versus Common Law. For us, agreements appear more regular and binding when rendered in standard script. For human beings in general, all sociological factors aside, commitments appear firmer and more real that way, as well. We are also less likely to become diverted from them when we have a documented means of reminding ourselves of them.

The Dhammapada states, "Let no man think lightly of good, saying in his heart, it will not come nigh unto me. Even by the falling of waterdrops a water pot is filled; the steadfast man becomes full of good, even if he gather it little by little." (Babbitt 2012, location 279, verse 122) The same analogy can be employed to describe the way in which our most cherished goals can be optimally realized.

When we set a bucket under a dripping pipe, there doesn't, at first, seem to be all that much happening. Yet we are likely to wake the next morning to find the bucket filled to the brim, perhaps even to overflowing. Most goals whose results are enduring, whether it be weight loss, game proficiency, or enlightenment are achieved in slow increments, by which the key to success is consistency. This steady, almost traceless, drop-by-drop consistency is the way of the Tao, as well.

Closely related to the establishment of written goals is the discipline of spiritual journaling. This is an extremely useful practice, as we are at first blinded by our flaws and later inclined to forget we ever had them. And each of us does, of course, have them, and for each of us they are different. Each flaw represents a groove that we can easily tumble into. Some of us are too shy, others too aggressive. Some of us are "anal retentive" while others are persistently rudderless. Maintaining a spiritual journal can serve as a reminder of what we need to change so that we can proceed to more effectively change it.

Chapter 86

When Fear is Positive

At the conclusion of Abraham's Biblical trials, the Lord acknowledged the sincerity of the former's commitment is exclaiming about him, "now I know that thou fearest God." (Bible Hub, n.d., King James Bible, Genesis 22:12)

I have always thought of fear as a strictly negative emotion, and in most cases, it is. Most fear is the flip side of greed's larger coin. It causes us to hesitate to act on behalf of truth in dread of the ensuing reprisals; through fear we hesitate to help others where our own physical hides are at stake. It is fear that causes us to miss our chance to do our best by our lives and souls, in terms both of worldly success and of spiritual liberation, through an inordinate dread of loss. Through fear we neglect the spiritual by taking refuge in the material mirage. Fear puts us at the mercy of effects rather than squarely at life's helm, generating new and better causes. Yet there is another type of fear that is not physical, that is not merely a chemical response or emotion, but an impulse that aligns with the very core of our being. It is a fear that hesitates to do wrong, recognizing the harm it could inflict on ourselves and others, an Avant Garde emotion that heads out on a raw winter's night, and uses the cold as a reminder that the desolation one is left with in in the wake of wrong-doing is far colder and darker.

Buddhism speaks of the great fear that comes when one senses palpably the colossal suffering inherent in the repeated cycles of birth, death, and rebirth. Nor is it necessary to believe in reincarnation itself to experience this "fear of death" within the context of ordinary circumstances, amidst "the sufferings and vicissitudes of life." Where we would wish to freeze the moment at some pleasant and abundant time, knowing that we can't, knowing that it will transition onward, and that we are bound to experience the harsh chill of winter once again—but of course, a spring thaw afterwards—that makes us long eventually for the refuge that overcomes all such alternating states entirely, to put our faith in it, not merely in limited things, while not of course failing to appreciate them either.

Chapter 87

Could It Be That Simple After All?

When it comes to spiritual matters, we tend to get overly complicated and "legalistic." Too often, we are like those called-out Biblical hypocrites who think they will be heard because of their many words. Could it be that, in the final analysis, whether we choose to call ourselves Hindus, Buddhists, Muslims, or Christians, that the Truth is as basic and simple as loving God and loving one's neighbor, as Christ, Himself, advised? In a universe where all is one, showing respect and consideration for your neighbors is enough to make you the beneficiary of Life's natural abundance; to actually love them is to stream that abundance in torrents. While peace and economic sufficiency seem tragically rare; rarer still, is a love that dares to extend beyond the boundaries of self, family, race, and nation. Should that latter, rarer, condition be realized, perhaps the aforementioned state of abundance can be too.

In similarly direct and basic terms, the Bhagavad Gita states that, "if you avoid lust, wrath, and greed, then you will do what is good for your soul." (Mascaro 1974, 111) As for our innate interest and desire for the things of this world, including sex and material possessions, the Gita further clarifies:

> Those who with confidence and faith shall constantly follow this teaching shall be made free even by works and action. But those who reject the teachings of Truth and act contrary thereto shall suffer the fate of the senseless and deluded ones and be confused and lacking in Peace/ But the wise man also seeketh that which is in harmony with his own nature and endeavors to fit his life according thereto, rather than to seek after things contrary to his nature. Let each do the best he can, in his own way, and in accordance with the highest within his own character. (Yogi Ramacharaka 1930, 50)

In short, enjoy life fully, but don't make anything besides God, God. While living in the material world, keep your spiritual center true. This is, of course, harder to do for people who are not aware that they have a spiritual core, to begin with.

So, what, in truth, did Christ die for? What was that "original sin" for which he was reputedly crucified? Certainly, it was more than the consumption of an apple. The apple is a symbol of distancing. Christ, by his life as Man, bridged the gap between Man and God, and demonstrated what we need to do to recover our lost wholeness. That hopeful message, rooted in a most exemplary life, has since been misappropriated, mistranslated into a "you must believe" kind of tyranny to keep the pews—and collection coffers—filled. Yet Christ's sacrifice, one certainly made for all, remains real and beneficial, whether we outwardly add our voice to the chorus of His narrative, or not, as if it were not sufficient on its own merits. The disbelief is in our actions, and it is there that our commitment, our substantive consent, must likewise be demonstrated.

When we timidly scamper back into our Platonic cave of shadows and thereby shun the Light, we substantively disbelieve; we turn away from God, whether in the outward form of Christ, Buddha, Krishna, or any other. It is that, rather than any legalistic formulation of belief, pitifully unmatched by any genuine commitment, that keeps our souls from advancing and mired in darkness. Christ's sacrifice is true, as Truth is true, its benefits, real and boundless, regardless of what any of us thinks, believes, or verbally professes. Its value for us ultimately depends on what we think and do.

It is said, in the East, that a Master can assume the karma of a student, helping him to overcome it. It would be inconsistent to think that Christ couldn't do the same, and perhaps on a grander scale by his crucifixion. In a world where the Holocaust occurred, where countless other shockingly brutal atrocities have taken place, and continue to transpire, there remains a ponderous gap to bridge between our collective actions and the conditions necessary to secure our spiritual redemption. This may be a gap that someone with the stature of a Christ needed to fill. Individually we honor that sacrifice, whether as Buddhists, Muslims, Hindus, skeptical agnostics, or more explicitly as professing Christians, when we strive on a more basic, lesser level to live exemplary lives with enduring honor and kindness.

Chapter 88

Victimization

The Dhammapada states (as previously mentioned):

> There is an old saying, O Atula,—it is not only of today: "They blame him who sits silent, they blame him who speaks much, they also blame him who says little." There is no one in the world who is not blamed.
>
> There never was, there never will be, nor is there now, a man who is always blamed, or a man who is always praised. (Babbitt 2012, location 453, verses 227–28)

As it further advises, "patiently shall I endure abuse as the elephant in battle endures the arrow sent from the bow; for the world is ill-natured." (Babbitt 2012, location 587, verse 320) These statements combined coax us away from the slippery slope of victimization down which too many people slide when they feel that they are always deprived, that bad things happen only to them, and that the world "has it in for them," in particular. It is, of course, easy for the most selfish to think this way, for when the same misfortunes happen to someone else, they rarely notice.

The Tibetans compare the anguish we experience after someone insults us to our being cut by a knife, and then grabbing the knife away from our assailant to begin stabbing ourselves with it, over and over again in his place. The only way we can completely avoid this type of cyclic anguish is by recalibrating our center from opinions to Truth. Through the Law of Karma, we are assured that the good deed seemingly left unbalanced on the scales of a universal justice will weigh heavily there tomorrow. That conviction should encourage us to be more concerned about genuine consequences than about baseless opinions, however widely-held.

The leaders we most admire, faced many a hard decision before making an unpopular choice, doing so, ultimately, because that choice was right. Though nearly everyone around them at the time derided them for it, such admirable leaders had the courage to act as they did; thus we continue to praise and revere them. John F. Kennedy, in the Cuban Missile Crisis, had the courage to resist the pressure applied to him to go to war with the Soviets. For that, he garnered much immediate scorn and the world's enduring gratitude.

When people are excessively attached to others' approval, they routinely place themselves in the role of victim, hoping that those they cry to will arrive, like the cavalry, to caress and console them. In the process, they lose the ability to evaluate events accurately from the standpoint of an objective truth. This is a dangerous and destructive way to live; yet it remains perversely popular, and is a common and insidious trap. All the pity in the world, plus two dollars, may buy you a cup of coffee—but only if the two-dollar price hasn't risen, for self-pity is worth absolutely nothing. It may even be said to have a depreciative value, as it cannot help us to overcome our difficulties, but only compounds them to our detriment. So, avoid this dangerous obstacle. Shake the need for approval, especially the need to be pitied, in favor of courageous actions that are in keeping with cosmic law, and that you know in your heart to be right and effective.

Chapter 89

Egotism vs. the Glory of the Realm

I have enjoyed playing chess for a good many years. In the process, I have gained a respectable level of proficiency. Still, I know it is very unlikely I will ever go down in the annals of chess as one of the game's greats. Not by a long shot. But, you know, it doesn't really matter; nor does it in any way diminish the value this intricate game has for me. There is a feeling I get as I play chess of participating in a cultured realm of beauty, wonder and accomplishment, of being a part of something monumental that was here before I arrived and that will remain long after I am gone. Chess continues to captivate and challenge me, as the years march relentlessly on.

Much the same can be said of those who, while they may never compose a concerto, will sit enraptured for hours by the tones of a masterful performance. It is the way patriots feel when they put on their military, police, or engine company uniforms. Most people in the military who do feel that way won't attain the renown of a McArthur or a Patton; yet from the standpoint of what we are talking about, they are actually better off, for the latter have too much ego in the mix; for the former, it is pure, unalloyed devotion.

There is a blissful and exalted sense that comes from what *The Voice of the Silence* refers to as being, "lost among the host," (Blavatsky 2011, 31) where you become so much a part of your dedication, whether it be to patriotism, faith, knowledge, or beauty, that the line dividing personal ego from larger world blurs. This is the point in Zen at which the archer becomes one with his bow, the worker in the Gita, one with his craft. It is the junction on life's whistle-stop tour at which action and meaning intersect. It is just about the best place to be, as we make our way home.

Chapter 90

The Obstacle of Moral Superiority

In a seemingly odd statement, the Tao Te Ching exclaims, "Away with the kind ones;/ Those righteous men too! / And let people return/ To the graces of home." (Tzu 1983, 81)

One of the subtle guises under which egotism hides is the mask of moral superiority. Committed, as we are, to spiritual progress, we no longer regard ourselves as superior, based on wealth, social status, or intellectual attainments; so, our egos find a more obscure refuge in a peculiar form of vanity. We become pompously convinced that we are simply better people, people whose character is more honorable, whose virtue is more pristine, whose lives are more purposeful and worthwhile. Here the ego usurps that righteousness which is an attribute of God alone or, in Buddhist terms, but the natural expression of the Dharma, and weaves it into a garment of delusion for us to flaunt. Like Don Quixote, we mount the saddle of our moral high horse (which is really just a mule) and sally forth on our personal crusade against all the evils surrounding us. They are those same evils which, in similar form, we ourselves have—or think we have—just recently overcome. And so many of those who do this have their "fingers stuck in everyone else's pie," ready to litigate, ready to disrupt, ready to angrily condemn, whether a valid cause exists or not.

We are meant to be serviceable beings. We are meant to help one another. What we are not meant to do is to make a big deal about it. Such willingness to assist is part of our genuine nature, stripped of the ego's posturing and contrivances. Zen Master Suzuki made a parallel statement in Zen Mind, Beginners Mind, when he said that "pride is extra." (Suzuki 2005, 59) It damages our work through distortion and excess. It is like taking a perfect painting and slapping on some extraneous brushstrokes at the end to garishly accentuate its patterns.

I have always had a visceral distrust of most advertising for this very reason that, too often, it takes what should properly be regarded as the superior end—friendliness, humor, kindness, standing opposite the quest for monetary gain, and inverts them, using the former as a tool for securing the latter, and seeing value in it predominantly—if not entirely—as such. All too often in our rabidly extroverted society does style stand in for substance, ritual for truth, rather than enhancing or accentuating it, as it was originally meant to do. The cartoon character on the box is what makes the cereal inside desirable, in the absence of any nutritious ingredients, we would otherwise—and reasonably—expect to find there.

When we pursue virtue for its own sake, it is not only its own reward, but a reward beyond comparison. But we need to know, feel and appreciate this. We need to taste the flavor of virtue, in the form of supernal peace and bliss, through which all our worldly activities harmoniously blend and effortlessly fall into place. Until then, we may think we are pursuing virtue for its own sake, but are really after fame, fortune, approval, vindication, or a "something else" that's truly something less.

As asserted in the "Elegant Sayings," "The Supreme Path of Altruism is a short-cut, / Leading to the realm of the conquerors . . . / The selfish . . . know not of it." (Evans-Wentz 1967, 65) Many of the problems we face individually loom inordinately large because we are disproportionately focused on ourselves, on our own isolated plans and neurotic preoccupations. Service to a higher cause, be it to the nation, the community, or God, mitigates the burden of egotism, and thus the problems and pitfalls associated with it. But if all we are doing is projecting our own problems upon what we would prefer to see as a problematic world, then our efforts will bear the taint of these personal distortions. We will hate where we should love; we will be angry where we should be patient; we will be proud where we should be humble, and we will assume, more than anything else, that the universal clock should be set by the timing of our individual schemes.

The untrimmed forests of the world, though they remain a significant concern, are no excuse for neglecting the weeds growing rampant in our own gardens. To the extent that the latter still flourish there, they need to be uprooted, if not entirely at first, at much the same time as we are confronting the world's more intransigent problems, and not ignored.

What remains after all the pomp and pretentiousness have exited the stage of our spiritual strivings is what Christmas Humphreys calls, "a busy minding of one's own business." (Humphreys 1962, 167) That business may be saving the world, like Mother Theresa's, or building a nation, like Gandhi's. But it might just as well be baking bread or repairing roofs. Either way, it will be done in simple harmony, without a lot of fanfare, and without the bitter seasoning of a righteous indignation, one which builds your ego up, while implicitly taking others down. In relation to this theme, the Dhammapada praises the man, "who does his duty is tolerant like the earth . . . ," (Babbitt 2012, location 234, verse 95) also one" . . . who is just, speaks the truth, and does what is his own business, him the world will hold dear." (Babbitt 2012, location 436, verse 217)

As we gingerly approach life's problems and groaningly assume its burdens, we shouldn't be surprised that others have them too. We are born and die alone in a complex world, constant companions to impermanence and loss. It is a world where we are dodged by far more questions than answers, where we can trace in the furrows of a stranger's brow, the plight of our common humanity. So how, then, can we presume to judge, when dukkha is our mutual predicament?

Chapter 91

Two Types of People

There are two types of people in the world. The first are those who have found their purpose, what Napoleon Hill terms a "definite chief aim." That aim could be winning a sports pennant, composing a novel, or sculpting an artistic masterpiece. It could be serving the poor at a food kitchen, rescuing homeless pets, engaging in political action, or crafting the perfect bow. It is even okay to have more than one purpose, so long as the drive to achieve your primary goal isn't diluted in the process.

The second category of people have no aim. Should you ask them what they are all about, or what they intend to do with their lives, they will typically say "I don't know." The distinguishing characteristic of the first group is that they have no time in their busy schedules for "crap," for all the drama involved in unproductively mucking around in other people's lives. Should you ask them to engage in such useless and intrusive behavior, they would say as much directly. Yet for those who have no purpose, time is all they have; thus, their lives are distinguished by an exaggerated amount of interpersonal drama, and by a self-righteous focus on other people's business rather than upon their own. They worry about what "so-and-so" said a week ago that supposedly hurt their feelings. They are too preoccupied with lying on the ground to get up. And they fail to recognize how they are, in the direction they are headed, their own greatest obstacle.

The solution to this problem is to find and embrace your motivating passion, a passion tied to your purpose, and to pursue it with all the rabid intensity with which you are capable. Would you rather be "a pillar or a parasite?" If the former, then assiduously undertake what you came to this world to do.

Chapter 92

Compassion

The means to entering, as well as the method of treading, a bona fide spiritual path is an enhanced level of simplicity. By simplifying our lives, we stop tying ourselves into knots—intellectual knots, financial knots, neurotic knots, and toxic relationship knots alike, and begin to unravel those we've already tied. One knot spiritual people tend to tie only after having entered the path, one unlikely to have been there before, is a concern over their level of loving. Since the extent of their compassion is not nearly as deep as that of Jesus or Buddha, they must, they feel, be doing something wrong. This obstacle is nothing other than needless posturing on the part of the ponderous ego, and should be recognized as such.

As Joseph Goldstein asserts: "love is the natural expression of oneness." (Goldstein 1983, 238) The assumption that "I" am being loving is, at basis, a contradiction in terms, for it is the "I," the ego, that separates us from that unity which is the essence of a conjoining love. In a sense, we can say that God is love and to the extent that we have God we have love too, with love being a divine attribute, and not a facet of our separate personalities.

That being said, there are ways of strengthening the factor of loving kindness in a practice known in Buddhism as metta. The Tibetan take on this is interesting. We first direct our love toward someone that we care about easily and unconditionally. For most people, that person would be their mother. We then imagine this cherished individual being engulfed by an angry tide, and drawn frightened and helpless downstream. Our hearts would naturally reach out with love for her, and a with fervid desire to help her. The Tibetans then say, in an intriguing twist of reincarnation logic, that "all beings have been our kindly mothers." This idea, one somewhat strange to most of us who weren't nourished on an Oriental diet (of either food or ideas), is that we have been seeking substance from illusion, security from change, permanence from impermanence for a very, very, very long time. During that very long time, each being has at one point or another been our kindly mother. Though a bit of a stretch for Western minds, this startling viewpoint emphasizes the more basic and accessible idea that love derives from a palpable sense of interconnectedness with the lives and destinies of others. Anything that reinforces the structure of that universal bond will elicit affirmations of an abiding Love that has been there all along.

Chapter 93

What Success Is and What It Is Not

What if I told you I knew of someone who was arrested by the authorities for a crime against the State, someone who was subsequently tried and executed, with that humiliating event widely publicized. He's probably someone you wouldn't want to meet—right? Well, the person I am describing is Jesus.

What if I were to refer instead to someone else, someone who was lavishly affectionate toward his dog, very patriotic, a courageous and decorated war hero, and a strict vegetarian to boot. Probably a really good guy, right? Yet the individual I am describing here is Adolf Hitler.[1]

There is only so much we can tell about the character and integrity of an individual by his outward circumstances or ostensible status in life. Yogananda's autobiography speaks of towering spiritual figures who, unbe- knownst to the world, bestow their abundant benefits from the sidelines. (Yogananda 2003, 347) In encountering them on the road you might consider them to be outright losers or good-for-nothing bums. Yet the "method to their madness" is that they have not lost, but are simply not playing your game. They are playing their own at a higher-stakes level, and, by their own stan- dards, winning.

Too often, we define success in terms of ownership, or by the titles that a pompous and self-infatuated world deigns to bestow upon us. No doubt those that have their awards and degrees worked very hard to attain them; yet there are many PhDs who have problems making their way through life, and many intelligent and cultured people without degrees, whose character is worthy of our praise and regard. With each new moment, we are newly defining our- selves, either winning fresh battles against our immediate and persistent chal- lenges and obstacles, or losing precious ground. In each flickering instant, we actively restate who we are. Time and Life do not carry our degrees and other accolades along with them; only society does.

Still, in a crass and commonplace way, we routinely gauge people's "worth" by the amount of money they have in the bank, by the value of their concrete assets, or by the static influence of their degrees. Yet these are indicators only, broadly descriptive at best, and often vastly misleading. They are essentially external to the individual and to the substantive level of his attainment. They do not reveal character or drive like a patch or insignia.

It has been argued that if you take a successful person's good fortune away, he will quickly reacquire it, while the statistics of those who win the lottery reveal that many of them lose their wealth—and often their health and reputation too—in very short order. They are like casual drinkers who can't hold their booze in a protracted drinking bout. As the Dhammapada states, "riches destroy the foolish, if they look not to the other shore." (Babbitt 2012, location 673, verse 355) Here the trappings of success are but outward effects that don't always correlate directly to their causes, or to the ultimate source of success within.

If one had to define success, it may best be characterized as an attitude, as an optimal way of confronting life with all of its challenges and obstacles. It is an approach interwoven with character that is upbeat and undaunted. It is a calm, silent swagger that looks around at all the chaos, carnage, loss, and disappointment, and says "I am better than this; this I shall endure." As Winston Churchill is reputed to have said, "Success is not final, failure is not fatal: it is the courage to continue that counts."

Another valid measure of success is simply being happy, in a deep, true, and abiding way, for if you are following your purpose in life, you are travelling the road to success, whereas if you are on the wrong path, you may, as Rousseau described it, know only "pleasure without happiness," honor, accolades, and wealth, without true satisfaction or meaningful accomplishments. (Rousseau 1964, 245)

It seems obvious that failure is the opposite of success, but in some ways, success is its own opposite too. How can that be? It is because the time we dedicate to one thing is time we must withhold from something else. As has been wisely observed, "success is measured not so much by what you are willing to give forth as by what you are willing to give up." It is here that our very enthusiasm for life can cause us to insidiously fail. It can lead us to randomly dabble rather than to productively focus. The common analogy of the magnifying lens demonstrates this clearly. When a beam is sharply concentrated, it generates a searing heat that can vaporize matter. Dispersed, the beam has little effect. When our thoughts and energies are similarly concentrated, we can reach towering heights. Lacking focus, our efforts invariably fail or fall short. The Gita speaks to this issue in observing how "many branched and endless, are the thoughts of the man who lacks determination." (Mascaro 1974, 52)

There are ways in which our ostensibly separate goals can be mutually supportive. Games that develop our minds can sharpen them for other tasks, tasks more essential to our growth and survival. Staying physically fit can keep us mentally strong too. Such examples are patently obvious. At the opposite extreme are all those useless activities whose fat can be trimmed from the streamlined structure of our lives. If we are at all serious about success, success in any form, we will jettison these time-wasters quickly. But then there are moments, invariably sad and poignant moments, when we reach a fork in the road, a juncture where we realize we can't succeed at everything we hope to do at once. It is then that we must choose what is most important to us, among a number of competing pursuits—all of them worthwhile, each of them jockeying for our time and attention. Bobby Fisher became world chess champion, but only at the cost of his sanity, having lived a life almost exclusively dedicated to the royal game. Was it worth it? As he realized an enduring fame, and remains a cultural icon, some would say, "yes"; but others would quickly disagree. Then it remains to be noted that had he balanced chess with other activities, the way Magnus Carlson has, Fisher's reign might, like Carlson's, have been more enduring. He might also, like Carlson, have set a better, more holistic example for the rest of us to follow.

Only you can decide what is most important to you. Eliminate what is superfluous, then make your defining choices, for as the Dhammapada asserts, "many good things may be achieved by a mortal once he is born." (Muller 2009, 29) The people who are most successful, ultimately, make choices on a predominantly spiritual basis, for they realize that, among all the goals that can be achieved, the Spiritual endures when all else fades.

NOTE

1. This is a famous comparison, not original to this work.

Chapter 94

The Conclusion of Our Journey

The idea of acceptance is based on Pope's notion that "whatever is, is right,"[1] right at least from the standpoint of being true or factual, and thus to be factually regarded, as such. An exam response is said to be "right," not because we like or dislike the question, the exam environment, the teacher, or even the fact that we must sit and take a test that day. Yet even in terms of this second, more expository meaning, we still have cause to wonder how certain events can ever be right in themselves. How can they even occur without God or Truth being negligently absent from the field of human striving?

This is the root of the verbal paradox, "God is all powerful/ God is all compassionate/ Evil exists." How can He be enthroned, how can He be concerned, and certain horrible things still happen? And how, moreover, can we ever forgive God or embrace life unconditionally, in the wake of such monumental tragedies, especially when we are the ones directly impacted by them? How, in any way imaginable can the Holocaust or 9/11 be right? How can God be good and such heinous Evil be allowed to exist?

Six million people died in the Holocaust at the hands of a regime of almost unthinkable malice. Yet those six million have vacated this earth as those six billion plus who inhabit it today (with the hypothetical exception of a few legendary immortals, like Babaji) will in 120 years or less. As the Bible bluntly asserts, we are all just sojourners in this world, whether that temporary stay be pleasant or unpleasant, short or long. While the existence of Evil is noteworthy, it need not contradict the ultimate benevolence or justice of Life or God.

The problem with the above paradox, and the key to its resolution, is that it denies an absolute good on the basis of a relative evil. If we be souls, entities of subtle, luminous energy, subtly tied to our Source, then it is easy to see that by their release in death, those six million, and those who suffered at the hands of the terrorists on 9/11, will have moved on to other states, conditions, or worlds where their hopes and dreams, once shattered here on earth, can finally and fully be realized. Those who destroyed those lives and shattered those dreams are most likely to be suffering now in dire realms of hideous retribution, perhaps without hope, and for a very long time. Since we lack the critical overview, God's overarching perspective, we are not equipped, any more than Job, to render our paltry judgments on life as being false or godless simply because we can see that Evil exists.

An illuminating koan of sorts is to imagine a stick with one end. You really can't do it. Once you have established a beginning you have determined an end as well. It is the same with all relative happenings, with all the transient beauty in this world, with all created things in what, in our perpetual bewilderment, we falteringly term "life," that which exists for a time but which is not the end-all or be-all of Being.

What remains when the relative vanishes, in not being relative anymore, is an essence no longer bound by time or limitation. It cannot be expressed, any more than that black dot on a black page can be seen. Yet far from being unreal, the Absolute is the most real thing of all, the "Unbecome, Unborn, Unmade, Unformed" by which we are freed from that which is "become, born, made, and formed." The disciple who asked the Buddha, in the "parable of the poisoned arrow," whether the soul survived after death, received no answer, for he revealed the thickness of his delusion attempting to drag Truth down to his own conceptual level. He demanded that the Absolute be expressed in relative, earthly terms. His inquiry thus met with silence, as did Pilate's question to Christ, "What is truth?" and for much the same reason. It is but shadows sparring with shadows. This is what made Thomas's doubting wrong—not the fact that he questioned—but that he expected a definitive answer to come through his own limited senses. The faith on which he was called upon to rely had a higher and more enduring basis in a greater, more substantive form of understanding.

In a similar and reassuring way, the obstacles and difficulties we are each likely to face, far less burdensome than the Holocaust or 9/11, and likely even less severe than what other people we know have already had to endure, will eventually dissipate too, like thin mist in the sweltering heat. They will morph into a memory, encapsulated in a lesson whose value will beneficially persist and which can sustain us in our forward journey toward our ultimate and ultimately satisfying end. As we face our own less exacting challenges, we too shall learn, and be equipped, as a result, to understand that we can eventually move beyond our obstacles to a higher and better place. We can leap over and past each hurdle; we can finally make our way home.

NOTE

1. This line is contained in Epistle 1 of Alexander Pope's "An Essay on Man."

Chapter 95

How it Concludes

The Ideal Person

Well-makers lead the water (wherever they like); fletchers bend the arrow; carpenters bend a log of wood; good people fashion themselves.

—Dhammapada (Babbitt 2012, location 317, verse 145)

As we study the Bible, the Dhammapada, the Tao Te Ching, and the Bhagavad Gita, a strikingly consistent portrait of the ideal person emerges. This is not to say that at all times and in all places, all people are meant to be alike. Yet like leaves that change color, directly before they fall, those on a spiritual path will exhibit certain traits as they approach their journey's end.

The ideal person is dutiful; he tends to his responsibilities productively and efficiently. While constantly seeking to improve his craft, his means of contributing to life, he knows that God is the source of all excellence and that he is merely the temporary custodian of those gifts he has been privileged to share. He is consistently committed, hard-working and serviceable; yet he doesn't carry his serviceable attitude to an unserviceable extreme, a flaw exhibited by those for whom work itself has become a distraction from those nagging personal issues they are fearfully reluctant to address. In Japanese, there is a term for working oneself to death—karoshi. It has no place in the ideal person's vocabulary.

The ideal person is efficient and economical in his use of speech. He'll most often let his accomplishments speak for themselves. The phrase "still waters run deep" applies well to him. He is knowledgeable on matters of the highest substantive importance, but because he doesn't flaunt his knowledge, the true depth of his understanding may well go unnoticed, and particularly by those who forever feel the need to draw attention to themselves. The ideal person knows that virtue is its own reward, and that the results of his actions will return to him in keeping with their intrinsic quality. This is a destiny determined, not in accordance with the uncertain whims of others, or with fickle social norms, but through alignment with the Magnetic North of Truth.

The ideal person is tolerant; he doesn't intensify an argument but seeks to resolve his disputes amicably. He is slow to anger, knowing that the universe doesn't calibrate its time by his personal watch, that the Divine Watchmaker has His own plans to which he may not be individually privy.

The ideal person is humble, yet conscious of the nobility and value of his purpose. Edward Arnold's translation of the Bhagavad Gita refers to this as being "modest, and grave, with manhood nobly mixed." (Arnold n.d., 70) Not infatuated with his own ideas, he allows his understanding to naturally and fluidly evolve, and his intellect to accommodate new knowledge. He does this without the obstruction of an undue personal bias. Quick to recognize his faults, he rapidly improves.

The ideal person is conscious of the larger world and its needs. He embodies the perspective of John Donne, who famously observed that "no man is an island alone unto himself." The ideal person is respectful of tradition, but not enslaved by it. He knows that we are what we are because of what others in the past have contributed, but that what we add with today's understanding will amplify that benefit exponentially. He knows that we the groundbreakers, the idealists, the progenitors of the future norm, have our own contributions to make, and that the greatest wonders are those which are yet to be unveiled.

The ideal person is a citizen of the world, a denizen of all places and times, not of one place and one time only. Having realized the perspective of the Absolute, he can sharply identify the bias and imbalance inherent in all relative trends, and not be unduly swayed by any of them. The ideal person, while living in the Light is sagaciously aware of the Darkness and its snares. He does not confuse naivete with virtue. He is aware of evil's ways while not being evil himself.[1] He would not confuse an illegitimate moral compromise with "peace in our time." When Christ's enemies tried to trap him with his own words, he was quick to acknowledge both sides, to "give to Caesar what belongs to Caesar and give to God what belongs to God." (Bible Hub, n.d., New Living Translation, Mark 12:17) He did not innocently fall into any cannily-laid trap.

The ideal person respects both others and himself. He maintains his body in good condition without pandering slavishly to its urges. The ideal person is, more than anything else, sincere. This sincerity allows him to live in harmony with the laws of existence, and with those of his own being. In constant alignment with Nature, he is, as a result, never confused as to his proper role in life. He knows that the tendency to be insincere, proceeds from a desire to manipulate outcomes through force or deceit. While this may result in temporarily favorable outcomes, in being opposed to the laws of life, it sets into motion the cause of its own undoing. As noted by David Hawkins and others, the power that arises from sincerity ultimately works, while the manipulative force generated by the insincere and conniving person is met by a counter-force that drives away his victory.[2]

The ideal person never judges, but constantly and incisively evaluates. He learns from the example and experience of others in both what to do and in what to avoid. The ideal person is affectionate and kind to all beings, but is particular about his associations, knowing that his own nature and tempera-ment will be molded by the company he keeps. The ideal person is coura-geous, but not foolhardy. He knows that "the world is won by those who let it go . . . ," (Tzu 1983, 119) and that "he who would save his life shall lose it." (Bible Hub, n.d., King James Bible, Matt. 16:25) So, he proceeds toward his good without clinging, yet with a storehouse of knowledge and wisdom in play, applying due consideration to whatever choices he ultimately makes.

The ideal person regards life's obstacles and challenges as opportunities to grow. He neither seeks problems, nor avoids them. He knows that in a uni-verse where what he sows is what he reaps, he accepts his rewards as given, without that gratuitous sense of shame and guilt that derives from others' envy and scorn. He accepts his problems without complaint as ultimately self-created. He strives for success, but doesn't depend on it or on the larger world's approval. He knows that the ultimate value of his attainments resides in a realm beyond them, a realm which is the ultimate beneficent end of all of his strivings. The ideal person seeks joy in the Source of joy, success in the Source of accomplishment, before seeking it elsewhere.

The ideal person knows how to laugh, but isn't careless or flippant. Having secured the shelter of the harmony within, he naturally and, as it would seem, effortlessly, gives to each of his external activities the proper measure of his concern and attention.

The ideal person is thankful for all he has received. He knows that life is a gift that has come to him unearned, and that it is incumbent upon him to make the best of it, despite its annoying constraints, and to face and surmount its attendant obstacles through wisdom, experience, and love. He knows that in a compassionate universe, those obstacles exist to beneficially mold him, and not to thoughtlessly destroy him. He sees how everything is useful, in the end.

NOTES

1. Quoting directly from the *Tao Te Ching*, "Be aware of the white all around you;/ But remembering the black that is there,/You shall be to the world like a tester,/Whom the Virtue eternal, unerring,/Redirects to the infinite past."

2. As described by Hawkins, "Force always creates counterforce; its effect is to polarize rather than unify. Polarization always implies conflict; its cost, therefore, is always high. Because force incites polarization, it inevitably produces a win/lose dichotomy; and because somebody always loses, enemies are created. Constantly faced with enemies, force requires constant defense. Defensiveness is invariably costly, whether in the marketplace, politics, or international affairs." (Hawkins 2002, 133)

Bibliography

Alexander, David, dir. *Star Trek: Plato's Stepchildren.* 1968. Film.

Almine. n.d. The Seer Almine. Accessed January 28, 2019. https://www.alminediary.com/solitude-is-the-price-of-greatness/.

Archon, Sofo. n.d. The Unbounded Spirit. Accessed January 20, 2019.

Arnold, Sir Edwin. n.d. The Bhagavad Gita. Amazon digital Services LLC.

—. 2012. The Light of Asia, Kindle Edition. Amazon digital Services, LLC.

Augustine. 2012. The Confessions of Saint Augustine. Amazon digital Services, LLC.

Babbitt, Irving trans., ed. 2012. The Dhammapada. Cambridge, MA: New Directions.

Bach, Richard. 1977. Illusions, The Adventures of a Reluctant Messiah. New York: Dell Publishing Co., Inc.

Berg, Yahuda. 2004. The Power of Kaballah, Technology for the Soul. New York: Kaballah Center International.

Berg, Yehuda. 2009. Tune-Ups: A Day-to-Day Guide to Making Your Life Better. New York: The Kaballah Center.

n.d. "Bible Hub,." https://biblehub.net. Accessed January 23, 2019.

Billington, James H. 1967. The Icon and the Axe: An Interpretive History of Russian Culture. Toronto: Random House.

Biro, Brian D. 2001. Beyond Success: The 15 Secrets to Effective Leadership and Life Based on Legendary Coach John Wooden's Pyramid of Success. New York: Berkeley Publishing Group: A Division of Penguin Putnam Inc.

Blavatsky, Helena Petrovna. 2011. The Voce of the Silence (Zen and Now Book 1). Edited by Translated and Annotated by H.P.B. River Drafting.

Braff, Cindi Sansone-. 2009. Grant Me a Higher Love: How to Go from the Relationship from Hell to One that's Heaven Sent by Scaling The Ladder of Love. Amazon Digital Services.

2007. Star Wars: The Legacy Revealed. Film. Directed by Kevin Burns.

Burtt, Edwin, ed. 1955. The Teachings of the Compassionate Buddha. New York: New American Library.

1991. Terminator 2: Judgement Day. Film. Directed by James Cameron.

Campbell, Joseph. 2008. The Hero With a Thousand Faces (The Collected Works of Joseph Campbell). San Francisco: New World Library.

Capra, Fritjof. 2010. The Tao of Physics: An Exploration of the Parallels Between Modern Physics and Eastern Mysticism. Boston: Shambhala Publications, Inc.

Chinmoy, Sri. 1988. Beyond Within: A Philosophy for the Inner Life. Jamaica, New York: Agni Press.

1968. Star Trek: Day of the Dove. Film. Directed by Marvin J. Chomsky.

Cope, Stephen. 2014. The Great Work of Your Life: A Guide for the Journey to Your True Calling. New York: Random House LLC.

Das, Ram. 1987. Grist for the Mill. Berkeley, CA: Celestial Arts.

—. 2004. Paths to God, Living the Bhagavad Girta. New York: Three Rivers Press.

—. 1971. Remember: Be Here Now. New York: Crown Publishing.

Dwoskin, Hale. 2009. The Sedona Method. Sedona, AZ: Sedona Press.

Dyer, Wayne W. 2004. The Power of Intention: Learning to Create Your World Your Way. Carlsbad, CA: Hay House, Inc.

n.d. "Edgar Cayce's A.R.E. Association for Research and Enlightenment." https://www.edgarcayce.org/the-readings/akashic-records. Accessed 2018.

Evans Wentz, W. Y., ed. 1969. Tibet's Great Yogi Milarepa: A Biography from the Tibetan. London: Oxford University Press.

Evans-Wentz, W. Y. 2000. The Tibetan Book of the Dead. New York: Oxford University Press.

—. 1967. Tibetan Yoga and Secret Doctrines. Edited by W.Y., ed. Evans-Wentz. London: Oxford University Press.

F. Max Muller, ed. n.d. The Upanisads: Part II. New York: Dover Publications.

Fast Company. 2005. The Rules of Business. New York: Doubleday, A Division of Random House Inc.

Feuerstein, Georg. 1989. The Yoga-Sutra of Patanjali: A New Translation and Commentary. Rochester, Vermont: Inner Traditions International.

Floyd, Pink. 1973. "Breathe." The Dark Side of the Moon. Sound Recording.

Francis, Gary Zukav and Linda. 2001. The Heart of the Soul: Emotional Awareness. New York: Simon & Schuster Source.

Goldstein, Joseph. 2014. "Mindfulness: What it is and is Not." CFM Guest Lecture Series. Shrewsbury, MA. https://www.youtube.com/watch?v=3Uqoxo_jPXQ.

—. 1983. The Experience of Insight. New York: Random House.

Hallett, Garth. 2011. Guideposts to the Heart: Observations from the Spiritual Path. Indianapolis: Dog Ear Publishing.

Hallett, Garth J. 2015. Humanity At the Crossroads: Technological Progress, Spiritual Evolution, and the Dawn of the Nuclear Age 2015. Lanham, Maryland: Hamilton Books.

Hawkins, David R. 2002. Power vs. Force: The Hidden Determinants of Human Behavior. Carlsbad, California: Hay House.

Hawley, Jack, ed. 2011. The Bhagavad Gita: A Walkthrough for Westerners. Novato, CA: New World Library.

Hesse, Hermann. 1963. Steppenwolf. New York: Randon House, Inc.

Hesse, Hermann. 1968. Beneath the Wheel. Translated by Michael Roloff. New York: Farrer, Straus and Giroux.

Hicks, Esther and Jerry. 2006. The Amazing Power of Deliberate Intent: Living the Art of Allowing. Carlsbad, CA: Hay House, Inc.

Hill, Napoleon. 2008. The Law of Success. New York: Penguin Group.

1965. Holy Bible: Containing the Old and New Testaments, New King James Version. Nashville: Thomas Nelson Publishers.

1982. Poltergeist. Film. Directed by Tobe Hooper.

Humphreys, Christmas. 1962. Zen: A Way of Life. Boston: Little, Brown and Company.

Isherwood, Swami Prabhavananda and Christopher, ed. 1972. The Song of God, Bhagavad-Gita. New York: The New American Library, Inc.

Joel, Billy. 1977. Only the Good Die Young. Sound.

Joplin, Janis. 1971. Me and Bobby McGee. Comp. Fred Foster, Kris Kristofferson. Sound.

Kempis, Thomas A. 1985. The Imitation of Christ. New York: Catholic Book Publishing Co.

1980. Star Wars: Episode V - the Empire Strikes Back. Film. Directed by Irvin Kershner.

Krishna, Gopi. 1970. Kundalini: The Evolutionary Energy in Man. Berkeley, CA: Shambala Publications, Inc.

2014. Der Anstandige (The Decent One). Film. Directed by Vanessa Lapa.

1992. I Borg (Star Trek: The Next Generation, Season 5; Episode 23). Film. Directed by Robert Lederman.

Lama, Dalai. 2008. Freedom in Exile: The Autobiography of The Dalai Lama. New York: HarperCollins.

Lee, Johnny. 1980. "Looking for Love." Urban Cowboy. Sound Recording.

Liu, Da. 1991. T'ai Chi Ch'uan & Meditation. New York: Schocken Books.

1977. Star Wars: Episode IV - A New Hope. Film. Directed by George Lucas.

1968. Star Trek: Elaan of Troyius. Film. Directed by John Meredyth Lucas.

M. Scott Peck, M.D. 1978. The Road Less Traveled. New York: Simon & Schuster, Inc.

Maclaine, Shirley. 1986. Out on a Limb. New York: Bantam.

1983. Star Wars: Episode VI - Return of the Jedi. Film. Directed by Richard Marquand.

Mascaro, Juan, trans. 1974. The Bhagavad Gita. Middlesex, England: Penguin Books, Ltd.

McWilliams, Peter. 1995. You Can't Afford the Luxury of a Negative Thought. Los Angeles: Prelude Press.

Merritt Y. Hughes, ed. 1981. John Milton: Complete Poems and Major Prose. Indianapolis: The Odyssey Press Inc, A Division of The Bobbs-Merrill Company, Inc.

Michael F. Roizen, M.D. and Mehmet C. Oz., M.D. 2007. You Staying Young: The Owner's Manual for Extending Your Warranty. New York: Free Press, A Division of Simon & Schuster, Inc.

Milton, John. 2011. Paradise Lost, Kindle Edition. Amazon digital Services.

Montaigne, Michel de. 1965. The Complete Essays of Montaigne. Stanford, CA: Stanford University Press.

Moody-Blues, The. 1986. "The Other Side of Life." The Other Side of Life. Comp. Justin Hayward. Sound Recording.

Muller, Friedrich Max, ed. 2009. Dhammapada. New York: Fall River Press.

Nikhilananda, Swami, trans. 2003. The Principal Upanishads. Mineola, New York: Dover Publications.

Northcutt, Wendy. 2002. The Darwin Awards, Evolution in Action. New York: PLUME, a member of Penguin Putnam Inc.

Pound, Ezra. 1968. The Literary Essays of Ezra Pound. Edited by T.S. Eliot. New York: New Directions Publishing.

Prabhavananda, Swami. 1972. The Sermon on the Mount According to Vedanta. New York: Mentor.

Prem, Sri Krishna. 1948. The Yoga of the Bhagavat Gita. London: John M. Watkins.

Reid, Daniel P. 1989. The Tao of Health Sex and Longevity: A Modern Practical Guide to the Ancient Way. New York: Simon & Schuster.

Roberts, Jane. 1972. Seth Speaks: The Eternal Validity of the Soul. London: Prentice-Hall International, Inc.

Robinson, Edwin A. 1997. Edwin Arlington Robinson: Selected Poems. Edited by Robert Faggen. New York: Penguin.

Roman, Sanaya (Channel for Orin). 1989. Spiritual Growth. Tiburon, CA: HJ Kramer, Inc.

Rousseau, Jean-Jacques. 1964. The Social Contract and Discourse on the Origin of Inequality. New York: Simon & Schuster.

Salisbury, Harrison. 1970. The 900 Days: The Siege of Leningrad. New York: Avon.

Saraswati, Swami Satyananda. 2009. Kundalini Tantra. Bihar, India: Yoga Publications Trust.

Shakespeare. 2012. Hamlet. New York: Simon & Schuster, Inc.

—. 1994. The Tempest. New York: Simon & Schuster.

Sivers, Derek. n.d. "Siverse.org." https://siverse.org/horses.

Smith, Huston. 1991. The World's Religions. New York: HarperCollins Publishers.

Solnado, Alexandra. 2011. The Book of Light: Ask and Heaven Will Answer. New York: Simon & Schuster.

1966. Star Trek: Shore Leave. Film. Directed by Robert Sparr.

Suzuki, Shunryo. 2005. Zen Mind, Beginner's Mind. Boston: Weatherhill, An Imprint of Shambhala Publications, Inc.

Taylor, Sandra Anne. 2011. The Hidden Power of Your Past Lives: Revealing Your Encoded Consciousness. Carlsbad: Hay House, Inc.

The RV Forum Community. n.d. Accessed February 27, 2019. http://www.rvforum .net/SMF_forum/index.php?topic=7085.0.

Thirumoolar, Siddhar. 1993. Thirumandiram: A Classic of Yoga and Tantra, Vol. 2. Montreal: Babaji's Kriya Yoga and Publications, Inc.

Tolkien, J.R.R. 2013. The Lord of the Rings. Boston: Houghton Mifflin Harcourt.

Trungpa, Chogyam. 1985. Shambhala: The Sacred Path of the Warrior. Shambhala.

Twin Flame Connection: Twin Flame Guidance and Insights with Twin Flame Psychics. n.d. Accessed January 24, 2019.

Tzu, Lao. 1983. Tao Te Ching. Edited by R.B. Blakny. New York: New American Library, A Division of Penguin Group.

Vogler, Christopher. 2007. The Writers Journey: Mythic Structures for Writers, 3rd edition. Studio City, California: Michael Weise Productions.

Voltaire, Francois Marie Arouet De. 1981. Candide, Zadig and selected stories. New York: Penguin Putnam, Inc.

Vonnegut, Kurt. 1991. Slaughterhouse Five. New York: Bantam Doubleday Dell Publishing Group.

Walker, Brian. 1992. Hua Hu Ching: The Unknown Teachings of Lao Tzu. New York: HarperCollins Publishers.

Watts, Alan. 1975. Tao: The Watercourse Way. New York: Pantheon Books.

—. 1999. The Book on the Taboo Against Knowing Who You Are. New York: Random House.

Wilde, Oscar. 1995. The Picture of Dorian Gray and Other Stories. New York: Barnes & Noble Books.

Yogananda, Paramahansa. 2003. Autobiography of a Yogi. Los Angeles: Self-Realization Fellowship.

Yogi Ramacharaka, trans. 1930. Bhagavad Gita. Chicago: Yogi Publication Society.

Zukav, Gary. 1989. The Seat of the Soul. New York: Simon & Schuster.

Index